Keeping a Watchful Eye

Keeping a Watchful Eye

The Politics of Congressional Oversight

JOEL D. ABERBACH

The Brookings Institution
Washington, D.C.

Copyright (c) 1990 by
THE BROOKINGS INSTITUTION
1775 Massachusetts Avenue, N.W., Washington, D.C. 20036

Library of Congress Cataloging-in-Publication data

Aberbach, Joel D.
  Keeping a watchful eye: the politics of congressional
oversight / Joel D. Aberbach.
    p.   cm.
  Includes bibliographical references.
  ISBN 0-8157-0060-1 (alk. paper)
    1. Legislative oversight—United States.   2. Bureaucracy—
United States.   I. Title.
  JK585.A63   1990
  328.73'07456–dc20   89-25232

9 8 7 6 5 4 3 2 1

The paper used in this publication meets the minimum
requirements of the American National Standard for Information Sciences—Permanence of Paper for Printed Library
Materials, ANSI Z39.48-1984.

Composition by Monotype Composition Co.
  Baltimore, Maryland
Printed by R.R. Donnelley and Sons, Co.
  Harrisonburg, Virginia
Book design by Ken Sabol

THE BROOKINGS INSTITUTION

The Brookings Institution is an independent organization devoted to nonpartisan research, education, and publication in economics, government, foreign policy, and the social sciences generally. Its principal purposes are to aid in the development of sound public policies and to promote public understanding of issues of national importance.

The Institution was founded on December 8, 1927, to merge the activities of the Institute for Government Research, founded in 1916, the Institute of Economics, founded in 1922, and the Robert Brookings Graduate School of Economics and Government, founded in 1924.

The Board of Trustees is responsible for the general administration of the Institution, while the immediate direction of the policies, program, and staff is vested in the President, assisted by an advisory committee of the officers and staff. The by-laws of the Institution state: "It is the function of the Trustees to make possible the conduct of scientific research, and publication, under the most favorable conditions, and to safeguard the independence of the research staff in the pursuit of their studies and in the publication of the results of such studies. It is not a part of their function to determine, control, or influence the conduct of particular investigations or the conclusions reached."

The President bears final responsibility for the decision to publish a manuscript as a Brookings book. In reaching his judgment on the competence, accuracy, and objectivity of each study, the President is advised by the director of the appropriate research program and weighs the views of a panel of expert outside readers who report to him in confidence on the quality of the work. Publication of a work signifies that it is deemed a competent treatment worthy of public consideration but does not imply endorsement of conclusions or recommendations.

The Institution maintains its position of neutrality on issues of public policy in order to safeguard the intellectual freedom of the staff. Hence interpretations or conclusions in Brookings publications should be understood to be solely those of the authors and should not be attributed to the Institution, to its trustees, officers, or other staff members, or to the organizations that support its research.

In loving memory of my father, Isidore Aberbach

Foreword

CONGRESSIONAL OVERSIGHT activity has increased dramatically since the early 1970s. Congressional committees now spend more of their time holding hearings to review the activities of federal agencies, and committee staff members are busy collecting information about what goes on during program implementation.

This book examines the reasons behind the surprising growth of congressional oversight. Using original data collected for this project, Joel D. Aberbach documents the increase in oversight activity and links it to changes in the political environment. He explores the political purposes served by oversight, the techniques Congress uses to uncover information about the activities of the federal bureaucracy, and the reasons why topics get on the oversight agenda. He concludes that even though the U.S. government system was not designed with a large administrative sector in mind, its ability to expose bureaucratic behavior to public scrutiny is impressive, and that Congress plays a vital role in this endeavor.

Joel D. Aberbach, a former senior fellow in the Brookings Governmental Studies program, is professor of political science and director of the Center for American Politics and Public Policy at the University of California, Los Angeles. He gratefully acknowledges the cooperation of the representatives, senators, and congressional staff members who agreed to be interviewed for this project. They gave generously of their time and knowledge. Assurances of anonymity prevent thanking them by name.

The author thanks the many colleagues who commented on the manuscript at various stages. Thomas E. Mann, Daniel B. Mezger, Morris S. Ogul, Paul J. Quirk, and Bert A. Rockman provided detailed suggestions on the entire manuscript. Martha Feldman, John E.

Jackson, John W. Kingdon, Mathew D. McCubbins, Russell D. Murphy, Paul E. Peterson, and Jack L. Walker critiqued particular chapters or sections.

The author is particularly indebted to those who assisted him in the research. Katherine H. Dolan and Deborah P. Kelly were dedicated research assistants and interviewers. William R. Katovsky and Paul J. Kennedy did much of the coding of the survey of staffers. Paul J. Kennedy also conducted some of the follow-up surveys and provided valuable administrative assistance. Steve Anderson, Robert Copeland, and Bill McGee assisted in the data analysis reported in this book. Jeffrey Cohen, Cynthia Engquist, Merle Feldbaum, Celinda Lake, Darlene C. Steil, and Susan Van Alstyne coded data from the *Daily Digest* of the *Congressional Record*.

John R. Chamberlin, Mary Corcoran, Thomas L. Gais, Lynn Gale, Robert Mare, and Lincoln Moses generously supplied statistical advice. Judy Jackson and Sylvia Goodwin provided secretarial assistance. Theresa B. Walker edited the manuscript, and Peter Dombrowski verified it. Max Franke prepared the index.

Much of the work in chapter 4 appeared in "The Congressional Committee Intelligence System: Information, Oversight, and Change," *Congress and the Presidency*, vol. 14 (Spring 1987).

This material is based upon work supported by the National Science Foundation under Grant No. SES 78-16812. In addition, the author gratefully acknowledges funding from the Institute of Public Policy Studies and the American Institutions Program at the University of Michigan, and the Academic Senate, the Center for American Politics and Public Policy, and the Institute for Social Science Research at the University of California, Los Angeles. The author also benefited immensely from a year spent as a fellow at the Center for Advanced Study in the Behavioral Sciences, where he did much of the analytical work reported in this book.

The views expressed in this book are those of the author and should not be ascribed to the persons and institutions acknowledged above or to the trustees, officers, or staff members of the Brookings Institution.

Bruce K. MacLaury
President

December 1989
Washington, D.C.

Contents

Figures

Keeping a Watchful Eye

Chapter 1

Governing the Bureaucracy

IT IS commonplace these days to acknowledge the tremendous power of bureaucracies in modern governments. Max Weber, in a classic essay, contended that the specialization endemic to a fully developed bureaucracy normally puts it in an "overtowering" position of power relative to its nominal political masters, who often find themselves mere dilettantes confronting the expert officials of the state administration.[1] More recently, Robert D. Putnam introduced an insightful article on the political attitudes of senior civil servants with the following question and answer:

> Can there really be much doubt who governs our complex, modern societies? Public bureaucracies . . . are responsible for the vast majority of policy initiatives taken by governments. . . . Bureaucrats, monopolizing as they do much of the available information about the shortcomings of existing policies, as well as much of the technical expertise necessary to design practical alternatives, have gained a predominant influence over the evolution of the agenda for decision.[2]

Putnam's article analyzes signs of a trend toward a more "political" bureaucracy in several Western European nations. Political bureaucracies are composed of officials who "recognize the need to bargain and compromise, yet at the same time [do] not necessarily shrink from advocating or even fighting for [their] own preferred policies." In closing, Putnam notes some of the dangers accompanying this trend, including "the danger that as a politically aware bureaucracy comes to play a more active role in the policy-making process, the ability of the representative institutions of government to control that bureaucracy may be weakened."[3]

The research reported in this book addresses an aspect of the important problem Congress faces in governing, that is, in directing and controlling, the complex and highly political (though not necessarily partisan) bureaucracy found in the United States. Governing the bureaucracy is difficult everywhere, but especially in the American polity because of the nature of American institutional structures and traditions. This book deals with one critical element of Congress's effort to control administration and policy: congressional oversight.

Appendix A contains a full discussion of my definition of oversight. Briefly, I define it as congressional review of the actions of federal departments, agencies, and commissions, and of the programs and policies they administer, including review that takes place during program and policy implementation as well as afterward. Oversight, then, is a significant facet of congressional efforts to control administration and policy.

Congressional oversight in the United States is part of a dynamic system. Many others characterize oversight as an uncommon activity, low in political payoff to individual legislators. I demonstrate the conditions under which Congress oversees actively. Under the circumstances delineated in this book, the institutional features of American government encourage the growth of oversight activity. Understanding the conditions that encourage oversight activity, however, does not tell us about its nature. Much of this book, therefore, is devoted to detailing how Congress secures information about administration and policy, how items get on the oversight agenda, who decides what oversight is to be done, what forms oversight takes, the political context in which oversight occurs, and the implications of oversight behavior for democratic control of administration and policy. Oversight is a big subject, but it is a vital one for understanding democratic life in the contemporary era.

The Special Problem in the United States

The structure of American government and the assumptions behind it make congressional oversight of administration important but problematic. The American system of government is one, to use

Richard E. Neustadt's classic characterization, of "separated institutions *sharing* powers."[4] The framers of the Constitution, fearing the ill effects of the concentration of power and authority, partitioned them with great care. One major reason for this was a deep-seated suspicion of power. The Convention delegates, to use Robert A. Dahl's words, "shared a hard-headed, unsentimental, skeptical view of the ability of human beings to withstand the temptations of power. They took it for granted that individuals are easily corrupted by power. . . . The best way to prevent the abuse of power, then, was not to trust in human character but to limit the legal authority allocated to any person and to set one power against another."[5] As James Madison said in *Federalist no. 51*, "Ambition must be made to counteract ambition."[6]

The grand design of the system the framers devised was one in which every actor or institution would be checked by another. Power would be diffused, individuals and institutions would be forced to accommodate one another, and the ambitions of political actors would be harnessed, the framers hoped, for the public good. James MacGregor Burns quotes Richard Hofstadter's cogent observation that the Madisonian aim was "a harmonious system of mutual frustration."[7]

Where was the administrative apparatus of the state to fit into this system? Clearly, this question is important from the contemporary perspective, but it did not take up much time in the work of the framers. As James Q. Wilson says in "The Rise of the Bureaucratic State," "The Founding Fathers had little to say about the nature or function of the executive branch of the new government. The Constitution is virtually silent on the subject and the debates in the Constitutional Convention are almost devoid of reference to an administrative apparatus."[8] Not much thought was given to the problems of administrative responsibility and accountability in a complex bureaucratic state because a large administrative apparatus was not envisaged at the time.

I emphasize the nature of the American system of separation of powers because it introduces a unique element into the problem of legislative control of the executive. To quote Herbert A. Simon and others, "The separation of powers in this country between legislative and executive somewhat beclouds the right of the chief executive to control administration."[9] Neustadt says it even more strongly in a stimulating essay on politicians and bureaucrats. "Congress, constitutionally, has at least as much to do with executive administration as does an incumbent of the White House."[10]

In a system where there are multiple masters, "most agencies have need for men of passion and conviction, or at least enormous powers of resistance—near the top. American officialdom may generate no more of these than other systems do, but it rewards them well: they rise toward the top. And there they tend to set the tone of bureaucratic views about all comers from 'outside,' not least the President."[11]

So one sees an ironic interplay. The American version of separation of powers, designed to check and tame the powers of governmental officials and institutions, gives the legislature enough freedom from the executive to allow it an independent role in the control of administration. The growth of the administrative sector, and the power that accrues in the hands of administrators because of the complexity of policy and administration in the modern state, has made control by representative institutions, including the presidency, increasingly important. But in the U.S. system of separation of powers, where sources of authority are uncertain because they are multiple, top career bureaucrats "often are impelled to become political entrepreneurs [in order] to push favored proposals or, more often, to protect their programs."[12]

Thus efforts by Congress to review and control can be counterproductive. When there are multiple overseers, those being overseen have ample incentive to be very active players in the process. And since usually no one set of institutional actors has clear control and signals often conflict, it is difficult to hold the bureaucracy, or any other institution, reasonably to account.

The U.S. administrative personnel system is another source of complexity.[13] In part because of tradition, but also because great emphasis is given to political control in a system lacking clear lines of control, the American career civil service is superintended by a large layer of noncareer, politically appointed officials.[14] Some noncareer officials are appointed by the president with the consent of the Senate, and others do not require Senate confirmation. The literature of American political science is replete with studies of the role of these appointees and of their conflicted status as administrators facing pressure from the president and his staff, from Congress, from the interest groups affected by programs under their jurisdiction, and from the career administrators who run the agencies of government.[15] Appointees are subject to cooptation by their more knowledgeable and experienced subordinates, and many develop strong ties to the relevant committee personnel in Congress, not to mention ties to client groups. These phenomena frustrate the president and those around him. Such dissatisfaction has led presidents to try a variety of strategies to gain control over the administrative branch, including the aggressive "administrative presidency" strategy of placing loyal subordinates lacking independent status in political appointee slots and bypassing Congress in every way possible.[16] The system ebbs and flows in terms of presidential leverage with administrators, but in the end institutional design and its accompanying incentives confirm Norton E. Long's account of administrative authority in the United States. "The unanswered question of American government—'who is boss?'—constantly plagues administration."[17]

American Bureaucracy: Some Comparative Perspectives

Top American career bureaucrats, to an extent unmatched in the Western world, are responsible for shoring up their own bases of political support. Their bosses tend to be inexperienced, short-term appointees, "a government of strangers" to use Hugh Heclo's words, who often leave office just as they learn the job.[18] But the key members of congressional committees with jurisdictions in their areas are likely to hold office much longer, longer even than the president, and to have a better idea of what they want. Wise career administrators, therefore, are responsive to congressional committees. Members of congressional committees, however, often do not agree with the political administrators in the career bureaucrat's department or with the president. Committee members may not even agree with one another, since the ordinary agency is overseen by at least two committees in each chamber. (One authorizes expenditures, and another appropriates funds.) This pattern of multiple authority and diverse views presents both a problem and an opportunity for those who administer the U.S. government.

Cabinet government, that is, government by a coordinated team, is an elusive goal proclaimed but not achieved by each new American administration.[19] By contrast with other systems, U.S. political parties are weak, providing little unity, especially when the branches of government are controlled by the different parties. A strict division between politics and administration is not found anywhere, but the notion that the function of the bureaucracy is merely to implement authoritative decisions rests on an assumption that is often totally unrealistic in the United States—reasonably clear, consistent signals. By institutional necessity, then, reinforced by the party system and by the organization of Congress, it should not surprise anyone that American bureaucrats, career and noncareer, are more oriented toward traditional political roles such as protecting the interests of client groups than bureaucrats in Western Europe, and that American legislators are more oriented to traditionally bureaucratic roles such as applying specialized knowledge to policy problems than parliamentarians in Europe.

Evidence from a comprehensive study of bureaucrats and politicians in seven Western democracies, a study I did in the early 1970s with colleagues at the University of Michigan, graphically demonstrates the validity of these statements. Data collected from top-level administrators and parliamentarians in the United States, Great Britain, France, Italy, Germany, the Netherlands, and Sweden led to a clear conclusion. "The distinctiveness in role focus between civil servants and legislators throughout Europe is conspicuously absent in America. . . . Whereas bureaucrats and politicians in Europe conceive their roles quite differently, bureaucrats and politicians in America conceive their roles quite similarly."[20] Terms like "American exceptionalism" and "the American aberration" came naturally as descriptions of ways in which the U.S. data contrasted with data from the other nations.

American bureaucrats and members of Congress are unique not only in their role conceptions but also in their communication patterns. The picture is complex, but the modal case in parliamentary systems is the "mediated linkage" model. Senior civil servants in parliamentary systems apparently do most of their communicating with parliamentarians through the minister, even in nations like the Netherlands where ministers are not necessarily members of Parliament. In these systems "ministerial responsibility, collective cabinet government, and a party-centered parliament are most fully developed."[21]

The contrasting model is the direct linkage model, where civil servant-parliamentarian contacts are not mediated. Direct linkage is found where "parliamentary institutionalization is more advanced, and the system of governance more fragmented." The country that is most unlike the mediated linkage nations is the United States. In the United States one finds the "end-run model," a unique case in which members of Congress and senior civil servants report more frequent contacts with one another than with department heads.[22] Indeed, analysis of the pattern of contacts leads to the conclusion that "while congressmen and bureaucrats are mutually dependent, Congress' constitutional powers and independent staffing make bureaucrats somewhat more dependent on congressmen than the reverse. . . . In the American case, cabinet officials often are obstacles to be circumvented in accord with long-standing informal treaties among more durable actors."[23]

Thus the American bureaucracy is a likely political battleground. Presidents struggle to coordinate and control it, often devising elaborate techniques for ensuring compliance. Congress is tempted to assert control. In other democratic systems where the lines of political authority in relation to the bureaucracy are clearer, more ready acceptance of the influence that senior civil servants have on ministers' decisions prevails. Ministers and the cabinet are more comfortable about the power of civil servants, in part because of tradition but also because their authority is reasonably clear when disputes are to be settled or important decisions made. Bureaucrats will almost certainly cast their longest look "upwards" at key moments. In contrast, in the United States the system strongly encourages administrators to give at least as long a look "outwards" to Congress, especially its committee units controlling agency authorizations and appropriations, and even to interest groups representing agency clients.[24]

"Uncertain lines of authority encourage American bureaucrats to play political roles—to cut deals with congressmen who can protect their agencies from central executive control, to pursue the interests of clienteles who can help to protect their programs, and to act as advocates for interests inadequately represented through the ostensible channels of political representation."[25] As a result, the central executive authority (the president) often views the bureaucracy with suspicion and distrust; hence the extraordinary emphasis on elaborate methods to ensure compliance and the almost pervasive unease in the upper reaches of the executive about the policy influence of career civil servants.

In brief, the American constitutional framework provides, especially with respect to the bureaucracy, a set of opportunities, incentives, and lacunae that invites assertiveness and struggle. This invitation may not always be taken up, but it is always open, a permanent temptation.

Bureaucracy and the History of Democratic Development

In the United States, the bureaucratization of the state administration followed the development of democratic institutions.[26] In the other industrialized democracies, though the time of bureaucratization varied, professional bureaucracies "emerged prior to the flowering of mass democratic politics and its instruments, the modern mass political party and the supremacy of elected assemblies."[27] Partly as a result of this sequencing, the tendency to connect conservatism to state authority, which is common in Europe and Japan, is not present in the United States. However, for the same reasons, the American top career bureaucracy also lacks the great prestige as a bastion of a traditional high-status elite found in polities where administrative development preceded that of democratic institutions. This lack of prestige is reinforced by the unimportant role it is thought that the state and, therefore, its administrative arm played in economic development in the United States.

In those polities in which the bureaucracy preceded the full development of democratic institutions, there is commonly a tradition "that emphasizes a unitary corporate will . . . [and] a government strong enough in its collective authority to make collective decisions."[28] The democratic struggle has been, as Richard Rose notes, to subordinate that "government" authority, including bureaucratic authority, to the popular will. The mechanism chosen, which I call the "cabinet government model" for convenience here,[29] features a popularly elected Parliament with a cabinet as its powerful executive committee. It emphasizes clear lines of authority to the cabinet ministers, an opportunity for strong central direction of policy and administration by means of the cabinet, and only limited "interference" in the operations of government, the workings of the bureaucracy, or in policy evaluation from backbenchers in Parliament.[30] The system provides a powerful mechanism allowing cabinet members to control the activities of career administrators and the policies they administer if cabinet members have the inclination to exert such control.[31]

The American bureaucracy is relatively less prestigious and more politicized than its counterparts in the other democratic states. It does not have a legacy of representing a unitary corporate will—the bureaucracy is certainly not a symbol of the American state. One strength of the system is that many actors have the potential to oversee the bureaucracy. There is no strong tradition of bureaucratic prestige or function to block the realization of that potential. However, because of the absence of clear hierarchy and effective coordination, the oversight that does take place becomes part of a complex political game in which bureaucrats are important participants. In the American system the struggle, most often lost, is to subordinate the free play of politics ("the representation of conflicting demands," in Richard Rose's terms) to the needs of government ("resolving these conflicts authoritatively and to a nation's benefit").[32] In large part because of the history of its development and the institutional setting in which it was born, the bureaucracy in the American system is more a part of politics as Rose defines it than it is in other systems.

Cultural Influences

Cultural influences are difficult to describe in precise terms and even more difficult to analyze. Suffice it to say that the American state was born in a late eighteenth-century rebellion by a people in a new land relatively unencumbered by traditions. It was a time of intellectual ferment that yielded classical liberalism with its individualistic premises. And that liberalism seems to have become an ingrained part of American tradition, taking root in the relatively unworked soil and deeply affecting notions about human behavior and institutional design. As Kenneth Dyson says, "The American liberal tradition is profoundly individualistic and anti-bureaucratic; it begins with the autonomous individual and with a populist belief that all authority emanates from the people. A dispersal of public power was seen as necessary in order to maintain the supremacy of the popular will and to protect the individual."[33]

This liberal political culture of the United States emphasizes the supremacy of individual rights over institutional authority. The government, and certainly its bureaucracy when it developed, embodies institutional authority and so is always suspect to some degree. People do not easily defer to state authority. They expect their elected representatives to press their claims and grievances. When Richard

F. Fenno asked, "If, as Ralph Nader says, Congress is the broken branch, how come we love our Congressmen so much?" he was touching on a basic dilemma inherent in the American political system.[34] In essence, "the balance between demand making and rule making, between representation and authority, between politics and government is necessarily delicate. But the first element of each of these pairs is given more weight in the United States than in other advanced industrial democracies."[35]

The American cultural tradition supports the individual against the state and exalts the role of the elected representative as agent for the citizen in struggles with the authorities. It is a tradition that makes legislative "interference" in the workings of the bureaucracy very attractive to members of Congress because the benefits are highly celebrated and the possible costs understated. Indeed, one prominent scholar has built a theory of congressional dominance of public policy around the notion that Congress gains advantage from nurturing old programs and creating new ones, thereby giving benefits to constituents and organized interests, and from intervening in the administrative process in response to citizen and group frustration with bureaucratic processes and outputs. "Congressmen take credit coming and going," he says. "They are the alpha and the omega . . . the linchpin of the Washington establishment."[36] Members of Congress, in effect, using the status they have as part of a powerful separate institution, create the agencies of government, give them vague mandates, and reward them with funds and authority, all the while using their influence with the agencies on behalf of citizens and groups with grievances and denouncing "the bureaucracy" to public applause. It is a merging of institutional advantage and cultural biases against the authorities that benefits both those in Congress and the bureaucracy, although the costs in terms of government legitimacy and efficiency are not usually reckoned with the same precision as the immediate benefits to the actors involved. While this view may exaggerate the role of Congress, it does have a kernel of truth and demonstrates the interaction between cultural values and institutional design features.[37] Americans, at the same time, want small government with tightly checked bureaucracies *and* public programs of benefit to them. Elected officials take both facets of opinion into account in their relations with administrators.

Other Political and Institutional Features

The distinctive institutional architecture of the American system and its implications for legislative-executive relations have been discussed at some length, but there are three additional institutional and political facts I should highlight.

First, not only is Congress institutionally separate from the executive, but Congress also fragments power internally. It is organized into committees and subcommittees that are of great importance within the institution. Indeed, in the classic nineteenth-century account of Congress, Woodrow Wilson noted, "It is not far from the truth to say that Congress in session is Congress on public exhibition, whilst Congress in its committee-rooms is Congress at work."[38] And with the post-1960s "reforms" there has been a move from the strong committee government that increasingly characterized Congress after the 1910 revolt against Speaker Joseph G. Cannon to the current "system of subcommittee government."[39] In the 100th Congress (1987-88), for example, there were 140 subcommittees of standing committees in the House and 85 in the Senate.[40] Most had narrow jurisdictions matched to the organizational structure of the federal bureaucracy.

Second, "there is no party government, partly because there is no unified government and partly because U.S. political parties lack the will or ability to discipline their legislative officeholders."[41] The fragmented nature of the system and its institutional structure—with different terms of office for elected officials, constituencies of different scope and kind, and independent bases of institutional power—make it difficult to maintain party discipline. The primary system for selecting candidates and the open system of financing candidacies reinforce tendencies toward entrepreneurial politics. Further, with the increased professionalization of congressional politicians in the twentieth century,[42] people in Congress have a greater stake than ever before in protecting their institution's independence and reinforcing their chances for reelection. They have done so in part by building large and independent staffs as well as by strengthening agencies supporting congressional activity such as the General Accounting Office.[43] The buildup of personal and committee staffs has reinforced the power of the parts of Congress—individuals and committee or subcommittee units—as against the whole, further fragmenting the system and increasing the emphasis on the individual rather than the party.

Third, because the American system is so fragmented, with no unified government and a decentralized party system, strong subsystems for decisionmaking (so-called subgovernments) are encouraged. It is not the case that subgovernments are unique to the United States; far from it. What seems to be unusual in the United States is the relative balance of power between central authorities (the government) and subgovernments. Because there is no "government" and no party unity, "the American system . . . is best described as lopsided because the power of sub-governments is so great in relation to collective authority."[44] Congressional committees are organized so that their subcommittees match bureau-level structures in the administrative agencies. The committees, in turn, encourage, and often require through statute, an organization of the bureaucracy that meshes with congressional organization and needs. Narrowly focused interest groups that mirror and support these bureaus and congressional interests are key actors in the process. Because subgovernments often have such a powerful influence over policy and administration, and because it is unusually difficult for central authorities—either the president or Congress as a whole—to successfully assert their authority over them, attribution of responsibility for policy and administration is more difficult in the United States than even the formal elements of the system of separate institutions sharing powers would lead one to expect.

Overview

To recapitulate, the structure of American government and the assumptions behind it make congressional oversight of administration and policy important—to aid in the review and the control of administrative officials and to maintain Congress's role as a coequal branch—and problematic. Efforts by Congress to review and control may even at times be counterproductive from the standpoint of the balance of power between elected and nonelected officials and of coordinated control of policy and administration. While the U.S.

system was originally designed to increase the ability of government to act beyond the level likely under the Articles of Confederation, it emphasized liberty (avoiding tyranny) over efficiency and integration. Since its designers did not envision either a large state or a large corps of administrators, little thought was given to problems of democratic control of bureaucracy. The system the United States has, structurally (separate institutions sharing powers) and by culture and extraconstitutional institutions (weak parties, fragmented power in the Congress, and so on), provides multiple masters of the large bureaucracy that has developed. When public opinion or interest groups demand it, or intra- or interinstitutional rivalries inspire it, or even when the spirit is there for idiosyncratic reasons, congressional actors in the U.S. system are unusually well positioned to respond by playing an active role in relation to the bureaucracy through various means, including oversight of policy and administration.

The latter is the main focus of this book. In studying congressional oversight, my aim, of course, is to understand the phenomenon better—its causes, correlates, and consequences—but my final goal is broader and deeper. The study of oversight is an avenue to understanding the complex problem of democratic control of bureaucracy and the even more complex world of politics and policy in the United States.

The core of this book examines oversight in a systematic manner, using historical (longitudinal) and interview data focused on committee behavior. The book raises, and goes some distance in answering, a series of questions about oversight behavior and about the theories that political scientists have used to explain it. It concludes with a broad consideration of the role of congressional oversight in the American political system.

Appendix A describes in detail my study design and the methods I used to gather the data analyzed in the book. The study concentrates on committee oversight behavior because most oversight activities are committee centered. I analyze longitudinal data drawn from the *Daily Digest* of the *Congressional Record* on committee oversight activities for the years 1961 to 1983. Interviews with congressional personnel—primarily key committee staff but also elected members—complement these data. The interviews focused on oversight in its many forms, ranging well beyond the formal hearings and meetings listed in the *Daily Digest*. I also used other information sources, including roundtable discussions held at the Brookings Institution with executive branch and congressional personnel, to broaden and deepen my understanding of oversight.

Most scholars agree that, despite the import of the congressional oversight role, there has been little formal oversight activity by Congress (such as hearings that review programs or policies).[45] They also agree that other types of oversight are mainly reactive in nature, with Congress waiting for information to come to it.[46] This pattern of behavior is explained primarily in terms of the electoral incentives experienced by members of Congress. In the academic literature, and in the view of many inside observers, members are seen as reelection-seeking political entrepreneurs who spend their time and resources on activities yielding the greatest electoral payoff. It is argued that to those in Congress the cost-benefit ratio of oversight activity is low relative to the alternatives (such as gaining credit for enacting new programs). Therefore, formal oversight is infrequent and other types of oversight activity are overwhelmingly passive, involving little time or effort. However, in this book I demonstrate and analyze a dramatic increase in one type of formal oversight activity (hearings) since the early 1970s. And I present significant evidence to suggest that Congress is now much more active than before in searching out information about the executive branch.

My analysis emphasizes the fact that Congress acts in a dynamic political environment. Changing environmental factors interact with the institutional characteristics of American government to shape congressional oversight behavior. The changed political environment beginning in the early 1970s increased the payoffs of oversight relative to other activities, and Congress responded accordingly. In essence, in this book I retain the underlying logic of theorists who view congressional behavior in terms of member incentives. I look at behavior, however, from a dynamic perspective in which changing context alters the relative payoff to be gained from various activities. In describing such a perspective, Joseph Cooper and Cheryl D. Young note "self-interest per se has no definitive or absolute meaning as a guide to action. . . . The concrete, operational meaning of self-interest is always relative to context and informed by context."[47] When members of Congress see a pressing interest or political advantage to interjecting themselves into the administrative side of government, they can do so—in contrast to legislators in other countries—with relative ease. There is a potential for substantial oversight activity inherent in the American governmental system, and conditions since the early 1970s have stimulated Congress to increase the level and aggressiveness of its oversight.

Part One
Trends in Congressional Oversight

Chapter 2

Changing Congressional Oversight

THIS CHAPTER is an introduction to the history and dynamics of congressional oversight. The first section provides a broad historical and institutional perspective on the amount and nature of oversight, giving special emphasis to the reasons why there is so much dissatisfaction with oversight both inside and outside Congress. The second section looks at trend data on congressional oversight behavior. It documents changes in the amount of oversight and looks at linkages between changes in the environment and changes in congressional behavior. The data suggest that Congress increases oversight activity in response to changes in its environment, thus realizing, when conditions are right, much of the potential for active oversight inherent in the American governmental system. Indeed, such factors as a growing perception on the part of congressional personnel that the citizenry felt increasingly burdened by government's growing size and complexity, a related scarcity of resources, a heightening of the normal tension between the president and Congress stimulated by the aggressive posture of the Nixon administration on policy control, and the effects of internal changes in Congress seemed to work together to increase the attractiveness of oversight. By the mid-1970s the level of oversight had increased dramatically, reaching and sustaining very substantial levels.

A Historical and Institutional Perspective

Prior to the emergence of a more powerful government in the late nineteenth century and certainly before the changes wrought by the New Deal, there was little concern about congressional oversight of administration and policy. In part, this inattention to the issue prevailed because of the small size of the American state and its relatively minor impact on daily life. In part, the unconcern reflected the power Congress actually exerted over the bureaucracy.

The early federal bureaucracy was not very numerous. As James Q. Wilson points out, while the number of civilian federal employees increased eightfold from 1816 to 1861 (from 4,837 to 36,672), "86 percent of this growth was the result of additions to the postal service."[1] After the Federalist period, when the details of running the executive branch were left to the administration, Congress reacted (with the cooperation of President Thomas Jefferson) with more energetic attempts to control administration.[2] Allen Schick catalogues a series of restrictions Congress imposed or attempted to impose in an effort to control the particulars of administration and policy. He emphasizes that

> Congress was the dominant branch through most of the nineteenth century (wartime was the major exception) as its increasingly powerful and specialized committees imposed their preferences on the White House and executive agencies. In those years, Congress initiated and drafted most legislation—the president's role as "chief legislator" was not fully developed until the New Deal—and it often legislated in very great detail. Individual positions and their salaries were itemized in law; post roads were plotted by Congress; tariff schedules were enacted for hundreds of imported goods; pensions were voted for designated soldiers and their survivors. In the context of contemporary legislation, it is hard to imagine the extent to which Congress got involved in administrative matters; . . . These legislative practices alarmed a young scholar—Woodrow Wilson—who in his influential 1885 book, *Congressional Government*, charged that Congress "has entered more and more into the details of administration until it has virtually taken into its own hands all the substantial powers of government."[3]

As the state expanded its functions in the second half of the nineteenth century as promoter, military power, and regulator, the size of the federal bureaucracy grew accordingly. Wilson points out that "between 1861 and 1901, over 200,000 civilian employees were added to the federal service, only 52 percent of whom were postal workers."[4] This increase in the size of the federal establishment (it reached 550,000 by the 1920s) made it more and more difficult for Congress to play the rather comprehensive controlling role assumed for most of the nineteenth century.[5] Even though Congress became more "institutionalized" during this period[6] (as the government influence shifted from the state to the federal level, long-term congressional careers became more attractive, which in turn contributed to increased congressional expertise), and more decentralized after the revolt against Speaker Joseph G. Cannon (an event related to the growing career aspects of congressional life), Schick convincingly argues that the scope of Congress's traditional control tasks overwhelmed the legislative body.[7] The growth of government in size and complexity, coupled with such factors as the influence of efficiency doctrines advocated by the Progressive movement, led Congress to cede much of its influence over the bureaucracy to the president in the Budget and Accounting Act of 1921.

However, Congress did not fully cede its influence. A strong committee structure remained in place with experienced, senior members firmly in control. This, coupled with acts of omission in the Budget and Accounting Act, such as Congress's rejection of the "proposal that it bar itself from appropriating more than the amounts recommended in the president's budget,"[8] led to a system of cooperative control under the Republican presidents of the 1920s. As Schick says, "The president willingly served Congress because his interests were closer to those of the legislative branch than to those of the executive agencies. No less than Congress, the White House felt helpless in the face of agency expansion."[9]

This fairly tranquil relationship of cooperation between the president and Congress was short-lived. To quote Schick again, "The New Deal and World War II changed the relationship between the executive and legislative branches and made the president chief executive in his own right, not merely as the agent of Congress. These critical events fueled an enormous expansion of the federal government and a redistribution of power between the two branches."[10]

The Roosevelt period and its aftermath saw presidential leadership institutionalized.[11] A large staff was built up. Equally important, the leadership role of the president was fully legitimated. Franklin D. Roosevelt shaped the modern office and our conception of it. Though he certainly did not enjoy continuous smooth sailing in his relationship with Congress, indeed Congress clearly continued as the world's most powerful legislative body with great influence over agency behavior, there is little question that by the time Roosevelt died, presidential leadership was celebrated as "the embodiment of national political leadership and benevolence."[12] Again, Congress continued to have great influence, but compared with earlier periods it was less influential than the president and his direct agents. Congress now "meddled" less in foreign affairs than before and in the domestic sphere granted wider discretion to many of the executive agencies within a context of enhanced presidential oversight capability.

Though this is the governmental system that most Americans who came of political age before the late 1960s were weaned on, one must remember that it was a fairly recent phenomenon, related to changes in the scope and size of government and to increasingly effective presidential leadership. For these generations it was the natural way the system operated, but it was at odds with Congress's more traditional role vis-à-vis the presidency and the bureaucracy and with the institutional power base given Congress by the constitutional framework. Not surprisingly, Congress started to fight back, weakly at first and then with increasing vigor.

The Legislative Reorganization Act was passed in 1946. The act streamlined the congressional committee system by reducing the number of committees in both chambers, clarifying committee jurisdictions, establishing a new budget process (which failed in a short time), and providing additional staff for the standing committees to give them expertise independent of that available through the executive branch. The act also provided the first formal congressional endorsement of oversight, directing the committees to maintain "continuous watchfulness" over the activities of the executive agencies.[13]

As Roger H. Davidson and Walter J. Oleszek point out in their excellent study of House reforms, "The reformers of 1946 believed that strengthening the committee system strengthened Congress itself. That was necessary because congressmen were concerned about the growing power of the executive branch and recognized the imperative of reestablishing Congress' role as a co-equal branch of government."[14]

A dilemma, however, accompanied this belief in strengthening Congress in relation to the executive branch. The interests of individual members of Congress and those of the institution as a whole did not (and do not) mesh very well. "The central dilemma of the contemporary Congress," as Davidson and Oleszek note, "is that individual legislators' careers are separated from the collective product of the institution. Performance is collective but accountability is individual."[15]

This theme of individual versus collective interests guides much of the recent analysis of congressional reform. Lawrence C. Dodd's thesis in "Congress and the Quest for Power," and in subsequent revisions of the essay, is that the career-oriented people elected to Congress react to executive challenges to the power of the institution by enacting reforms to strengthen Congress, but they draw back from effectively centralizing congressional decisionmaking, and thereby assuring congressional power, because they entered Congress in the first place in hopes of building personal power through the congressional career. As a result, the reforms enacted are flawed by considerations of "personal power prerogatives."

> The attempt to protect personal prerogatives while centralizing power builds structural flaws into the centralizing mechanisms, flaws that would not be present were the significance of congressional structure for the national power of Congress itself the only motive. The existence of these flaws provides the openings through which centralization procedures are destroyed when institutional crises pass and members again feel free to emphasize personal power and personal careers.[16]

In essence, in 1946 Congress took a step (soon aborted) toward policy coordination through a joint committee on the budget, made its committee system somewhat stronger and probably more rigid because of the seniority system, increased its capabilities in comparison with the executive branch through increased staffing, and told itself to oversee the executive. Whatever else the reforms may have done, they did not solve either the problems of the committee system or of oversight. Many members chafed under the restrictions of the restructured committees, and the level of oversight was generally regarded as unsatisfactory.

The problems were manifold. With participatory opportunities limited by the senior southern Democrats who chaired the committees for most of the early postwar years, younger and more liberal members felt they lacked adequate influence. Bills opposed by the committee chairmen were easily bottled up in committee, and congressional influence over the bureaucracy was tightly held. A few prospered, the rest were told to wait and defer: "to get along, go along."[17] This created growing tensions within Congress, which eventually found expression in another spasm of reform.

The small academic literature on oversight that developed during the period between the passage of the Legislative Reorganization Act of 1946 and the wave of reforms in the early 1970s took two somewhat different tacks. One noted signs of a post-1946 increase in oversight and expressed concern about its often harmful consequences. The other emphasized the still low level of oversight activity (compared with other endeavors) and, while not ignoring the many problems involved, asked how Congress could be made a more active overseer.

Joseph P. Harris's 1964 study, *Congressional Control of Administration*, is the prime example of the first perspective. He reported an increase in the number and cost of investigations after passage of the 1946 act.[18] He also reported that standing committees, as opposed to special and select committees, were now the dominant investigators of administration and policy, a finding in line with the spirit of the 1946 act.

However, Harris was uneasy about the nature and implications of congressional, and especially congressional committee, activities related to administration and policy. Control before the fact of implementation through detailed statutes, prescription of administrative organization, and the like was proper, although best done in "close cooperation"[19] with the executive. After the fact oversight of administrative activities was undeniably legitimate but also "subject to serious weaknesses."[20] Given the political incentives of the legislative body, Harris said, "committees have often conducted such inquiries with more zeal than discretion, and have been guilty of unfortunate excesses and failure to act in a judicial manner."[21] He approvingly quotes George B. Galloway's statement that "inquiry is an instrument unsuited to frequent or continuous employment and justified only by grave circumstances."[22]

Harris's book gives clear evidence of an interest in ensuring some legislative control, but it is grounded in the dominant views of the period—both in the public administration literature and in the prevalent emphasis on presidential and administrative legitimacy. The chain of administrative command should be clear and lead to a powerful, well-staffed presidency. "Legislative controls which are unduly detailed stifle initiative; make for inflexibility and inefficiency in the conduct of governmental programs; sometimes result in imposing the will of individual legislators, or small groups, in matters in which they do not speak for the entire legislature and which are best left to executive officials; and end in frustrating the basic will of the legislative body."[23] Neither the president nor even administrators should be too encumbered because they represent the public interest far better than the narrow, insulated Congress with its rigid, unrepresentative committee structure and its parochial makeup.[24]

Congress did little to enhance its reputation during this period, in part made notorious by Senator Joseph McCarthy's reckless and ruthless inquiries in the early 1950s. Harris's book catalogues the weaknesses of many congressional investigations with their partisanship, harassment of officials, ill effects on agency operations, and the inefficient manner in which they were conducted because of the lack of congressional expertise.[25] He readily concedes the importance of legislative oversight in a democratic system but emphasizes that it "should not become excessive or encroach upon the executive function."[26]

There were academic pieces that had different emphases. While Harris noted the postwar increase in oversight hearings and "the leaps and bounds increase" in investigation funds "generated by the 1946 act," the most quoted characterization of the amount of oversight in this era comes from John Bibby's essay on "Oversight and the Need for Congressional Reform," subtitled "Congress' Neglected Function."[27] Bibby's analysis, based on a review of the limited number of scholarly works available, mainly case studies on oversight produced in the 1960s, and on his 1967 survey of House standing committees, concluded that there was "much less oversight being done than would be expected in the light of the official pronouncements of the Congress and the scholarly commentaries which assert the pervasiveness of the activity. Indeed, the House survey revealed such a limited amount of oversight that it raises the question of whether legislative oversight is not a phase of legislative behavior where scholarly generalizations have preceded description and analysis."[28]

Harris closed his book with a call for a joint legislative-executive commission "to re-examine the essential meaning of the oversight responsibility placed on Congress by the Constitution" and hoped that such an inquiry would lead to "an increasing cooperation between Congress and the Executive branch through which legislative oversight will be strengthened where it is needed and the kind of controls that hamper administration will be reduced."[29] But Bibby expressed little concern about such issues. He emphasized giving Congress "the tools and the necessary institutional arrangements to effectively perform the oversight job" and taking steps so that "Members of Congress . . . see more clearly their own and their country's stake in performing the oversight function."[30] Bibby's interest was in finding ways to make oversight more "comprehensive, continuing, and systematic," not in a delicate balancing of the need for oversight against the needs of the executive for a cooperative Congress.[31]

It is probably not surprising that Bibby was so firm an advocate of congressional oversight. He was writing, after all, for *The Republican Papers*, a volume edited by a traditional midwest Republican congressman, Melvin Laird, in a time following one of the great Democratic legislative outpourings of the twentieth century—President Lyndon B. Johnson's Great Society program. Many traditional Republicans were hoping for scrutiny of these programs, which they considered a great overreaching by the federal government. Active review by Congress also fit nicely with their Whig view of institutional roles.

However, the receptiveness to oversight was grounded in political events that made those on all sides of the political spectrum interested in a more active congressional role. The establishment of many new programs under Johnson further imbalanced the power of the two branches as the presidential role was enhanced. For a time, key congressional personnel were apparently satisfied with whatever share of the credit they received for the legislation they helped pass. But by the late 1960s there were problems mounting in these programs when it became apparent that the nation could not have a painless guns (Vietnam) and butter (Great Society) policy. Opposition to the war in Vietnam increased—a war that the Johnson administration could neither end nor insulate from domestic politics. The license granted by Congress to the president by the Tonkin Gulf Resolution was more and more resented in Congress. Johnson's coalition crumbled.

The net effect was to reawaken concern about Congress's role. This concern was stimulated by the administration of Richard M. Nixon who, lacking a majority in Congress, eventually devised his "administrative presidency" strategy.[32] In essence, Nixon more and more ignored Congress when it would not do what he wished. He impounded appropriated funds, harassed civil servants in programs favored by congressional committees, and prosecuted the Vietnam War as he saw fit. He challenged Congress in a clear and open way.

As part of its response, Congress continued to press itself to do more oversight. It implicitly accepted the assessment in the Bibby analysis that oversight was its "neglected function." In the oversight section of the report issued in 1974 by the Select Committee on Committees (Bolling Committee), the committee approvingly quoted a statement by a member asserting the following: "There is not sufficient oversight, and I doubt there is sufficient oversight in any committee of the Congress"; and "With all our efforts, therefore, what I am saying is that the Congress is just barely making a scratch on the oversight of the executive branch in any one year."[33] Several reform efforts were made and some reforms adopted.

In the 1970 amendments to the Legislative Reorganization Act of 1946, Congress attempted to stimulate more oversight by requiring that most committees issue biennial reports on their oversight endeavors. The act also "authorized additional staff assistance for all standing committees, . . . strengthened the role of CRS [the Congressional Research Service] and . . . empowered the General Accounting Office to do program evaluation."[34] In 1974 the House adopted a set of reforms (H. Res. 988) that made numerous changes in the rules about oversight. The Government Operations Committee was to issue a report within sixty days after a new Congress convened on the oversight plans of House committees and, in a vaguely specified way, it was to assist in coordinating the other committees' oversight plans. Special oversight authority (to conduct reviews of areas that cross committee jurisdictional lines) was granted to eight committees. Committees were encouraged to create oversight subcommittees.[35] Senate interest in increasing and improving oversight was indicated in the *Final Report of the Commission on the Operation of the Senate*[36] and by the Senate support for Sunset legislation in 1978. (Sunset is a review of programs on a periodic basis with termination possible unless Congress renews them.)

As was true of the 1946 congressional reforms, reforms adopted in the 1970s "seem to have cut in opposite directions"[37] because members were trying at one and the same time to strengthen Congress as an institution while protecting and enhancing their personal prospects in regard to power and career. The changes made to affect oversight were not insignificant, but they were watered down. The Bolling Committee, for example, proposed that the House Government Operations Committee be strengthened by allowing it to offer privileged amendments to other committees' legislation based on Government Operations' oversight findings. This proposal was intended to make membership on Government Operations and, therefore, oversight work more attractive. It was also meant to bring to bear on House policy decisions the objectivity and perspective of members of a broad-gauged oversight committee. The proposal was rebuffed. Instead, the House adopted a weaker provision that relevant oversight findings of the Government Operations Committee be included in committee legislative reports.[38] The Bolling Committee also considered but shied away from recommending various proposals to establish a leadership oversight agenda for House committees. The emphasis would have been on central coordination of committee priorities.[39]

Decisions protecting and even enhancing individual power were common in the way the House dealt with the Bolling Committee recommendations and marked other changes as well.[40] The so-called Subcommittee Bill of Rights enacted in the early 1970s gave a large number of members a big stake in protecting the status of their units.[41] (They were now chairs of subcommittees with real institutional authority from which they derived status and influence.) In the case just described, where the Government Operations Committee was to get to offer privileged amendments to other committees' legislation, and thereby gain some leverage over decisions, there was little incentive for those in other units who had a legislative power stake to cede any part of it. Davidson and Oleszek describe successful resistance to many of the jurisdictional changes proposed by the Bolling Committee in these terms.[42] The irony of the decentralization reforms is that they aimed to break the power, enhanced in the 1946 reforms, of the committee oligarchs who stifled democratic, collective rule in the House, and they unintendedly created a form of "sub-committee government" that also created problems for the House as a collectivity.[43]

It is not necessary to review the full record of the reforms here, both oversight and nonoversight,[44] other than to repeat that those adopted by Congress were not as sweeping as the reforms discussed or proposed in part because member and committee "self-interest often prevails over institutional welfare."[45] Members clearly wanted to see more and better oversight done, just as they wanted to strengthen Congress in other areas, but they tended to water down or not to adopt proposals that risked their prerogatives as individuals or as committee members. They were willing, however, to build up staff resources, both in-house and in the support agencies, to assist them in their oversight and other work. In the period following the oversight-related reforms of the early 1970s, the wherewithal was in place for much activity, although there was no guarantee that more oversight would occur or that it would meet high standards of quality.

Just as the reforms enacted in the postwar period as part of the original Legislative Reorganization Act were flawed from an institutional perspective by the desire to protect personal prerogatives, so the reforms enacted in the 1970s exhibited the same characteristics. As Dodd says in his summary of the postwar congressional reforms, some of which did strengthen the central leadership of Congress up to a point: "Underneath the centralizing reforms, which might seem to make Congress less attractive for particular individuals, the dispersion of power of the 1947 to 1973 era remains, institutionalized by a Subcommittee Bill of Rights and augmented by further decentralization decisions that occurred as part of the 1973–75 era. Numerous subcommittee chairs and the resources that go with them, as well as an appearance of power and status, all exist to draw members back to Congress."[46]

I will examine the impact of several of the reforms affecting oversight behavior in the next chapter (particularly the creation of oversight subcommittees and the decentralization reforms), but first I turn to a key issue. With the emergence of the American administrative state, Congress has prodded itself to do more oversight. Yet reformers inside and outside of Congress rarely seem satisfied with the results of this prodding, either in regard to the amount of oversight done or its nature and results. Why?

Dissatisfaction with Oversight

In 1946 Congress set a very high standard for itself. It mandated that each standing committee "exercise continuous watchfulness of the execution by the administrative agencies concerned of any laws, the subject matter of which is within the jurisdiction of such committee; and, for that purpose, shall study all pertinent reports and data submitted to the Congress by the agencies in the executive branch of the Government."[47] In purely quantitative terms, the mandate seemed to require congressional committees to maintain a steady watch—not necessarily day by day perhaps, but on a "continuous" basis—over the activities of all of the agencies under their jurisdictions. The implied standard calls for oversight to take up a significant share of any committee's time and effort. It requires active review of agency behavior defined in broad terms and comprehensive study of the reports and data that agencies submit to Congress— both formidable tasks.

Given the standard set, it is not surprising that people inside of Congress and out who believe that oversight is a vital congressional function would tend to think that it is "neglected." Harris, who was more ambivalent about the role of Congress than Bibby (or many of the congressional reformers), might look at the increase in congressional investigations in the postwar period and express concern. Others would look at the same increase and regard it as less significant, since formal oversight activities took up such a small part of Congress's time in this period.[48]

Indeed, in academic studies a little cottage industry grew up that attempted to explain why the level of oversight activity was so low. These studies put a heavy emphasis on political incentives. They argued that under most circumstances members of Congress found better political payoffs in endeavors such as sponsoring legislation to create new programs or using their contacts with the agencies to secure particular benefits and services for their constituents than in reviewing agency activities or evaluating the effectiveness and efficiency of programs or policies.[49]

In fact, the 1973 hearings of the Bolling Committee produced an exchange between academics and the congressional panel in which there was a wonderful role reversal, with the academics saying that oversight was infrequently done because there was usually little political payoff from it, a realpolitik explanation, and the congressional panelists asking them to rise above such explanations and offer suggestions for reform. The following exchange occurred between Professor Richard Fenno, one of the most eminent students of Congress, and Representative John Culver. Professor Fenno's comment was, "When the incentive isn't there, you are simply not going to get oversight," and Representative Culver replied,

> I am really at a loss to follow you when you say there is not adequate political incentive. I think there should be. What we need from you are suggestions as to how to strengthen the organizational design and shape and activities of the Congress and its members so that we can build into our system a far more effective program of congressional oversight.
>
> After all, it is our primary responsibility. If there is any disenchantment in the country, it derives from the validity of the thought that in this respect, Congress is pathetic.
>
> I hope we can get something more from you than the idea that there is not enough political incentive.[50]

Those academics emphasizing political incentives held that members of Congress might well oversee programs when a blatant scandal in an agency made review almost unavoidable and promised considerable publicity for the overseer. Members might also want to oversee when complaints by constituents or agency clientele groups were severe and personal intervention on a case-by-case basis by the member had not remedied the particular problem. Or members could be interested in some program for idiosyncratic reasons. But, in the main, analysts said, key committee members were advocates for "their" programs and did not see much benefit in scrutinizing them too closely unless pressed. Many members of Congress seemed to agree when they spoke frankly. (The incentives framework, of course, had been derived from studies using congressional informants.) In the Bolling Committee hearings, for example, Representative William R. Poage, who was the chairman of the House Agriculture Committee and a veteran of the House, voiced this view very clearly. In answer to a comment by Representative David Martin of Nebraska that "many of our committees have been negligent in this area in follow-through on how programs are working," Poage said,

> We have been somewhat slow. . . . But I would point out that the alternative is to stir up a political "porridge pot" where you simply have things boiling all of the time, . . . to drag out some issue every 2 years for the campaign, . . . About all we would accomplish, as I see it, is to create hard feelings. . . . Maybe we are too critical at times. Maybe we are not critical enough at other times. But I think that you must bear in mind that if we do overdo this we destroy the effectiveness of the administrative agencies. I think by and large our Department of Agriculture has been doing a pretty fair job.[51]

It is not too surprising, therefore, in light of the standard set for oversight quantity and the apparent reasons for failure to achieve that standard, that reformers were dissatisfied with the nature of the oversight done and with its results.

Implicit in the 1946 call for "continuous watchfulness" and for scrutiny of agency reports and data submitted to Congress, and in the consequent strengthening of the analytic capacities of congressional support agencies, was a style of oversight as well as a quantitative expectation. Good oversight should be comprehensive and systematic. Academics writing on the subject stressed this, but so did those within Congress attempting to reform the oversight process.

In the Bolling Committee report, for example, the section on oversight stressed that in the extensive hearings held by the committee "representatives and other witnesses were virtually unanimous in acknowledging the inadequate oversight being done by congressional committees."[52] And some of the comments of members reproduced after this statement make clear that the authors meant more than quantitative inadequacy. For example, "I think that Congress has been derelict to a great degree by not having the force or the means at its command to do the type of oversight that should have been done in the past."[53]

Students of oversight made similar judgments. Bibby, for example, while noting that oversight was rarely "continuing," also stressed that it was not "comprehensive" and infrequently involved "systematic reviews of policies and performances of administrative agencies."[54] Morris Ogul's book flatly asserts that "there is consensus in the Congress that comprehensive and systematic oversight *ought* to be conducted," even though this rarely happens.[55]

Later I will examine the reasons why it is unusual for oversight to be comprehensive or systematic. For now, it is enough to say that congressional style, even for most active overseers, clashes with the norm of comprehensive and systematic oversight work. Congress most often uses an incremental, error-correcting strategy. Evidence generated in a "systematic" manner—assuming for the moment that an incremental, error-correcting style is not systematic, an assumption that clearly fits the norms of those using these terms in reference to oversight—may well be used, but it is likely to be used selectively.

If the nature of congressional oversight is neither comprehensive nor systematic, what does this mean for the way oversight results are employed? The oversight reformers hoped that Congress would use oversight results to ensure "that scarce resources are expended wisely and that programs that are not working as anticipated would be modified or even terminated."[56] This theme was not an isolated one, since it was implicit in the Congressional Budget Act of 1974 and explicit in many of the Sunset reforms suggested in later years.[57] Congress was to use oversight to consider trade-offs, make hard choices, even make big changes or cutbacks.

Institutional power might well be enhanced by a process that used comprehensive and systematic oversight results for trade-off decisions, but the power and reelection prospects of the senators and representatives serving on most of the subcommittees of Congress would be lessened. Not surprisingly, therefore, the members of the committee units of Congress doing the oversight often had very different things in mind than the oversight reformers. As we shall see, committee members usually wanted to protect the basic integrity of "their" programs, tinkering with them for their own purposes and those of their constituents perhaps, but only the rare committee unit was willing to see the programs in its jurisdiction cut in favor of another unit's programs. Oversight, for them, was not greatly valued as an input to a centralized decisionmaking process.

To recapitulate briefly, after the first century of the Republic, as the government grew to the point at which it consumed significant resources and had a large presence in American life, Congress's very powerful role in relation to policy and administration was called into question. Power previously held by Congress was ceded to the presidency, which, slowly at first and then rapidly in the New Deal and World War II eras, became more and more important in American political life. Congress gave the president great budgetary powers and increased staff. A consequence was increased presidential influence over policy and program administration. Some of Congress's influence was thus offset in an attempt to rationalize the policy process. The uncoordinated, complex relationships implied by the system of separate institutions sharing powers was challenged even in Congress by a concern about central political control over the rapidly expanding government, an emerging orthodoxy of efficiency, and a doctrine holding that the president was the natural "chief administrator."

However, the relative congressional passivity of these years (and I stress the word relative, since Congress ceded only some of its influence) was short-lived. The postwar period witnessed a definite concern by Congress to redress the balance of influence on administration and policy. It has acted to achieve this goal, but Congress's actions often "cut in opposite directions" because members try to balance their personal needs against the needs of the institution.[58] Indeed, in a weak party, entrepreneurial legislative system like that in the United States, individuals' needs are rarely neglected.

Because of the standards set for oversight (a high level of activity carried out in a systematic and comprehensive way and contributing to a "rational" process of congressional priority setting), those who advocate oversight as a mechanism for enhancing congressional control of administration and of policy made as part of administration have rarely been content with what is done. The incentives of the elected members, it seems, do not mesh well with behaviors expected by many advocates of an enhanced congressional oversight role.

Trends in Congressional Oversight

Is there any evidence, in light of the prodding to do more, that the amount of congressional oversight behavior has changed? In this section I focus on changes in one type of oversight behavior—congressional committee hearings and meetings devoted primarily to

TABLE 2-1. *Hearings and Meetings of Congressional Committees,
January 1–July 4, 1961–83*[a]

Year	Total days[b]	Oversight days[c]	Oversight as percent of total
1961	1,789	146	8.2
1963	1,820	159	8.7
1965	2,055	141	6.9
1967	1,797	171	9.5
1969	1,804	217[d]	12.0
1971	2,063	187	9.1
1973	2,513	290	11.5
1975	2,552	459	18.0
1977	3,053	537	17.6
1981	2,222	434	19.5
1983	2,331	587	25.2
		Percent change	
1961–71	15.3	28.1	11.0
1961–77	70.7	267.8	114.6
1961–83	30.3	302.1	207.3

a. Hearings and meetings held by Appropriations, Rules, Administration, and Joint Committees are excluded. See appendixes A and B for details on the *Daily Digest* data. The 1979 data are missing because they were not coded.

b. Total days means a count of the total number of days that committees met for any purpose during the time covered.

c. Oversight days means days committees devoted to primary-purpose oversight. Day is shorthand for a hearing or meeting. The typical event lasted two or three hours on a given date.

d. Large number of oversight days occurs mostly because of one unusually long series of hearings (33 days) on a single topic.

oversight. This is just one example of oversight behavior and has its limitations.[59] However, it is one of the better established indicators of formal committee activity and is the most reliable way of looking at trends.[60]

The data in table 2-1 display the raw facts on congressional committee hearing and meeting activity for the first six months (January 1 to July 4) of each odd-numbered year from 1961 to 1983 (except for 1979).[61] This period covers the years of the 1960s when oversight was described as Congress's "neglected function," through the period of heightened internal congressional reform and external conflict with the president, and ends with the first two Congresses of the Reagan administration.

The data (described in detail in appendixes A and B) include the meetings and hearings of all House and Senate committees except Appropriations, House Rules, House Administration, and Senate Rules and Administration.[62] The committees dealing with rules and administration were excluded from the analysis because of their preoccupation with internal chamber business. The Appropriations Committees were excluded for reasons of comparability. Until the 93d Congress, the House Appropriations Committee followed a unique tradition: it reported very few of its hearings or meetings for inclusion in the *Daily Digest*, the source of these data.

A look at the total days column in table 2-1 shows that the overall level of hearing and meeting activity did not vary much from 1961 to 1971. The mean for this period (1961–71) is 1,888 days a year, and the totals for all years are within 10 percent of the mean. In 1973, however, the total number of days of activity jumped by 450 from the preceding year coded 1971, which was the highest of the previous period. This total remained approximately the same in 1975 (2,552) and then jumped by 501 in 1977. In the Reagan administration, total days fell back substantially but stayed above the 1971 total by 159 days even in 1981 and climbed again in 1983. The pattern is clear: a steady level of overall hearing and meeting activity in the 1961–71 period followed by big increases first in 1973 and then in 1977, and a diminution in the 1980s but not back to the levels of the 1961–71 period.

The pattern for oversight days is somewhat more complex but can be summarized briefly. The average number of days of oversight was 149 in the years 1961–65, 192 in the years 1967–71 (but only 181 with an unusually long series of hearings held in 1969 removed),[63] and then climbed to 290 in 1973, and up to 587 in 1983. Growth over this period is quite apparent, with some increase starting in 1967 over the three previous data points, but the most marked increases occurring in 1973 and 1975. Starting in 1975, the total number of oversight days never dips below 434 and averages 477, more than three times the 1961–65 average.

Not only did oversight increase in absolute terms during this period, it more than held its own as a percentage of total activity.

Oversight averaged 7.9 percent of total activity for the three years' observations from 1961 to 1965, 10.2 percent from 1967 to 1971 (9.6 percent with the 33-day series in 1969 removed), 11.5 percent in 1973, and up to 18.0 percent in 1975. Even though the number of days of hearing and meeting activity rose to more than 3,000 during the first six months of 1977, oversight just about kept pace at 17.6 percent of total activity. It seems, in fact, that by the mid- to late 1970s it is hard any longer to justify calling oversight Congress's neglected function. And in the somewhat less active congressional sessions of the Reagan period (averaging about 2,275 days of total activity), oversight stayed at about the 1977 level or higher, so that it reached the highest percentages of the total recorded in these data: 19.5 percent in 1981 and 25.2 percent in 1983.

Perhaps these data are somehow atypical. It is posssible that the measure used is flawed by the considerations discussed in appendix B (for example, lack of clarity in some entries in the *Daily Digest*), and other indicators would lead one to a different view. Or maybe, even if the indicators all lead in one direction, inside observers would have a very different interpretation of what they mean.

However, other indicators do point in the same direction. Table 2-2, for example, shows the number of public bills enacted in each Congress beginning with the 87th (1961–62), and the number of pages per statute. The data support the interpretation that oversight-related activities are on the rise.

The data are best understood by examining legislative output for Congresses after presidential elections (1961–62, 1965–66, . . .) separately from output after off-year elections (1963–64, 1967–68, . . .). The number of statutes passed is generally greater right after a presidential election when the president's position is strongest and his program, therefore, stands the best chance of adoption.[64] Midterm election results and politics tend to dim the president's luster, create greater interinstitutional deadlock, and diminish legislative output somewhat.

If one looks at the immediate postpresidential election Congresses, one sees a steady decline in the number of statutes passed, from 885 in 1961–62, to 810 in 1965–66, down to 633 in 1977–78, and a low of 473 in 1981–82.[65] A weaker version of the same pattern is found for post-midyear election Congresses, where the relevant comparable entries are 666, 640, 588, and 623. The trend is clear, with the

TABLE 2-2. *Number of Public Bills, Pages per Statute,*
Oversight Days, 1961–84

Congress	Number of public bills enacted	Pages per statute	Days of oversight in first six months of odd-numbered years
87th (1961–62)	885	2.3	146
88th (1963–64)	666	3.0	159
89th (1965–66)	810	3.6	141
90th (1967–68)	640	3.6	171
91st (1969–70)	695	4.2	217
92d (1971–72)	607	3.8	187
93d (1973–74)	649	5.3	290
94th (1975–76)	588	7.0	459
95th (1977–78)	633	8.5	537
96th (1979–80)	613	8.1	n.a.
97th (1981–82)	473	9.2	434
98th (1983–84)	623	7.8	587

Correlations (r)
Number of bills and oversight days -0.58
Pages per statute and oversight days 0.95

Source: Norman J. Ornstein, Thomas E. Mann, and Michael J. Malbin, *Vital Statistics on Congress, 1987–1988* (Washington: Congressional Quarterly, 1987), p. 170.
n.a. Not available.

discrepancies between postpresidential and post-midterm statutory output decreasing over time as overall statute output drops, and even reversing themselves in President Reagan's first term.

However, while the number of statutes may be decreasing, the number of pages per statute is on the increase. It peaked in 1981–82 but still was higher in 1983–84 than in any previous year.

The number of data points (eleven) for the series is small enough so that one would want to interpret a correlation coefficient between either of these two indicators and the number of days of oversight with caution, but the relevant statistics are highly suggestive. The correlation between the number of statutes and the number of oversight days is -0.58. Oversight has been increasing while the number of statutes passed has declined. Considering the apparent effects of the electoral cycle on the number of statutes passed described above, this relationship is quite substantial. And the correlation between pages per statute and oversight days is 0.95. Oversight has increased very much in tandem with the increase in the number of pages per statute.

Allen Schick, in his discussion of the phenomena represented by the statute data in table 2-2, is confident that the trends presented reflect an underlying change in American politics. He argues that "whether only in perception or in reality as well, American politics was transformed in the 1970s from affluence to scarcity."[66] As a consequence, politics became more conflictual, with a gain for one group more and more seen as implying some cost to others. Legislating has become more difficult, groups demand to be heard more, Congress spends more time to do less, and the character of its product changes. "Where members are willing to entrust the fate of their policies to administrators, they are apt to legislate in broad terms. The laws can be brief, with little bickering among members over the details. Not so, however, when members are skeptical about whether executive agencies will perform according to their expectations."[67]

Because of new political pressures, Schick argues, legislators want to maintain as much influence as they can over the actions of administrators. The pressures come from changes in the economic environment that, in the 1970s, sowed discord in the "pluralist harmony" of the postwar era. In addition, executive-legislative tensions were exacerbated by Vietnam and Watergate, reinforcing the legislators' desires to play a more important role in program implementation. Changes in the way Congress works owing to democratization at the floor level (making it easier to secure recorded votes and amendments) and changes in committee processes (decentralization, staff increases) also gave more people an opportunity to participate and a greater stake in particular outcomes. More legislators have become involved and want to influence administration and current policy because they have fewer chances to create new programs and more pressures to justify and improve the old. These changes contributed to a whole series of related changes in congressional activities: more oversight hearings of the type measured in table 2-1, certainly, but also more detail in statutes as partially represented by the increases in pages per statute in table 2-2 (and by fewer statutes), more short-term (as opposed to permanent) program authorizations, increased limitations in appropriations bills, and more legislative veto provisions.[68]

Committee insiders agree that oversight activity has been increasing. In my survey of top congressional committee staffers, done for this book and described in appendix A, respondents were asked to evaluate the perception that there had been a "great increase in congressional oversight activity since the early 1970s." They were close to unanimous in agreeing that it had increased greatly. Almost 90 percent of the top staffers, both House and Senate, were comfortable in endorsing the statement in the survey item.[69]

Sometimes respondents, even elite respondents, will simply accede to a suggestion in a survey item. However, the top committee staffers interviewed were willing and able to articulate the reasons why they felt that oversight had increased greatly since the early 1970s. (The question was asked as part of the first round of the interview, so most people were looking back over the decade from the perspective of 1979.)

Table 2-3 presents answers to the question asked of respondents who perceived a great increase in oversight activity: "To what do you attribute the increase in congressional oversight activity?" Entries in table 2-3 are grouped crudely into two categories for presentation purposes: those explanations labeled external, which refer to factors in the broader (external) political environment in which Congress operates, influenced by Congress to be sure but not controlled by Congress alone; and those explanations labeled internal, which refer to factors directly under congressional control in the sense that they are totally within the province of Congress to determine—for example, organizational and internal staff issues. Let me turn first to the external categories.

Explanations based on the increasing size and complexity of government were given by more than 50 percent of the respondents. These explanations focused on public reactions to growing government (its size and perceived inadequacies in performance) and on problems accompanying government growth (complexity, the proliferation of programs and consequent issuance of numerous regulations by the bureaucracy, and so on). Another large explanatory category (mentioned by 22.1 percent of the respondents) is negative congressional reactions to the executive's accrual and/or abuse of power. Like increasing government size and complexity, it involves factors external to congressional operations and not subject to Congress's sole control (although clearly affected by Congress). Congress was

TABLE 2-3. *Top Staffers' Explanations of Why Oversight Has Increased*
Percent[a]

Explanations	All top staffers	Top House staffers	Top Senate staffers
External factors			
Increasing size and complexity of government	55	52	57
Negative reactions to the executive's accrual or abuse of power	22	24	20
Increased publicity value of oversight	7	7	6
Influx of new members interested in oversight	5	7	3
Internal factors			
More or better staff, support agency personnel	27	24	31
Impact of internal congressional reforms	17	26	6
Other (miscellaneous)	14	17	11
N	(77[b])	(42)	(35)

a. Entries are percentages of respondents giving the answers coded under each category. Since some respondents gave multicause explanations, the totals do not add to 100 percent.

b. The number of top staffers indicated (N) is less than 95 because the percentages were calculated on a base excluding those who did not agree that oversight had increased greatly (N = 10), or who said they did not know the answer to the question (N = 4) or were not asked it (N = 4). In other tables throughout this book, Ns may also differ from 95 because of contingency effects or missing data. Explanations of Ns less than 95 will be given only under special circumstances.

described by respondents coded in this category as using increased oversight to offset increasing executive power and assertiveness. The focus was on the behavior of the president and his aides, with emphasis on abuses of the Nixon presidency, not on the actions of the agencies. No one said that the agencies had accrued too much power, a fact to bear in mind at other points in the analysis when we look at congressional views of the agencies.

Finally, note two smaller additional explanatory factors linked to the external environment, the increased publicity value of oversight during the 1970s and, closer to the border between the external environment and the internal, the influx of new members interested in oversight. It is a safe assumption that the increased publicity value of oversight seen by the staffers flows from aspects of the first reason discussed—the increasing size and complexity of government, and perceived reactions to this fact by the broad public and even by program clientele. Likewise, those who cited the influx of new members interested in oversight were, in large part, hypothesizing that the members elected in the 1970s were particularly attuned to the new-found political benefits of oversight owing to factors connected to governmental growth and complexity and to revised notions in the attentive public about the role of Congress in the wake of Nixon administration abuses of power.

This brings me to the second set of factors in table 2-3, those directly under congressional control, which I call internal factors in contrast to the external factors just discussed. Responses focusing on internal factors were also prominent in explaining the great increase in congressional oversight. Indeed, the second largest set of responses to the question focused on more and/or better staff and congressional support agency (Congressional Research Service, General Accounting Office, and so on) personnel. In explaining the increase in oversight, these answers emphasized the role of committee and even personal staff, not the support agency personnel, although the emphasis on committee staff might be expected given the fact that the respondents are committee staffers. About a third of the staffers coded in this broad category, just under 9 percent of the total respondents, even talked spontaneously about increases in staff size leading to efforts by staffers to justify their positions by seeking out oversight assignments.[70]

Finally, there was also a smaller but still sizable emphasis on the impact of internal congressional reforms—oversight reforms in particular, but also decentralization of authority in Congress brought about by the reforms of the early 1970s (increasing the number of subcommittees and the independence of subcommittee chairs, for example). These mentions, particularly the former, were concentrated among House respondents, probably because both oversight and decentralization reforms occurred primarily in the House.

In sum, top committee staffers believed that oversight had greatly increased since the early 1970s and had little trouble finding explanations for the increase. Their explanations emphasized the size and complexity of government, and they also gave quite a bit of weight to negative reactions to executive accrual or abuse of power. Smaller numbers mentioned the increased publicity value of oversight and the influx of new members interested in oversight. These explanations reflect changes in Congress's broader (external) political environment discussed in the first part of this chapter—changes caused by growth in government and greater tensions in congressional relationships with an increasingly imperial presidency. Other explanations offered by top staff cited what I labeled internal factors, such as congressional reforms and staff buildup, as reasons for the increase in oversight. These internal factors were surely influenced by changes in the external environment, but they are subject to direct congressional control in that Congress decides definitively and, in that sense, independently whether or not to increase the size of its staff or to change its rules and procedures.[71] As a result, one might well expect such internal factors to affect institutional behavior patterns such as the amount of oversight done by committees independent of the effects of external factors.

Figure 2-1 charts trends in congressional committee staff size and days of oversight from 1961 to 1983 (excluding 1979 as before because it was not coded).[72] Committee staff size increased at a more even rate than oversight days until 1973, but then it took off rapidly, paralleling the trend in oversight days.[73] Though these two indicators may well show common patterns of movement because of common outside forces influencing each (growing government complexity, for example), it is clear that they do move roughly together and it is at least possible that staff size exerts some independent influence on oversight activity.

Not only do the size of staff and number of oversight days move together in roughly the same manner, the correspondence between a crude indicator of the complexity of government and of its penetration into citizen life—the number of pages in the *Federal Register* each year—and the number of oversight days is equally strong. The *Federal Register* contains the text of final federal regulations, proposed regulations, official notices (notices of agency meetings and the like), and presidential proclamations and orders. It has not been stagnant over the years. Indeed, "as the average length of statutes increased in Congress in the 1970s, the number of pages in the *Federal Register*—

FIGURE 2-1. *Oversight Days and Number of Congressional Committee Staff,* *1961–83*

which among other things displays regulations mandated by these statutes—jumped correspondingly."[74] The pages indicator was selected for the analysis because of the large number of staff respondents who saw a link between the increasing size and complexity of government and increases in the amount of congressional oversight.[75]

Figure 2-2 charts the trend over time in the number of pages in the *Federal Register* and the number of days of oversight coded for congressional committees.

It is evident that there was a very rapid upturn in the number of pages in the *Register* in the early 1970s. From an average of about 20,000 in the late 1960s and in 1970, the number of pages each year began a steady climb, from 25,442 in 1971, to 28,920 in 1972, to 35,586 in 1973, and rapidly upward to 63,629 in 1977, dropping off in the Reagan years in response to a concerted effort to hold the length of the *Register* down as a symbol of the administrations in combating the growth of government. As was the case in the figure 2-1 for staff, 1973 is the turning point in the series. It is here that both indicators evidence their first steep upturns from previous years.[76]

I should make certain points about my argument clear, since the previous pages may suggest a line of reasoning that goes beyond

FIGURE 2-2. *Oversight Days and Pages in the Federal Register, 1961–83*

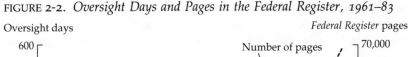

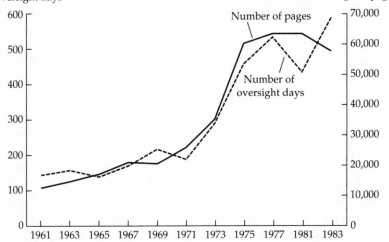

what I mean to convey. I argue that much identifiable internal and external change has affected congressional oversight behavior. This change and its impact on oversight is recognized, at least in retrospect, by many of those working in the area—in particular, the top committee staffers interviewed for this study. It has also been the subject of much recent academic writing as scholars seek to come to grips with its causes and implications. The environment that Congress confronts externally has changed with accompanying changes in the ways Congress operates internally. As a result, the incentives and resources affecting the behavior of congressional actors have also changed over time and congressional oversight behavior has changed with them.

An increase in pages in the *Federal Register* is an indicator of an important change in Congress's external environment. It almost certainly does not cause an increase in oversight in some simple direct sense, even though the relationship over the limited time period examined is so close. However, it is part of a set of environmental stimuli affecting the nature of congressional behavior—its pattern and its sources.[77] The external environment has changed significantly, thereby creating an environment for change in the pattern of congressional behavior. In the oversight area, the changes are reflected in the rising overall level of primary-purpose oversight hearings and in other manifestations of oversight concern discussed earlier such as growth in the number of short-term authorizations, more detailed statutes, and, until the Supreme Court dealt a blow to the practice, a greatly increased number of legislative veto provisions. As a result, by the mid-1970s one could no longer reasonably repeat the simple phrase "Congress's neglected function" and thereby summarize the level of formal congressional oversight activity.

Overview

In the postwar period, Congress showed a pronounced concern with the degree of its influence compared with the president's over administration and policy. This concern was expressed in many ways, including advocacy of more congressional oversight as one means to redress the balance of influence.

There were many skeptics about the likelihood of greater oversight and some who doubted its desirability. One argument put forth by scholars was that Congress did not oversee more often or vigorously because it lacked the incentives to do so. Members of Congress found greater political payoffs in other activities. And they would continue to do so.[78]

Starting with the same basic assumption as the incentives theorists, that those in Congress act mainly from self-interest, I argue like them that the political environment shapes what Congress does in oversight. My argument, however, stresses that in the American separation of powers system Congress has the potential to be an active overseer, a potential significantly realized when conditions are favorable.

This chapter documents a rise in congressional oversight activity, a rise linked by the explanations of congressional personnel and by objective data to a set of changes in the political environment. Under the circumstances outlined, with the relative payoff of oversight apparently up compared with the payoffs from other activities, Congress has displayed a much greater inclination to oversee than it did in earlier years.

As one ambitious Democratic representative said colorfully, and maybe a bit too emphatically, in explaining the politics of the increase in oversight activity:

I think the people of the United States are saying: "We don't want any more new programs. We want existing programs to work better." . . . How does that impact up here? It impacts up here politically. . . . In the 1960s I suspect you could not get any credit for going home and saying, . . . "I'm making this program work better," but rather, you had to go back to your district and say, "I passed the new Joe Zilch piece of handicapped elephant legislation," something like that, right? And you've got a new bill on the wall, and that was what you wanted. Well, that's not where the returns are now. The political returns are from oversight.[79]

However, the documented increase in the quantity of oversight does not guarantee increased satisfaction with what is done. Aside from a very high expectation of "continuous" oversight, an expectation that taken to its logical conclusion would require Congress to spend the vast majority of its time overseeing, many advocates of oversight also want to see it carried out in a systematic and comprehensive way. In this, they are usually disappointed because as chapter 8 in particular will demonstrate, congressional oversight most often is done in a context of program advocacy. Objective evidence may well be used, but it is likely to be used selectively to meet the political needs of committee overseers and their constituencies. So the increase in the level of oversight reported is not likely to satisfy many of the dissatisfied.

In brief, congressional committees are quite capable of reaching and sustaining high levels of oversight activity. The design of American institutions and the concomitant incentives of those in Congress make this possible.

Chapter 3
Why Oversight
Has Changed

F ROM ALL ONE can tell, the amount of oversight done by
Congress increased greatly beginning in the 1970s, and
the increase was linked to changes in the environment outside as
well as inside Congress. Given the explanations for the increases in
the amount of oversight by top congressional staffers, and the way
data on aggregate levels of oversight mesh with broad indicators of
changes suggested by these explanations, this linkage seems quite
plausible.

Drawing inferences from the aggregate data examined in chapter
2 is a reasonable beginning, but there are problems with resting the
argument at this point. There are only eleven data points (each odd-
numbered year from 1961 to 1977, and from 1981 to 1983), and the
congressional environment experienced numerous shocks during this
period. Linking the changes in oversight directly to any one of these
changes or even to a combination of them is risky. The argument is
appealing, since the underlying causes and hypothesized effect have
an intuitive connection, but with so few data points I cannot fine-
tune the analysis enough to have great confidence in it.

However, I can supplement the data presented in chapter 2 by
examining for individual years or clusters of years the relationships
between committee oversight behavior and variables thought to be
relevant to the level of oversight activity. How strong are these
relationships, and do they change over time? Changes in the strength
and pattern of the relationships can then be related to changes in the
broader political environment and to changes in the environment
within Congress (particularly in its organization, structures, and
resources). In essence, inferences about the connection between
environmental changes and changes in the level of oversight activity

48

can be refined and strengthened, although one cannot be fully confident that all of the inferences are correct. Much of the argument about environmental influences ultimately rests on the plausibility of the connections, but it can be buttressed by demonstrating a clear pattern of relationships logically linked to notions about changes in the environment.[1]

The main goals in this chapter, then, are to buttress and refine the basic argument that congressional oversight varies with changes in the environmental stimuli—both external and internal—affecting Congress. I want to understand better how and why the level of oversight changes. The underlying model is that the self-interest of those in Congress, defined in an institutional context, drives oversight behavior. Succinctly put, institutional design features (and related elements of the U.S. political culture) provide the environment in which congressional interests are defined. These design features interact with other environmental conditions in determining how those in Congress will define what it is in their interest to do. Behavior offering little payoff in one period may well be much more attractive in another. Therefore, one would expect congressional oversight behavior to respond to changes in the external and internal congressional environment.

The central analytic feature of the chapter is a multiple regression analysis pooling data from the *Daily Digest* for the years 1961 to 1977. Adjustments are made for years when the estimated regression coefficients suggest relationships that are not stable over time (that is, change appreciably).[2] The aim is to establish the impact of certain factors on the amount of oversight congressional committees do, to examine when and if changes in relationships occur, and to infer the origins of these changes.[3] Multivariate analysis (multiple regression) is the major tool, with some attention to simple (zero-order) relationships where appropriate.

Data from the years 1961 to 1977 are the focal points of this chapter primarily because they were collected and analyzed early in the project. The period covers sufficient years and environmental changes to accomplish the main goal of the chapter, that is, to buttress and refine the basic argument that congressional oversight varies with changes in the environmental stimuli affecting Congress. However, I do not want to ignore the Reagan period—both the facts about oversight in this period and the lessons those facts may teach us about the underlying principles governing oversight behavior. Therefore, after an examination of a model and related material developed from the 1961 to 1977 data, I will look at comparable material from the Reagan years. The goals will be to understand the contemporary environment better and to use the contemporary environment to verify, deepen, and if necessary amend the understanding gained from analysis of earlier data of why the levels of congressional oversight change.

Data, Indicators, and Approach

The data used in the analyses reported in this chapter are the *Daily Digest* data analyzed in the second half of chapter 2, only here the units of analysis are the standing committees of each Congress and major select and special committees. All standing committees except Appropriations and the internal housekeeping or disciplinary committees (Rules, Administration, Ethics) are included, along with Aging, Intelligence, Nutrition, and Small Business (some became standing committees during years covered).[4] In order to be included, committees had actually to meet, of course, though not necessarily for oversight, during the period the data were collected, that is, the first six months of each odd-numbered year. The number of committees qualifying in each year varied from a low of thirty-one in 1961 to a high of thirty-eight in 1975.

Variables employed in the analysis are indicators of two basic aspects of the congressional environment relevant to committee oversight behavior: relatively stable aspects of Congress as an institution and of the policy issues with which it contends; and readily changeable features of congressional structures and environment. There is also an indicator of total activity, originally chosen to provide a necessary statistical control but also of considerable substantive interest, and an indicator of political control—whether the same or different parties control Congress and the presidency. The variables were chosen on the basis of their presumed relevance to the frequency of committee oversight activity. Direct indicators of member and staff incentives are omitted by necessity, since they are available only in the survey data collected. These factors are considered in chapters 4 to 8.

Congressional Environment: Relatively Stable Aspects

The material is complex enough so that before turning to the analyses, it is best to discuss the variables employed and their presumed relevance to oversight behavior. First, I look at relatively stable aspects of Congress as an institution and of the policy issues with which it contends.

The most obvious influence to consider is chamber. The U.S. Congress is a bicameral legislative body. Much ink has been spilled about the unique aspects of each chamber. Charles O. Jones summarizes these differences, with emphasis on the Senate as a "debating" chamber where, compared with the House, committees are relied on less, parties are less important, and debate and floor activity more important. He says in summary, "While both chambers have changed through time . . . the differences remain more striking than the similarities."[5]

Because of the relative importance of committees in the House and the consequent specialization of its members, a function of the larger size of the House and the fact that its members serve on fewer committee and subcommittee units, the obvious expectation is that House committees will be more active in all areas, including oversight, than Senate committees.[6]

Congress contends with a great variety of policy issues, but these fall into certain broad categories. Scholars have struggled for years to link these broad categories to distinctive patterns of politics.[7] It is likely that the oversight behavior of congressional committees is influenced by the types of policy issues (policy domains) that are dominant in their jurisdictions. Certainly, it is important to allow for this possibility in any analysis.

The literature on policy types and related issues (styles of conflict resolution, for example) is extensive, widely criticized, and widely used. All of these schemes present problems for analytical work because it is quite difficult to categorize actual policies in terms of the policy typologies developed.[8] I employed Theodore Lowi's classification scheme as an aid in selecting the committee sample for the survey part of the study because Lowi's scheme is basically compatible with its competitors, and the existing literature contains a useful mapping to congressional committees of the three basic policy arenas it identifies—distributive, redistributive, and regulatory. Using the

Lowi scheme in the analysis in this chapter is, in part, a form of insurance. Perhaps the nature of policy, even crudely classified, is a crucial determinant of congressional oversight behavior.

The Lowi scheme has the virtue that some students of relations between Congress and the bureaucracy have speculated about the impact of policy type on committee oversight behavior.[9] The speculations are mainly qualitative in nature (for example, that there is greater disagreement between Congress and the executive branch—meaning by executive branch primarily the president and political appointees—in regulatory and redistributive than in distributive arenas, especially when there is split partisan control of Congress and the presidency), but there are quantitative implications also. For example, while Randall Ripley and Grace Franklin believe that oversight is relatively infrequent in any policy arena,[10] their scheme implies that committee oversight behavior will be very unimportant and infrequent in the redistributive arena because that arena, much more than the others, is the province of the presidency, broad-based liberal and conservative coalitions, and Congress as a whole.[11]

The difficulty of assigning committee units to any policy arena makes one cautious about the results of any exploration of the relationship between policy type and oversight activity. However, the committees were coded into dummy variables based on George Goodwin's assignment of them to the various policy arenas. Then zero-order correlations for each of the dummy variables were run with the frequency of committee oversight activity.[12] The zero-order results were not very promising. They were weak and positive in the average year for both the distributive and regulatory committees, and weak and negative on average for the redistributive committees.[13] These were basically as predicted, but of such low magnitude and poor consistency that I was tempted to drop them completely. However, later multivariate tests indicated that the redistributive committees were such consistent "underperformers" in oversight when other factors were controlled that the redistributive dummy was included in the regression analysis reported in this chapter.

Congressional Environment: Readily Changeable Features

Now let us turn to more changeable features of the congressional environment—factors that can change readily because of decisions made by Congress as a whole or of its committees or because of broader changes in Congress's political environment.

In the postwar era of concern about oversight, no structural reform has received more attention than the creation of separate oversight units—committees or subcommittees having oversight as their major purpose, with few or preferably no other tasks competing for their attention. There are several related assumptions that underlie this desire to create separate oversight units:[14]

—Oversight is less attractive to members of Congress than other activities; it has less political payoff and greater political risk.[15] If possible, members would prefer to create new programs or add to what already exists. Committees with jurisdictions largely restricted to oversight are a good idea because they restrict the options open to members and, therefore, encourage oversight activity.[16]

—Oversight activity is done best, and is more likely to be done, by those with specialized skills. By defining oversight as the organization's principal mission and limiting options for alternative activities, members and staff will be more likely to do oversight and, in the process, to build up the expertise needed to do it well. Building expertise will also give them an incentive to continue doing oversight. It will, in addition, encourage members to hire staff with the requisite skills—either investigative skills in the narrow sense of ability to ferret out wrongdoing or problems in programs or agencies, or evaluative skills of the type used to determine program effectiveness in achieving goals.

—Members and staff of oversight units will be more objective than those in other units. Lacking serious responsibility for the creation or nurturance of programs, and, by implication, lacking ties with the interest groups that support the programs, they will look at programs with fewer preconceived notions about their value.

In sum, separate oversight units would encourage Congress to do more oversight and to do it well. This chapter focuses on the quantitative aspect of this hypothesis. In later chapters, I will look at the qualitative side.

Decentralization of committee decisionmaking has long been identified as a factor encouraging greater amounts of oversight.[17] The hypothesis is that "in committees where subcommittees are accorded a prominent and autonomous role in policy-making there will be greater opportunity for oversight activity than is the case in committees where subcommittees play a more restricted role."[18] Behind the hypothesis lies the assumption that chairs of highly centralized full committees have limited time to devote to oversight given the press of other business, and few incentives to do so. What they want from administrators they can almost always get through private channels. They are usually identified with programs in "their" committee jurisdictions and, given the great personal influence they possess and the press of other tasks, have neither time nor incentive to disrupt the flow of agency or committee business with inquiries about overall program effectiveness or efficiency.

But when committees are decentralized "power over money, staff, and program is largely in the hands of subcommittee chairmen or others [and this] enhances the opportunity for oversight simply because decision-making is dispersed."[19] Dispersal of decisionmaking authority, by this argument, means that there is a greater chance in a decentralized decisionmaking environment that a member with an interest in doing oversight will have influence over a part of the committee's agenda. "A highly centralized committee is unlikely to conduct much oversight without the active approval of the chairman,"[20] and the chair is likely to give oversight a very low priority if the arguments in the previous paragraph are correct. This line of argument rests on the assumption there is greater interest in oversight in the broader body than among the set of chairs of centralized committees. Otherwise one would not expect committee decentralization to make much difference after controlling for the total level of committee activity in Congress. That is, if decentralization increases the level of committee activity because it creates newly autonomous decisionmaking units, each holding hearings and meetings, and if the decentralized units behave more or less like their centralized forebears, then the absolute level of oversight activity would rise only in proportion to the increase in activity. In essence, there would be more decisionmakers under a decentralized system and more activity of all types, but no more oversight activity than before once one takes account of the rise in total activity.

If, however, decentralization has a more profound impact, one would expect it to have an effect on oversight even after controlling for total activity. And, indeed, this is the thrust of the argument just presented about the lack of incentives that committee chairmen have to engage in oversight in a highly centralized environment. A statistical test, it should be clear, requires that the relationship between decentralization and oversight be examined with total activity controlled; otherwise, a positive relationship between decentralization and oversight activity might be masking the fact that decentralization drives up activities of all types and has no independent effect on oversight.

The literature on oversight cites several factors as oversight stimulants that would seem to be encompassed by or strongly related to decentralization. Morris S. Ogul, for example, mentions sufficient expertise to understand the subject matter and the likely visibility of the issue as stimuli to oversight.[21] A subcommittee chair and affiliated staff have less of the committee's subject matter in their hands than the comparable full committee personnel. Therefore, they have greater opportunity and incentive to build expertise in a narrow area than does the chair of the full committee. Possessing a narrower jurisdiction, they also have more incentive to seek as much visibility as they can in their particular areas. This does not necessarily mean crude publicity seeking in the mass media. Visibility with attentive clientele groups is a more achievable goal, and oversight is one way to achieve it, especially when fairly narrow jurisdictions limit possibilities for new legislation and push unit chairs to look for alternative activities. Oversight to show support for a program or to help make the case for its expansion is especially likely in such a setting.

Another variable feature of the congressional environment is staff size. Congress increased the size of its staff over the years for multiple reasons, but in large part as an attempt to give it resources necessary to counter the expertise available to the executive branch.[22] Staff increases for these purposes are evident in the numbers of employees of the congressional support agencies (Congressional Research Service, General Accounting Office, Congressional Budget Office, and Office of Technology Assessment), but most especially in the staffs of the congressional committees.[23]

As chapter 2 demonstrated, there is a definite coincidence in the upward trends of the aggregate days that congressional committees devote to oversight and of the total staff available to them. The literature on oversight emphasizes that adequate staff resources are a necessary, but not a sufficient, condition for oversight. Ogul contends, "Access to staff and the willingness to use it are often important preconditions to substantial oversight. Oversight without effective staff work is normally impossible. But the amount of oversight performed does not depend mainly on the size of the staff available. Adequate staff is a necessary precondition to oversight but it is not a sufficient one."[24]

In this chapter I will look at the zero-order association of committee staff size and committee oversight activity. This will yield an estimate of staff effects on committee oversight behavior more precise than that suggested by the crudely aggregated data in chapter 2, where totals for committee staff size and oversight days were simply plotted against one another. But the major emphasis in the analysis will be on the independent effects of staff in influencing oversight activity once other factors are taken into account (staff as a slack resource). In other words, taking into account the other indicators used in the analysis, including the overall level of activity of the committee, is there any sign that "excess" staff resources are translated into oversight activity? If there is a significant residual effect of staff on oversight after all other variables (including total workload) are taken into account, this will not establish that staff is a strong independent force influencing the committee agenda (a live issue among those who are concerned about the growth of staff and its implications for congressional behavior), although it will offer some supplemental evidence to use in chapter 5, which, through analysis of interviews, looks at staff influence in committee decisionmaking. What the analysis will provide is a better handle on the question of whether slack ("excess") staff somehow gets translated into oversight, and under what conditions this may happen.

The number of pages in the *Federal Register* is a crude indicator of the complexity of government and of its penetration into citizen life. Informed respondents, as seen in chapter 2, associate increases in the amount of oversight with the increasing size and complexity of government, and a strong correlation between the *Federal Register*'s bulk and the level of oversight activity was revealed. The preliminary analysis included the pages in the *Federal Register* indicator. It was later dropped for statistical reasons (see appendix C). However, the substantive argument presented in the chapter takes account of the underlying phenomenon the indicator represents.

Finally, I included two important additional variable features of the congressional environment in this analysis. The first, total level of committee activity, has been mentioned several times in the discussions of decentralization and staff size. Total level of committee activity has value for interpreting the effects of decentralization and staff size on the level of committee oversight activity. But it is important for other reasons as well. Its presence enables one to test the hypothesis that oversight is a constant function of committee behavior: that is, determine how active a committee is in any year, and then one can know how much oversight a committee does in that year because oversight is always the same proportion of total committee activity. If this is so, the rise in oversight behavior over time would likely be caused by exactly the same forces leading to a rise in the overall level of committee activity; and differences in oversight activity among committees at any one point in time would simply be a function of how busy the various committees are. If it is not so, the changing relationship between total activity and oversight activity may help in interpreting the sources of change in oversight activity. Taking account of total level of committee activity also provides an important control needed to interpret results other than those for staff and decentralization—it enables one to say, "Holding constant the level of committee activity, variable X or variable Y has the following effect on oversight activity."

The second, split partisan control of the presidency and Congress, has become a frequent occurrence in the contemporary era.[25] One of the most common hypotheses in the field is that "if different parties control the presidency and Congress, the majority in Congress has an incentive to harass and embarrass the executive for partisan gain."[26] Or, as Ogul says, "A congressman of the president's political party is less likely to be concerned with oversight than a member of the opposition party."[27]

Several variables of potential importance are not directly considered in this analysis. "Member priorities," widely identified as key elements in the decision to oversee,[28] are not included because of the nature of the *Daily Digest* data. Inferences about priorities will be made, as they were in the discussion of decentralization and other factors. Indeed, priorities as an aspect of self-interest is an important part of my underlying model. However, the interview data analyzed in later chapters provide a more direct examination of the political psychology of oversight.

A factor that can be directly linked to these data, but is not considered here in any detail, is the political stance of committee unit chairs, at least as measured by such standard indicators of congressional voting as Congressional Quarterly Presidential Support Scores and indicators of liberalism or conservatism such as Americans for Democratic Action (ADA) or Americans for Constitutional Action (ACA) scores. Data were gathered for the House and matched to the relevant committee units. The expected negative relation between presidential support and frequency of oversight (higher support, lower level of oversight) was found in seven of the nine years between 1961 and 1977 where data were coded, but the relationships are very weak (the average correlations in these seven years is −0.05). Those chairs who scored high on the ACA support scale were more likely to engage in oversight, the expected finding again, but here the average positive correlation is only 0.06 (and that excludes the one year where the correlation is negative.)[29]

Partisan factors do play a role in oversight decisions, as shall be seen when data on split partisan control of the presidency and Congress are considered in the analysis, but overall indicators of committee chair support for the president in voting on the floor of the House or of liberal or conservative voting records do not have power as explanations of the frequency of oversight activity. Split partisan control tends to increase committee oversight activity, but that tendency is only slightly depressed by the propensity of a chair to support the president in floor votes or increased by a tendency to support conservative causes. The probable reason for this tendency, as indicated in chapter 8, is that committee chairs tend to be advocates for their committees' programs and to oversee them within an advocacy context. They also tend to be affected by concerns about their institutional prerogatives. Therefore, though Democrats may have a tendency to push a Republican president more than a president of their own party, in the oversight domain it is quite likely to be a push to assist the program in some way or to maintain committee influence—factors independent of their broader support for the president's program or of liberal or conservative floor voting.

To reiterate, the principal goals of this chapter are to buttress and refine the basic argument that congressional oversight varies with changes in the environmental stimuli, both external and internal, affecting Congress. In a dynamic environment, one changing over time, the level of congressional oversight changes. Behavior that was once relatively unattractive can grow more attractive, or vice versa, and relationships to variables associated with behavior can also change. The previous pages looked at aspects of the congressional environment and at their expected relationships to oversight. Now I will build a model of committee oversight behavior and how it works, with special attention to the inferences that can be drawn from changes over time in the relationships between variables in the model and oversight.

The model is based on pooled data for the years 1961 to 1977. From it emerges a better understanding of the sources of committee oversight behavior and the forces determining changes in oversight behavior over time. This understanding can then be tested and refined by applying the model to data for the Reagan years.

Some of the more technical aspects of the approach and details on the measures are described in appendix C, but the basic elements are reasonably straightforward. I want to understand committee oversight behavior better, why it is greater for some committees than others and why it has increased or decreased over time. I have constructed a regression model of committee oversight behavior using pooled data for 1961 to 1977, making adjustments for years in which a slope of an independent variable indicates a marked change from other years. In that way stable relationships and changes in relationships over time can be seen and interpreted.

Since the dependent variable used in the analysis is the days of oversight done by each committee, transformed by taking its natural log, standard units can be used in interpreting the regression coefficients (see appendix C). One can talk about the percent increment in committee days of oversight for a unit change in the independent variables. Or for dummy variables such as the chamber of the committee holding a hearing or meeting, one can convert the regression coefficient to say that (all else held constant in the multiple regression case) committees in one chamber spend X percent more of their time on oversight than committees in the other chamber.

Changes in Congressional Oversight: 1961 to 1977

Table 3-1 presents the results of the regression analysis. First, table 3-1 shows that split partisan control of the presidency and Congress does indeed have an impact on committee oversight behavior. Holding

TABLE 3-1. *Regression Coefficients for Pooled Committee Oversight Data, Odd-Numbered Years, 1961–77*[a]

Variable	Summary estimates (when appropriate)[b]	Year-by-year estimates (when appropriate)[c]			
		1961–71	1973	1975	1977
Intercept	0.294*	. . .	. . .	. . .	. . .
Total days	. . .	0.006	0.013	0.007	0.012[†]
Staff	. . .	0.011	−0.007	−0.002	0.004
Oversight unit	. . .	1.203**	0.556	0.500	0.088
Committee decentralization	. . .	0.004**	0.015	0.021	0.018[†]
Chamber	−0.366*	. . .	. . .	. . .	. . .
Redistributive policy issue	−0.398*	. . .	. . .	. . .	. . .
Split partisan control	0.233*	. . .	. . .	. . .	. . .
$R^2 = 0.58$					

*Significant at $p \leq 0.05$.
**Significant differences ($p \leq 0.05$) from the 1977 baseline.
†Baseline coefficients significant at the $p \leq 0.05$ level.
a. The dependent variable is the log of committee oversight days in each odd year plus one. For descriptions of the independent variables, see appendix C. The analysis is based on 305 cases. The Senate Judiciary Committee was dropped in all years. Senate Government Operations was dropped in 1973. See appendix C.
b. Stable coefficients are given a single estimate. See appendix C.
c. Unstable coefficients are estimated by year. See appendix C.

the other factors in the equation constant, congressional committees averaged 26.2 percent more oversight in years of split partisan control (in these years, Republican presidents and Democratic Congresses) than in years when both institutions were controlled by Democrats.[30]

Second, committees with a heavy concentration of redistributive policy issues in their jurisdictions averaged 32.7 percent fewer days of oversight over the years than other committees. As mentioned, the hypothesis was that committee oversight behavior will be relatively infrequent in the redistributive arena because that arena, much more than the others, is the province of the presidency, private sector peak associations, and Congress as a whole. Nothing in these data leads one to question the hypothesis.

Third, holding all other variables constant, House committees on

TABLE 3-2. *Regression Coefficients and Percent Interpretations of Logged Oversight Days on Chamber, by Year*

Item	1961–71	1973	1975	1977
Chamber regression coefficient	0.166	0.398	0.643	0.707
Percent interpretation[a]	18.1	48.9	90.2	102.8
N	(198)	(34)	(38)	(35)

a. Positive = average percent by which oversight behavior is greater for House than for Senate committees.

average spend 30.6 percent less of their time on oversight than Senate committees. The expectation was that the House would be a more active overseer than the Senate, given the fact that committees are more important in the House, House members have fewer committee assignments, and House members, consequently, are more specialized. The actual results appear to be quite different.

The statement "holding all other variables constant" is the key. Table 3-2 presents the zero-order (no controls) regression coefficients for the logged oversight days variable regressed on the chamber dummy variable. House committees are indeed more active than Senate committees in oversight. In the early years, when oversight was a relatively infrequent activity, House-Senate differences were small. House committees averaged about 18 percent more days of oversight than Senate committees. As the years progressed and the number of days of oversight took large jumps starting in 1973, the percentage differences between the houses increased markedly so that by 1977 House committees averaged more than twice as many days of oversight as Senate committees.

Not surprisingly, a control for total days of committee activity (rising rapidly during this period) reduces the differences between House and Senate rather markedly. Table 3-3 presents these data. The figure is slightly negative in 1961–71 (down from plus 18.1 percent with no control) and in 1977 merely taking account of total days of activity reduces the estimate of the average percent by which House committee oversight behavior is greater than Senate committee oversight behavior from 102.8 percent to 28.0 percent. If one goes one step further and controls for total days and committee decen-

TABLE 3-3. *Percent Interpretations of Logged Oversight Days Regressed on Chamber, Controlling for Total Days and Total Days and Committee Decentralization, by Year*

Item[a]	1961–71	1973	1975	1977
Average percent by which oversight behavior is greater for House than for Senate committees after accounting for:				
Total days	−4.0	5.1	18.2	28.0
Total days and committee decentralization	−11.0	−31.8	−31.5	−24.9

a. Positive = average percent by which oversight behavior is greater for House than for Senate committees.

tralization (which is more marked in the House than the Senate), the figures are negative in each year.

In other words, the final figure for chamber differences (with everything controlled) produces a significant estimate of lower overall House activity. Merely controlling for level of total committee activity reduces the differences between the chambers quite a bit, and adding in just one more control, for decentralization, reverses the zero-order sign of the coefficient in every instance. In fact, if one looks at the pooled data, and adds in one control after another, House committees average an estimated 39 percent more oversight than Senate committees in the zero-order relationship, dropping to 19 percent less oversight with total days and decentralization controlled, and 33 percent less oversight with total days, decentralization and oversight unit controlled.

Two possible and complementary explanations come to mind. The first is that, as a consequence of its larger size and greater specialization, the House committee system is more decentralized, with a greater number of specialized oversight units (to mention just two of the factors included in the analysis in table 3-1). Once one holds decentralization and possession of specialized oversight units constant, the "remaining" Senate committees are more frequent overseers statistically because they are the only Senate units "available" to do the job when events such as scandal or conflict with the administration arise to stimulate oversight. The second is that senators (and, therefore, Senate committees) are more publicity oriented than their House colleagues and have a greater opportunity to secure media attention because of Senate visibility. All other factors held constant, they do more oversight because it is a rather attractive source of publicity.

In sum, of the stable features of Congress as an institution (chamber) and of the content of the policy issues in its committees' jurisdictions included in this analysis, one (redistributive policy issues) has the expected effect on committee oversight activity, even with all other factors considered, but the other (chamber) has just the opposite effect expected once statistical controls are instituted. Both effects are stable, however, in the sense that statistical tests indicate that, with all other factors controlled, the year-by-year changes in the regression coefficients are not significant. The summary estimate of effect, then, is best.

The more variable features of the congressional environment—factors that can change readily because of decisions made by Congress as a whole or of its committees—must also be examined. First I look at the total days variable. This variable is used as a control, but it is also an important indicator of a change in the congressional environment. The average number of days of committee activity rose markedly over this period (from 53.9 per committee over the 1961–71 period to 82.3 per committee in 1977).[31] More interesting, however, the percentage yield of oversight days per day of total activity also rose over this period. In 1961–71, with all other factors in the regression taken into account, each day of additional activity per committee was associated with a 0.6 percent increase in days of oversight. By 1977, however, the comparable figure was double, or 1.2 percent. The coefficients do not rise smoothly over this period (1973 is higher than 1975), but every year has a higher coefficient than the 1961–71 period coefficient. Since this increase in the effect of the general activity (total days) on oversight frequency holds with all other factors controlled, it suggests a wider diffusion of oversight through Congress in the mid- to late 1970s than was the case in the early years of the series.[32]

Indeed, a look at the coefficients for the oversight unit variable in table 3-1 (translated into percentages in table 3-4) gives evidence of a wide diffusion of oversight activity. During the 1961–71 period, oversight was a very specialized activity in Congress. Oversight units

TABLE 3-4. *Percent Interpretations of Regression Coefficients for the Oversight Unit Variable in Table 3-1*

Item	1961–71	1973	1975	1977
Percent by which oversight days are greater for committees with oversight units than for committees without oversight units[a]	233.0	74.4	64.9	9.2

a. Comparable figures for the zero-order coefficients (no controls) are as follows: 1961–71, 352.2; 1973, 118.1; 1975, 89.6; and 1977, 54.8.

far outstripped all others in doing it. The academic literature on the period portrayed oversight as a rather unique occurrence for most committees, an event following a scandal or a severe policy dispute between a committee and an agency, and this portrayal was probably correct.[33] Most of the oversight in these years was done by committees with oversight subunits whose opportunities for alternative activities were limited. Other units sometimes did oversight but very infrequently.

In 1973, however, the data show a clear change. Committees with oversight units still did more than others (74 percent more controlling for other factors and 118 percent more at the zero-order level—see table 3-4), but the dominance of committees with oversight units had waned considerably. By 1977 the differences between committees with oversight units and those without were almost nil once other variables were considered (9.2 percent more oversight for the committees with oversight units), and relatively small even in the zero-order case (54.8 percent more oversight for committees with oversight units, down from 352.2 percent in the 1961–71 period). One might say that now almost every committee was getting into the act. A previously specialized activity was now widespread.

To make sure this interpretation is correct, it is useful to look at the data from some additional vantage points. The coefficient of variability is a standardized measure of variation expressed as a ratio of the standard deviation of a distribution to its mean. If one looks at coefficients of variability for congressional committees over time, the higher their value, the greater the variation of oversight activity across committees in any period or year; the lower their value, the

TABLE 3-5. *Cross-Committee Variability of Oversight Activity, by Year*

Year	Coefficient of variability[a]	Number of cases
1961–71	0.965	198
1973	0.621	35
1975	0.517	38
1977	0.374	35

a. The coefficient of variability is a standardized measure of variation expressed as a ratio of the standard deviation of a distribution to its mean, that is, $V = SD/X$. The higher its value, the greater the variation of oversight activity across committees. Means of the logged variables are presented for consistency. Coefficients using the unlogged data are as follows: 1961–71, 1.587; 1973, 1.054; 1975, 0.805; and 1977, 0.753.

smaller cross-committee variation in oversight activity. Table 3-5 shows that the level of committee oversight became more and more similar over the years. There was much greater variation in oversight activity across committees in the 1961–71 period than there was in the later years, with 1977 showing the lowest variation.

This finding holds even when the oversight measure is standardized by using percentages. Table 3-6 displays coefficients of variability for the percent of oversight activity. (Table 3-5 used logged days.) Committees were more and more likely to devote similar percentages of their time to oversight as the years progressed.

Finally, the percentage of committee units doing oversight increased dramatically over the years. Up to now, I have presented data using committees as the units of analysis. It is possible, however, to break the data down further so that organizational components of committees are the units of analysis; that is, a full committee is treated as an organizational unit separate from each of its subcommittees. That way, oversight subcommittees can be separated from their parent committees for analytical purposes.

If one separates the nonoversight units (those not having oversight as a major named function) from the oversight units and looks at the percentage of nonoversight units holding any oversight hearings at all, the change is very marked over the years.[34] In the 1961–71 period, an average of fewer than 20 percent of the nonoversight units did any oversight during the first six months of the year. The percentage

TABLE 3-6. *Cross-Committee Variability of the Percent of Committee Activity Devoted to Oversight, by Year*

Year	Coefficient of variability[a]	Number of cases
1961–71	1.529	198
1973	1.040	35
1975	0.839	38
1977	0.555	35

a. Coefficient of variability defined in table 3-6, note a.

was just over 30 in 1973, and by 1977 well over half (57.7 percent) of the nonoversight units were doing some oversight (5.6 times the 1961 figure).[35]

I noted earlier that oversight is no longer Congress's neglected function. These data pointedly round out the story. By 1977 oversight not only represented a sizable share of the total congressional effort, it was also a pronounced part of the agenda of the nonoversight units, engaged in by more than half of them. Indeed, if one groups the data and looks at differences in the percentages of active oversight and nonoversight committees doing oversight, the changing differences are marked. For example in the 1961–67 period, years of Democratic presidents and Congresses, the percentage of nonoversight units holding some oversight hearings was very small so that the average difference is a huge 52.3 percent. By 1977, also a time of same party control of the presidency and Congress, the difference in the percentages was down to a slim 13.7 percent.[36] And, finally, if one looks at the data from a different vantage point and considers the proportion of the total days of oversight done by nonoversight committee units (that is, the percentage of the total oversight done in Congress that is accounted for by the nonoversight committee units) it goes from an average of 52.6 percent in 1961–67 to a whopping 80.2 percent in 1977. And these figures, of course, take account of the increase in oversight units that occurred during the congressional reform period of the 1970s, since the days of oversight done by these units are in the denominator but not the numerator of the figures used to calculate the percentages.

The rapid increase in the number of committee units in Congress engaging in oversight hearings and meetings and in the overall level of oversight hearings and meetings are clearly established. It is quite possible that oversight spread to the agendas of congressional committee units in a manner suggested by some standard leaders and followers or the spatial "diffusion" model found in the academic literature (one unit imitating another),[37] but the *Daily Digest* data are not well suited to test whether or not this is so. They were gathered every other year (indeed, for the most part, for only the first six months of each odd-numbered year) so that it is difficult to determine the nature of the spread of oversight.[38]

What is evident is that oversight became a more and more prominent part of the agenda for units throughout Congress, and not just of specialized oversight units, at the same time that other changes were taking place in the congressional environment. Some changes took place within Congress (the decentralization of decision-making within congressional committees, for example). Other changes were aspects of the more general political environment (the increase in government size and complexity, for example) or of Congress's relations with other institutions (actions taken as part of its increasingly intense struggle with the Nixon administration). Many of these environmental changes are interrelated, of course, but the regression analysis suggests their independent effects.[39] Holding constant the effects of decentralization, for instance, one sees clear signs of the impact on congressional oversight behavior of the changing general environment and of changes in congressional relations with other institutions.

In 1973 the first significant changes (downward) in the slopes for the oversight units variable occur, and the total days regression slope also increases. This is precisely the moment that one would expect such changes if the environmental factors just discussed were having an impact. As mentioned earlier, the variable indicating the number of pages in the *Federal Register* did not survive tests done on the full regression model (all slopes allowed to vary in 1973, 1975, and 1977), but that is almost surely because the slope dummy variables for the three years are picking up changes in the political climate better than gross indicators of change such as the pages variable. An internal organizational factor like the existence or nonexistence of oversight units on a committee, once a key to understanding congressional oversight behavior, gave way starting in 1973 before an onslaught of pressures from the political environment. It is not that oversight units started doing less but that others were doing so much more.

An explanation drawn from organization theory helps to put these changes in perspective. Chances are that the increases in units doing oversight, and in the overall amount of oversight done, are the result of the coupling of a long-touted and widely advertised solution to the problem of congressional decline (oversight) and a set of problems that had become rather severe from the perspective of Congress (growth in government size and complexity, perceived public reactions to these facts, and blatant challenges to Congress from the president). John Kingdon says in his revision of the Cohen, March, and Olsen "garbage can" model of organizational choice, that the coupling of problems and solutions in the federal government occurs when a "problem is recognized, a solution is available, the political climate makes the time right for change, and the constraints do not prohibit action."[40] Here we probably have a good example of this model in action, although I would put less emphasis on the random elements of the process and more on the "ripeness" of the political climate as the key to a change in committee oversight behavior that had been advocated in Congress since 1946 at least.

Oversight had long been promoted within Congress as one solution to the rise of the administrative state and to the growing imbalance between the branches, but it took graphic evidence that the problems were growing out of control to affect significantly the profile of committee behavior (behavior by nonspecialized, that is, nonoversight committee units). Then the slow increase in oversight activity became a rush as oversight became a more regular and widespread part of committee agendas.

The general argument developed so far can be used to interpret the changes in the staff coefficients found in the regression analysis presented in table 3-1. In chapter 5 I will use answers to survey questions to examine the influence of staff on oversight decision-making. Here, after a brief look at the zero-order association of committee staff size and committee oversight activity over time (done to get a raw estimate of the effects of the size of a committee's staff on its oversight behavior before controlling for other influences), the emphasis will be on the independent effects of staff in influencing oversight activity once other factors are taken into account (that is, staff as a slack resource). Does "excess" staff somehow get translated into oversight, under what conditions, and what does this say about changes in oversight behavior over time?

A brief examination of the zero-order estimates of the effects of staff on committee oversight activity sets the stage for interpreting the role of staff in these terms. Each additional committee staff member was associated with a 2.4 percent increase in oversight for his or her committee in the 1961–71 period. However, this increase per additional staff member dropped to 1.0 percent in 1973, the year of transition in terms of the overall increase in committee oversight, and a rebound in the zero-order effect that started in 1975 (1.3 percent) reached only 1.5 percent in 1977.[41] While still indicating a formidable effect, the 1977 figure was only five-eighths of the 1961–71 figure.

The coefficients for staff with other factors controlled in table 3-1 offer some clues about what has happened. In the 1961–71 period, each additional committee staff member was associated with approximately a 1.1 percent increase in committee oversight, even with the effects of other variables in the equation taken into account. In that sense, staff was a slack resource and it yielded a sizable increment in oversight activity. In 1973, however, the year when the number of days of oversight took its first major jump, the coefficient for staff is actually negative. It remains negative, although closer to zero in 1975, and only in 1977 does it become positive again.

The year 1973 was one of transition for Congress. There was a big increase in the overall level of committee activity. Total days of hearings and meetings went to 2,513 during the first six months of 1973, up from a mean of 1,888 (standard deviation of 133) during the comparable months from 1961 to 1971.[42] Oversight kept pace with this increase. There is ample evidence presented in the previous pages that more committees were holding oversight hearings and meetings. The negative coefficient for staff in 1973 found in the pooled regression results in table 3-1 indicates that this was true even for, in fact especially for, committees whose staff resources were modest. The 1973 coefficient for total days in the pooled regression went up quite a bit (from 0.006 in 1961–71 to 0.013 in 1973) at the same time that the staff coefficient became negative and the oversight unit coefficient dropped from 1.203 to 0.556. In 1973 more committees than in earlier times were striving to assert themselves as overseers, even those with small staffs.

By 1975 the staff factor was still negative but very close to zero, and in 1977 it became positive once again but at a lower level than for 1961–71. Staff sizes, of course, were increasing rapidly during this period and by 1977 enough balance was restored so that there was a small positive effect (0.004) of staff on oversight with other factors controlled (each added staffer typically yielded a 0.4 percent increase in oversight for his or her committee), and a larger zero-order effect (0.015) than in the previous two years included in my data (1973 and 1975). The overall impression for 1977 is one of widespread oversight activity, with most committees active. At the level of staff resources and committee activity present in 1977 there is little evidence of "excess" staff as a slack resource translated into oversight.

With some caution, I would say that in the 1970s committee staff resources did not lead (indeed, may well often have followed) the drive for more oversight and, in this sense, were not dominant factors in oversight behavior. With great confidence, I reiterate that the evidence is overwhelming that by 1977 oversight had a wide appeal in Congress. It had become a significant part of the general agenda and not a specialized activity concentrated almost exclusively in a few committee units designated for the task.

Committee decentralization is the last of the variable features of the congressional environment (features that can change readily because of decisions made by Congress as a whole or by its committees), represented in the regression equation (table 3-1). As mentioned, the hypothesis is that greater decentralization of committee decisionmaking should encourage greater amounts of oversight, and this finding should hold even when the total level of committee activity is taken into account (since decentralized committees should be more active). The decentralization indicator used is the percentage of committee hearings and meetings conducted by subcommittees.

The decentralization indicator was related to oversight as expected in the 1961–71 period. Each increase of 1.0 percentage point in the decentralization indicator was associated with a 0.4 percent higher level of committee oversight activity, even after controlling for the effects of all other factors including total days of committee activity. In 1973, the coefficient jumped to 0.015 (an estimated 1.5 percent increase in the level of committee oversight per increase of 1.0 percentage point in the decentralization score). It was higher still in

1975 (0.021, a 2.1 percent increase) and in 1977 (0.018, a 1.8 percent increase).

What caused this change in the coefficient? Though no one can say for sure, the change is coincident with a series of changes in Congress that most likely affected the power of the indicator as a measure of decentralization.

In chapter 2, I reviewed the changes taking place in Congress in the New Deal and postwar period. One was a solidifying of power in the hands of full committee chairs (highlighted by the 1946 consolidation of committee units). That set the stage for a slow building movement to decentralize committee control, which reached full flower in the early 1970s with passage in 1973 of the so-called subcommittee bill of rights in the House.[43]

As Norman Ornstein says, "Any description of congressional change in the 1970s begins with decentralization."[44] Roger Davidson notes that "between 1937 and 1971 the workgroups in both houses were dominated by a handful of senior leaders." This time was, Davidson says, "the zenith of committee government . . . when it seemed that Congress was ruled by a relatively small coterie of committee chairmen,"[45] but this domination waned gradually in the Senate beginning in the 1960s and more abruptly in the House in the early 1970s.[46] The changes are too complex to describe here, but, as the quotation from Davidson indicates, the literature makes it clear that the post-1971 dividing point used in the regression analysis is a sensible one.[47] Though much activity had already devolved to subcommittees earlier, in the early 1970s subcommittee autonomy flowered.[48]

The *Daily Digest* data fit nicely with this overall image of subcommittee influence. The mean level of committee hearings conducted by subcommittees did not change much in the period between 1961 and 1971 and the later years (it went up by less than 10 percent between the 1961–71 period and 1977), but the impact of the decentralization variable increased markedly as the regression coefficients make clear.[49] The highest coefficient was in 1975 (0.021), when coincidentally the House Democratic caucus deposed three inflexible committee chairs who had resisted change. But the coefficient for 1977 remained relatively high (0.018), even when taking into account the other variables in the equation, which indicates that oversight activity was now much more likely whenever subcommittees were more active. In the earlier period, the decentralization of hearings and meetings to subcommittees was based on the consent of committee chairs. By 1973 it was more a matter of right.

The decentralization of power from committees to subcommittees was accomplished by formal changes in the House rules but somewhat more informally and less completely in the Senate. Perhaps, then, decentralization effects should be analyzed separately by chamber.[50] Although the data confirm that the House is more decentralized by the measure used here, statistical tests show no evidence of an interaction between chamber and decentralization as they affect oversight. And the correlations between decentralization and oversight days are essentially the same for the House and the Senate considered separately.[51] Decentralization is the key variable, not chamber or chamber interacting with decentralization.

Overview

The regression analysis gives evidence of oversight as a concentrated activity in the 1961–71 period, with oversight hearings and meetings held very disproportionately by committee units lacking many other options (oversight units). Staff in excess of those required for other activities seemed to find their way into oversight, another sign of its low priority in most congressional committees. By 1973 this picture changed greatly. Evidence of the spread of oversight activity throughout Congress abounds. It was clearly more attractive as a committee endeavor, and therefore no longer largely confined to specialized oversight units, a finding fully consonant with the views of committee staffers on increased levels of oversight as expressed in the survey data analyzed in the closing pages of chapter 2. Nearly everyone was doing it, with the level of committee oversight a greater proportion of the overall level of committee activity than before. The measure of decentralized committee decisionmaking also had a more pronounced effect on oversight activity in these later years, as oversight achieved a prominent place on the agendas of committee units now more decentralized in fact as well as in appearance. Through the entire period, and controlling for all other factors of course, committees whose jurisdictions featured redistributive policy areas did less oversight. The same can be said of House committees and of Congress as a whole during years when the Democrats controlled the presidency as well as Congress.

The overall findings present a consistent picture. Oversight became an increasingly prominent part of the agenda for committee units throughout Congress just as important changes were taking place both in Congress's broader political environment and in its internal environment. The pattern of results in the regression analysis lends credence to the interpretation that each had an important influence in pushing up the level of committee oversight activity in Congress.

The Reagan Years: Continuity or Change?

Clearly, oversight varies with changes in the environmental stimuli, both external and internal, affecting Congress. In this chapter, I have discussed how and why the level of oversight changes. But, of course, social scientists also want to understand the contemporary political environment better and to use the contemporary environment to verify, deepen, and, if necessary, amend our understanding of political phenomena. Therefore, a look at any changes in congressional oversight behavior during the Reagan administration, and especially at the relevance of the model developed in this chapter to data for the Reagan years, is desirable.

Thus I collected and coded data for congressional committee activities during the first Reagan administration.[52] I have data on hearing and meeting activities for the period between January 1 and July 4 for each odd-numbered year of Reagan's first term, that is, 1981 and 1983.[53] These data can be used to compare the amount of primary-purpose oversight activity during the Reagan years to the activity of earlier years. They can also be used to examine stability and changes in the model of oversight behavior developed earlier in this chapter, taking account now of data from the Reagan years.

Consistent with his earlier rhetoric, and in tune with much of the prevailing rhetoric of his time, Ronald Reagan ran for president as an opponent of big government and many of its programs. He was mainly critical of the nondefense sector of the government and of its bureaucratic establishment. Reagan carried a Republican Senate into office with him. He also made important dents in the liberal majority in the House. Both were indications to the Washington establishment of a continuation, indeed an intensification, of public unease about the size and complexity of government. The climate, consequently, was favorable for a continuation of high levels of congressional oversight—few opportunities for new (nondefense) programs, controversy about existing programs, and the appearance of voter unease about large government.

And the data, as shown in chapter 2, do reveal a continued high level of committee oversight in both absolute and relative terms. By 1977 the total number of oversight days in the first six months of that year's Congress had climbed to 537, representing 17.6 percent of the 3,053 total days of committee hearings and meetings held by the congressional committees included in the data set.[54] In 1981 the total number of oversight days dropped to 434 (still the third largest total in the twenty-year period covered), but the percentage increased to 19.5 (the highest figure to date) because the total days of congressional committee hearings and meetings dropped to 2,222. In 1983 the total number of oversight days hit its all-time high in my data series, reaching 587. This figure represented 25.2 percent of the 2,331 days of hearings and meetings held in the first six months of 1983.

What these data make clear is that, despite the decline in total committee unit hearings and meetings during the Reagan administration (a decline, to keep these data in proper perspective, bringing the levels back to those of the mid-1970s in the House and the early 1970s in the Senate, and not to the lower levels of earlier periods),[55] oversight hearings and meetings remained very prominent items on committee agendas. They increased in relative terms in each of the years studied and even increased in absolute terms in one of them. The underlying factors that caused oversight activity to reach high levels in the mid-1970s, exacerbated perhaps by the slim legislative agenda and antidomestic program bias of the Reagan administration, seem to have kept oversight prominent during the Reagan years.

Even if the levels were high, perhaps a model different from the one explicated earlier in this chapter is necessary to understand committee oversight behavior. Some might expect, for example, that relationships between predictor variables and the level of oversight activity would be quite different in the Reagan and Carter administrations. To check this possibility, I used the coefficients for a regression equation estimated for 1977 to predict the oversight scores for committees in 1981 and 1983.[56] Correlations were run between the actual oversight scores for committees in 1981 and 1983 and their scores for those years as predicted by the coefficients from the 1977 model.[57] The correlations are very high. Using the 1977 equation to predict 1981 scores yields a correlation of 0.75 between actual and predicted scores. Using the 1977 equation to predict 1983 scores results in a still impressive correlation of 0.69. It seems that the basic 1977 model remained formidable in 1981 and 1983. Indeed, the coefficients estimated using data from the first year of the Carter administration were still effective in predicting congressional over-sight activity in the Reagan years.

Alternately, if one pools the data from 1977, 1981, and 1983 and tests to see whether the slopes for the independent variables in my standard regression model (table 3-1) should be adjusted for any of the years, one finds only one variable requiring a year adjustment.[58] That variable is the redistributive policy issues variable.[59] The year adjustment is necessary because committees with redistributive policy issues in their jurisdictions became more and more likely to oversee in the Reagan era as the administration challenged many of these programs.[60] Other than this response to a particular change in the environment, however, everything else remained much the same.[61]

To summarize, holding other factors constant, and comparing 1981 and 1983 to 1977, oversight is still very widespread, with total days of activity a statistically significant predictor and the existence of an oversight unit not significant.[62] An added staffer produces a margin-ally greater (but not statistically significant) amount of oversight. Decentralized committees remain more likely to oversee.[63] And the Senate is still more active than the House.[64]

Whatever else can be said about the Reagan era and Congress, it has had relatively little impact on congressional oversight activity. And, except for the change in the relationship of redistributive policy issues to the amount of oversight done, the model relevant to the Carter era is still applicable. Whether the qualitative nature of the oversight done during the Reagan era has been different is a subject discussed in chapter 8. To answer the question on the Reagan years posed in the heading to this section: continuity, not change, is the watchword when it comes to levels of congressional oversight activity.

Part Two
Processes and Politics

Chapter 4

The Committee Intelligence System

CONGRESS FACES A difficult task if it wants to do a good job of oversight. It has only 535 members, controls a numerically large but limited staff when compared with the legions of relevant agency personnel, and has priorities other than oversight competing for its attention. To facilitate its work, Congress is organized into committees, each with its own staff. One task these committees have is to oversee the activities of the agencies and to assess the effects of the programs and policies they administer. But how do committees find out what is going on?

Breaking Congress into committees and subcommittees with fairly well-defined jurisdictions is a help, but even these specialized units cover wide, complex areas and must face bureaucratic units with more personnel and the greater expertise and collective knowledge borne of intensive training and day-to-day administrative experience. How do committee personnel break through the maze to discover what is happening? How do they go about tracking down what goes on in the government? And what can be said, given their obvious limitations, about their capabilities and approaches?

Staffers and Administrators: A Surprisingly Good Match

Going back to Max Weber at least, it has been assumed that bureaucratic expertise creates a problem for elected officials seeking to oversee the work of administrators.[1] Studies of the membership of Congress present a mixed picture. Members are predominantly professional politician-lawyers, trained specialists in the form but not in the substance of legislation.[2] They compensate for any lack of training or experience in substantive areas and for the limited time

79

they can devote to committee work by building knowledge through long service on committees (recently compromised by subcommittee government with its tendency for more rapid turnover of subcommittee chairs)[3] and by hiring staff to assist them in their work. I will leave to chapter 5 a discussion of who has ultimate charge of the committee oversight decisions, but clearly the professional staff are eyes and ears for the committee leadership in their relations with the bureaucracy. If staff cannot do the job, the situation is often bleak.

A main function of staff is to lighten the burdens of committee members who have multiple responsibilities. The question is whether or not they are adequate to the task of overseeing the executive, or at least whether their records of experience and formal training indicate that they are adequate.

To illuminate the capabilities of committee staffers compared with administrators, I took a subsample from a survey of top American federal executives, career and noncareer, interviewed for a study done in the early 1970s and compared their backgrounds and experiences to those of the top committee staffers interviewed for this study.[4] The top executives came from agencies overseen by the committees represented in the staff study and in that sense are a rough match—a counterpart sample. What one has here is a broad comparative perspective.[5]

The comparison should reassure those who are concerned about congressional committee capabilities in relation to the executive agencies. Though top committee staffers do not match top career executives in expertise or experience, the data do not portray a hopeless contest of unequals.

First, and not surprisingly, neither group reflects the diversity of American society. Both are predominantly white, male, and exceedingly well educated. Ninety-nine percent of the top congressional staffers interviewed are white, 88 percent are male, and 99 percent have at minimum graduated from college.[6] Among top career civil servants, 98 percent in the comparable subsample are male, 96 percent white, and 93 percent have graduated from college. Top politically appointed executives are 92 percent male, 84 percent white, and all have graduated from college.[7] Both top congressional staffers and top administrators of both types, then, come disproportionately from a rarefied world of white males with very high levels of educational achievement.[8]

TABLE 4-1. *Undergraduate Majors of Congressional Staff and Counterpart Career and Noncareer Federal Executives*
Percent[a]

Major	Top congressional staffers	Top noncareer executives	Top career executives
Natural Science and Technology	17	18	52
Economics, Business Administration	19	35	10
Social sciences (other than Economics)	41	41	39
Humanities	24	6	0
Total	101	100	101
N	(91)	(17)	(31)

a. Totals may not add to 100 because of rounding.

More or less equal atypicality in the above respects does not necessarily guarantee a good match. A look at the nature of the education each group has received demonstrates subtle differences in educational backgrounds. As table 4-1 shows, congressional staffers resemble noncareer executives much more than they do career executives in the nature of their undergraduate training. Both majored in the natural sciences and technology to a far less extent than career executives. In this respect, top congressional staffers are liberally educated generalists much like the noncareer executives in the agencies they oversee. However, top staffers are even more liberally educated than noncareer executives. When comparing the two, notice the particularly strong representation among top staffers of humanities majors (24 percent versus 6 percent for top noncareer executives) and the small percentage of economics and business majors. This generalist bent in training is carried over into the postgraduate years where the strong representation of legal training among the top staffers (41 percent are lawyers) places them closer to the members of Congress who employ them (over 50 percent have legal training) than to administrators, either career or noncareer (both under 20 percent with legal training) in their counterpart agencies.[9]

Staffers are also much younger than administrators and have spent fewer years on the job. The available evidence indicates that career administrators are in a guildlike system (requiring long apprenticeship

TABLE 4-2. *Age and Years Respondent Has Worked for the Employing Committee or Agency, by Chamber and Role*

Item	Top congressional staffers		Top noncareer executives	Top career executives
	Senate	House		
Percent aged 49 and below	72	40	36	9
N[a]	(39)	(52)	(25)	(44)
Percent who worked less than or equal to 5 years for the committee or agency	67	42	84	23
N[a]	(42)	(53)	(25)	(44)

a. The numbers (N) in parentheses refers to the bases on which percentages are calculated.

within a single institution as a prerequisite for a position at the top). But top congressional committee staffers, particularly those working for the Senate, and top political appointees are more likely to share the characteristics of those in an entrepreneurial system. (An entrepreneurial system is "characterized by a high degree of lateral entry into the elite from outside careers and institutions."[10]) Top congressional staffers and political executives tend to enter the organizations employing them laterally, stay for a period of time shorter than the span of a career, and then leave for other endeavors.[11]

Table 4-2 illustrates some of these points. Top committee staffers, most especially top Senate committee staffers, are much younger than their counterpart career administrators (and younger than top appointees also) and, as expected from the entrepreneurial versus guild characterization, they have very limited experience on their committees in any capacity compared with the number of years that career civil servants have spent climbing the ladder of success in their agencies.[12] These are relative neophytes—particularly in the Senate where the greater shuffling of unit chairmanships than in the House helps to promote staff turnover.[13] In experience with the employing organization, then, top committee staffers match quite favorably with political appointees in the agencies but not with top career civil servants.

However, these young, relatively inexperienced, more liberally educated congressional committee staffers have an impressive record of experience in the specialized areas (fields) of the agencies their committees oversee. More than half of the House (56 percent) and the Senate (53 percent) staffers have had work experience in a relevant field.[14] This is work experience before the rather intensive experience gained in the Congress. And if one adds in those who have had some specialized education in the relevant area, the figures are even more impressive—more than 60 percent of Senate staffers and close to that in the House have had either work experience or specialized education or both in areas covered by their committee unit's jurisdiction.[15] These top congressional staff people, most especially the Senate staff even though it is younger, are not ill prepared to evaluate what goes on in the agencies. In fact, they match up surprisingly well considering their relative youth and lack of longevity in the committees employing them. Still, the job is formidable, given the gap in years of experience between top congressional staffers and top career civil servants and the broad coverage of most congressional subcommittees.[16]

Patterns of Communication

Top congressional staffers are clearly younger, less experienced, and less specialized in their educational training than their counterparts in the career bureaucracy and therefore are at something of a disadvantage. However, detailed data from the staff survey on contacts with agency personnel show that top staffers compensate in part for any training or experiential deficiencies by maintaining an extensive network of contacts with relevant members of the executive branch.

As table 4-3 demonstrates, top staffers in both chambers indicate fairly frequent levels of informal contact (discussions outside of formal proceedings such as hearings) with cabinet and subcabinet level policy officials (top appointed, noncareer executives) in the areas covered by their committee or subcommittee's jurisdiction.[17] Staffers were asked, "About how often do you have informal discussions with top cabinet and subcabinet level policy administrators in the area within your committee's jurisdiction: daily, more than once a week, weekly, fairly regularly, occasionally, never?" One-third of the Senate staffers and a somewhat smaller percentage of the House staffers report at least weekly contacts with top policy officials.[18]

TABLE 4-3. *Frequency of Informal Discussions between Top Staffers and Cabinet and Subcabinet Administrators, by Chamber*
Percent[a]

Frequency of informal discussions	Top Senate staffers	Top House staffers
Weekly or more[b]	33	27
Fairly regularly	31	27
Occasionally	33	44
Never	2	2
Total	99	100
N	(42)	(48)

a. Totals may not add to 100 because of rounding.

b. The first three categories of response—daily, more than once a week, and weekly—were combined in the table for ease of presentation. See text for question wording.

Given that the average tenure (two years or less) of top cabinet and subcabinet level policy administrators is so low, the contact is fairly impressive. Most of the respondents say that either they initiate the contacts (22 percent) or that both they and the top appointees initiate the contacts (72.5 percent). Senate staffers—who, after all, work for committees with confirmation powers whose bosses have more committee assignments and, therefore, typically devote less time to any given subject—report a bit more self-initiation as the dominant mode of contact.

Top staffers, as shown in table 4-4, say they have very frequent informal contact, much of which is self-initiated, with top career civil servants in the areas within the jurisdiction of their committee units. Staffers were asked, "About how often do you have discussions with supergrade career civil servants in the areas within your committee's jurisdiction: daily, more than once a week, weekly, fairly regularly, occasionally, never?" About two-thirds of the top staffers report at least weekly informal discussions with top civil servants. This finding is in line with notions of close subgovernmental links between Congress and the bureaucracy as well as with other comparative data showing exceptional levels of legislative-career executive contacts in the United States.[19] The level of assertiveness reported by top Senate staffers in their relationships with top civil servants is especially high—60 percent say they are the major initiators of informal contacts

TABLE 4-4. *Frequency of Informal Discussions between Top Staffers and Supergrade Career Civil Servants, by Chamber*
Percent[a]

Frequency of informal discussions	Top Senate staffers	Top House staffers
Weekly or more[b]	68	66
Fairly regularly	24	17
Occasionally	7	18
Never	0	0
Total	99	101
N	(41)	(50)

a. Totals may not add to 100 because of rounding.

b. The first three categories of response—daily, more than once a week, and weekly—were combined in the table. See text for question wording.

as opposed to just 35 percent in the House. This goes well beyond the slight Senate-House difference in reported self-initiated contacts with policy administrators just mentioned and attributable to a possible influence of the Senate's confirmation powers. It gives strong hints of an effort by the predominantly younger Senate staffers, who have relatively short tenure in their committee jobs, to compensate for deficiencies in experience by an effort to reach out through self-initiated contacts.[20]

Frequent informal contacts with supergrade career officials are not the only sources of information utilized by top committee staffers. When asked about contacts at "lower levels within the agencies who provide you with useful information for oversight," about 98 percent of the House and 93 percent of the Senate staffers report at least some contacts. More than one-third of each chamber, in fact, report that they have these contacts weekly or even more often. The pattern of contacts with informants splits about equally between regular contacts with the same individuals and ad hoc contacts.[21] And it is rare, according to the congressional staffers, that they find agency staff at any level unwilling to cooperate with their requests for information because of fear of reprisals by others in the agency.[22]

In sum, the data reveal a pattern of very extensive communication between top congressional committee staffers and the career bureaucracy, both those at the top and informants below the top who provide information useful for committee oversight. These data showing extensive congressional contacts with supergrade civil servants and less frequent, though still substantial, contact with political appointees mirror findings on the pattern of congressional-bureaucratic linkages from the University of Michigan comparative elites study done in the early 1970s. The Michigan comparative elites study delineated a U.S. pattern unique in the Western world. It was labeled the "end-run model" because civil servants and members of Congress reported more extensive communications with one another than either reported with department secretaries.[23]

The congressional staff communications data analyzed here fit nicely with the conclusion drawn from the University of Michigan study that the link between Congress and civil servants "reflects in part the independent strength of Congress and the consequent need for civil servants to maintain good relations with its members."[24] The staff communications data document the fact that the typical top committee staffer takes advantage of his (or, infrequently, her) position to maintain an extensive and intensive network of contacts, particularly with the top career civil servants who are the backbone of the executive branch. It is also apparent from answers to the explicit question asked that those below the top levels often provide information that congressional staffers find useful for oversight. I assume those at the top of the career civil service do likewise. Clearly, however, top career administrators, like their subordinates, would have many reasons to provide Congress with an incomplete view of the executive world, one most favorable to their particular interests. Maintaining a variety of contacts at different levels of the bureaucracy is a help in providing Congress with a more complete perspective. But how do staffers supplement the information they receive from those in the "official" world (and the cues given them by their education and work experience prior to Congress) so that they know better what questions it is in their interest to ask?

Keeping Track of the Executive Branch

Top congressional staffers were asked a simple set of questions: "Let me start by asking you to describe briefly how members and staff of your committee keep track of what's going on in the programs and agencies under its jurisdiction? Are any of these ways particularly valuable in bringing potential oversight topics to the attention of committee members and staff? Are there any other ways potential oversight topics come to the committee's attention?"

These questions were used as the basis for having coders score each respondent's "perception of the ways members and staff of the committees keep track of what's going on in the program and agencies under its jurisdiction." Staffers' answers were coded by using detailed categories grouped under the headings presented in table 4-5. Up to six responses per respondent were coded.[25] The entries represent the percentages of respondents giving at least one answer in the category.[26] Column totals do not equal 100 percent because many respondents gave answers codable into many more than one of the broad categories indicated.

The first thing of note about table 4-5 is what is not in the data. All top staffers reported that their units keep track in some way. More than that, the results contain evidence of a rich and varied set of activities or methods used to keep track of what goes on in governmental agencies and programs.

Top staffers reported that they or members of their committees were busy tracking what goes on in the programs or agencies under their jurisdiction by reading (or having their assistants read) news-papers and magazines, watching television, checking the specialized media, and reading government-produced reports and notices. Private, specialized media were one of the sources mentioned least often, and even these were said to be useful in keeping track of what goes on in governmental programs and agencies by more than 24 percent of the respondents. At least one nongovernmental media source (that is, excluding governmental publications and notices from the calculation) was mentioned by 53 percent of the top staffers, a figure smaller than the sum of the entries for mass and specialized media because there is overlap between the two.

Most committees are inundated with information at congressional hearings. As table 4-5 indicates, more than 40 percent of the respondents said that they keep track of what is going on in the programs and agencies by using information transmitted in this forum. These hearings are almost exclusively their own committee hearings. No one mentioned other committees' hearings and only 1 percent mentioned agency hearings.

Table 4-5 separately breaks down information about agencies or

TABLE 4-5. *Keeping Track of Agency Activities, for All Committee Units and by Chamber*
Percent[a]

Method of keeping track	All committee units	All Senate units	All House units
Media sources			
Mass media	31	29	32
Private, specialized media	24	33	17
Media, no indication of type	4	5	4
Government publications and notices	32	29	34
Hearings of all types	43	38	47
Complaints or criticisms about an agency or program			
From governmental sources			
Agency sources	35	36	34
Congressional sources	25	26	25
Other governmental sources	10	7	11
From nongovernmental sources			
Individuals	43	41	45
Groups	27	26	28
Other nongovernmental sources	3	2	4
Information (not specifically complaints or criticisms)			
From governmental sources			
Agency sources	56	67	47
Congressional sources	41	29	51
Other governmental sources	18	17	19
From nongovernmental sources			
Individuals	17	14	19
Groups	20	21	19
Other nongovernmental sources	4	0	8
Other	8	7	9
We don't keep track in any way	0	0	0
N	(95)	(42)	(53)

a. Totals do not add to 100 because of multiple responses.

programs received by committee units from sources other than the media or hearings. One category covers information respondents specified as conveyed through complaints or criticisms about an agency or program. Another covers statements about information per se, that is, where respondents did not specify that it consisted of complaints or criticisms about agencies or programs. Agency sources are tremendously important.[27] Fifty-six percent of the respondents mentioned information from agency sources and 35 percent cited complaints about agency performance or program content or administration coming from agency sources.[28]

Congressional sources are also widely used to gather information. As table 4-5 shows, complaints or just plain information about agencies is secured from other members, staff, committee reviews of agencies and programs (where no hearings were held), and informally from congressional support agencies (that is, not from their final written reports). The data under "congressional sources" in table 4-5 exclude information gained from hearings or directly from constituents (coded separately). They include such things as material gathered by staff on field trips or cases when "a staffer would come across some matter that he thought was worthy of an investigation or study by the subcommittee," or "members calling up requesting action on a problem they discovered" or "a member may [just] have a personal interest in the way something is operated."[29] Complaints from congressional sources were mentioned by 25 percent of the top staffers, information by 41 percent. Fifty-five percent cited congressional sources under one or the other, or both, of the headings.[30]

Complaints (10 percent) and information (18 percent) from "other government sources"—mayors, governors, and other state and local officials—are also important sources for many congressional committees in this era of grants to states and localities.[31]

Complaints and information from "nongovernmental sources" include tracking of agency activities through complaints and information received from individuals and groups in the society through direct communication to a member or staffer. Individual sources means constituents who write, telephone, or come in person to see members and staffers and information turned up through the servicing of casework requests. Not surprisingly, the bulk of such information comes in the form of complaints (43 percent of the top staffers mentioned complaints from individuals), although some respondents (17 percent) used more neutral terms to describe the information they receive from individual sources. The total mentioning individual, nongovernmental sources is 58.9 percent, almost the sum of the complaints and information entries since there is little overlap between the two.

Groups, interest groups, professional groups, and so on provide information on programs and agencies through visits by delegations and lobbyists and also through an important, often overlooked device. Members and staffers are often invited to attend and speak at group meetings.[32] While at the meetings, they are the targets of communication about government activities. Twenty-seven percent of the respondents reported that group representatives provide their committee units with intelligence about programs and agencies in the form of complaints, and 20 percent just give information. Slightly over 40 percent of the total reported receiving complaints, information, or both from groups, and this feedback is helpful in tracking agency or programs.

Chamber differences, as table 4-5 indicates, are not very great. Senate staffers were nearly twice as likely as House staffers to report that their committees rely on the private, specialized media for information about programs and agencies and somewhat more likely to receive information from agency sources—findings not too surprising in light of the shorter tenures of Senate staffers. But House staffers used hearings and other congressional information sources more often—probably because of greater familiarity with internal institutional sources and, therefore, somewhat less need to rely on the specialized media or the agencies.

The overall picture is one of an environment rich in sources of information about agencies and programs. Committees clearly rely heavily on the agencies; and the "complaints and criticisms" data from the agencies and other government sources are a sign of the extensive communication to congressional committees of "danger signals" about government programs from elected, appointed, and career officials at all levels. About 56 percent of the staffers reported that they keep track of government programs and agencies through complaints or criticisms from one type of official or another. Eighty-five percent mention complaints from some source.[33] Agencies are, however, only one source of information. Individuals, groups, the media, and the hearings held by Congress all provide information.[34]

Information Network Development

It is now abundantly clear that much information about programs and agencies is transmitted to congressional committees. However,

TABLE 4-6. *Information Network Development, by Committee Unit Type*
Percent[a]

| | Committee unit type | | | |
Information network development	Appropriations	Other[b]	Oversight[c]	Total
Well-developed network	82	46	18	48
Intermediate network	18	43	71	43
Poorly developed network	0	11	12	9
Total	100	100	101	100
N	(17)	(56)	(17)	(90)

a. Totals may not add to 100 because of rounding.

b. "Other" units are nonoversight, non-Appropriations committee units.

c. The oversight units in the survey consist of all House Government Operations and Senate Governmental Affairs units, and the specialized oversight subcommittees of House Commerce, House Public Works, and House Ways and Means.

it is still not entirely clear how well developed the typical committee information network is. For example, a relatively small number of committee units may have well-developed networks and a large number may have poorly developed networks. Certainly it is still unclear how aggressive committees are in their monitoring activities.

To shed some light on the first issue, respondents' answers to the tracking questions were coded to evaluate the level of development of each committee unit's information network.[35] There were three major categories. The first was for a "well-developed network," reserved for cases in which the respondents' answers gave "an image of a highly developed information network on agency activities— numerous sources, well used." The second code was for an "intermediate network," when there was evidence of "numerous sources, poorly used; or few sources, well used; or a medium number of sources [in] medium use." Finally, there was a code for a poorly developed information network when answers indicated "few sources, poorly used."[36]

The distribution of committee units on the information network development indicator is presented in table 4-6. The data reinforce the image gained from the information tracking data (table 4-5). Almost half of the top staffers (48 percent) gave answers indicating that their units had impressively developed information networks, rich in sources that they exploited well. Less than 10 percent had poorly developed networks where they both had few sources and did not give much evidence that the sources they had were well used. Forty-three percent fell into the intermediate classification between the two extremes.

The overall picture presented in table 4-6 is that congressional committee units have very impressive information networks keeping them posted on agency programs and activities. Slightly over 90 percent of the top staffers fell into the well developed or intermediate network categories. Those committee units in the dark about the programs and agencies under their jurisdiction were few and far between.

House and Senate differences are minor, with the House exhibiting slightly more-developed networks, as expected given the greater seniority of typical House staffers. Two groups stand out as having, on the one hand, particularly well-developed networks and, on the other, somewhat less well-developed networks. The Appropriations units shine in this respect, just over 82 percent scoring high on the indicator. Oversight units are lower than the norm, with most having intermediate networks. However, their distance from the distribution for the other units is not as great as that found for Appropriations.[37] The regular reviews done each year by the Appropriations Committees probably account for their especially well-developed information networks even though their jurisdictions are wide.[38] Committee oversight units, in contrast, are not constrained by the need to consider a yearly appropriation (or even, for the most part, periodic reauthorizations of the type most substantive committees handle) for the programs in their oversight jurisdictions, and there are numerous signs other than the information network scores of their more casual approaches. They are the most likely, for example, to rely on the mass media for information about the bureaucracy.[39]

The information network indicator combines two elements: number of information sources and quality of use. The notion is that to classify a committee unit as having a well-developed information network requires not only multiple sources of information but also some evidence that they are used well, that is, consulted with reasonable frequency, checked against other sources when appropriate, and so on.

The quantitative element is easy to demonstrate. All one must do is calculate the relationship between the information network development measure and a simple count of the number of information sources that each top staffer reported his or her committee unit used in keeping track of relevant agencies and the programs these agencies administer. The correlation (r) is -0.58; the greater the number of sources, the better developed the information network.[40] And committee units typically use a large number of sources (68 percent of the top staffers report that their units used five or more). In short, committee units usually employ many sources, a fact central to having a well-developed information network.

Proof that the quantitative element is vital to the network development measure, but not the whole story, is found in the pattern of contacts reported by top staffers for oversight units. Recall that oversight units score lowest on the information network development indicator. Yet they actually report a slightly larger number of sources overall used by their units than the average staffer reports.[41] Their relatively low scores on information network development are driven by the qualitative aspects of the measure, that is, how well sources are used.

In sum, committee units tend to have well-developed information networks, rich in sources that they exploit well. The large number of information sources described by top staffers is a key element in the impressive scores on the information network development measure, but so is the evidence that the sources are used well.

Active versus Reactive Monitoring

Clearly, congressional committees typically have well developed information networks. However, it is possible to have a good number of information sources and even to make good use of them without exhibiting an active approach to monitoring. Therefore, I developed another measure to round out this analysis of the congressional committee intelligence system.

This measure assesses each committee unit's approach to keeping track of agency activities. Based on each respondent's answers to the tracking question (and its probes), the coders assessed whether committees were best characterized as active or reactive monitors of agency activities. Choices were as follows: First, *active monitors*— marked by evidence of energetic monitoring of agency activities, including regular phone calls to agency counterparts, seeking out

TABLE 4-7. *Approach to Keeping Track of Agency Activities, by Committee Unit Type*
Percent[a]

Approach to tracking	Committee unit type			
	Appropriations	Other[b]	Oversight[c]	Total
Active monitor	63	27	29	34
Intermediate monitor	19	25	12	22
Reactive monitor	19	48	59	45
Total	101	100	100	101
N	(16)	(59)	(17)	(92)

a. Totals may not add to 100 because of rounding.
b. "Other" units are nonoversight, non-Appropriations committee units.
c. See table 4-6 for the definition of an oversight unit.

information wherever it can be found, and so on. Second was a category for *intermediate monitors,* whose activities are equally active and reactive. The third category, *reactive monitors,* involved a dominant mode of reactive monitoring of agency activities, finding out about things mainly from newspapers or as a result of constituent complaints or the like. Some respondents in this category claimed to follow the "squeaky wheel" approach, which in this context meant that the top staffer mentioned waiting for signs of trouble before reacting.[42]

The first point to note from the findings in table 4-7 is that the modal (most frequently occurring) approach to tracking category is reactive. This is more markedly the case when the responses of the Appropriations Committee staffers are separated out since they tend to describe a pattern of active monitoring, while those with the other committees, particularly the units specializing in oversight, are likely to report a more reactive style—responding to information that comes to them prepackaged (newspapers, the media) or arrives at the door.

Second, however, there is a sizable number of active monitors, although a majority only among the Appropriations units. More than 25 percent of both the oversight unit top staffers and top staffers for the other, non-Appropriations units described their units' approaches to keeping track of agency activities in ways that led my coders to code them as active monitors—units seeking out information on their own. And a sufficient number of respondents representing these "other" (nonoversight, non-Appropriations) units gave active enough descriptions of their monitoring approaches so that one-fourth were categorized as intermediate monitors. Therefore, more than half of the units are not scored in the reactive category.

The overall picture on monitoring style, then, is mixed. Reactive monitoring is more typical than other styles (modal) but not over-whelmingly so. Many committee units report a very active style, and the majority of all but the oversight units are active or intermediate monitors. I shall discuss this point at length next, but it should be clear now that the "fire-alarm" style identified by a very provocative analysis as typical of congressional committees is not dominant.[43]

Implications

Congress seems, on balance, well equipped to monitor executive branch activities. In recent years, committees have added staff to assist them in this task, so that there is now a sizable staff available. Compared with top career executives, top congressional committee staffers are relatively young, inexperienced, and liberally educated (that is, generalists), but they have an impressive record of job experience in the specialized areas that their committees oversee (and this prior to whatever familiarity they have gained in Congress). And top congressional staffers are clearly well matched to the political appointees at the apex of agency hierarchies. The monitoring task is, therefore, formidable, but not so far out of reach as staffers' youth and relatively brief experience on the job would lead one to expect.

Most top committee staffers are well enmeshed in an extensive informal communications network with top administrative officials. This is especially true of communications with supergrade career administrators. Top committee staffers who report extensive contacts with career administrators also tend to be the same individuals whose answers to an open-ended question on tracking what goes on in programs and policies indicate that their committees maintain active and well-developed information networks, a suggestion of the key role that top career people play in the congressional intelligence system.[44] While informal communications with top career adminis-trators are the most frequent, they are supplemented by extensive informal contact with political appointees and with officials below the top career level. Top committee staffers, as anyone who observes them can attest, have no shortage of communication with administrative officials.

Communication with the incumbents of top and lower-level official positions is clearly an essential requirement for a good intelligence network, but it would limit congressional committees to a narrow perspective on the administrative world—one seen through administrators' eyes only—if it represented a monopoly of committee information sources. Such is not the case, however, as the data on how members and staff keep track of what goes on in agencies and programs make abundantly clear.

Top congressional staffers present a picture of an environment rich in sources of information about agencies and programs. Aside from agency personnel (who, by all measures, are relied upon heavily by the committees), individuals, groups, the mass and specialized media, and congressional sources (for example, members, staffers, and congressional support agencies) all provide information. Some information is gathered through formal congressional proceedings like committee hearings or official agency reports. Informal sources and the media are also widely used.

This evidence that a great deal of information about the executive branch is transmitted to congressional committees is captured in the information network measure based on the interview protocols. It indicates that congressional committee units have very impressive information networks keeping them posted on agency programs and activities. The overwhelming majority of top staffers describe committee information sources and patterns of use that fit into the well-developed or intermediate-developed network categories, indicating that they either have many information sources, or exploit their sources well, or both.

The responses of top staffers suggest a committee approach to keeping track of agency activities that is surprisingly active. While reactive monitoring is the modal category characterizing the monitoring styles of the committee units studied, a majority of the top staffers give answers on tracking indicating either active or intermediate monitoring. These respondents present a picture of committee units characterized by a monitoring style involving a significant level of initiative to seek out information. These units do not merely react to information that appears in front of them at the initiative of others.

Though not everyone reports well-developed information networks or active monitoring styles, a significant share (27.3 percent) of the respondents indicate that both attributes (well-developed networks and active monitoring) characterize their monitoring activities. And a very high proportion (56.9 percent) give answers placing their units in either the top or intermediate categories on both monitoring attributes.[45] Add to that the backgrounds of the staffers and the extensive informal communication they report with agency personnel at all levels, and one must conclude that a majority of congressional committees are exposed to and often seek out a good deal of information about agency doings and program progress. They are also reasonably capable, given the data presented on staffers' backgrounds, of comprehending the technical as well as the political implications of what they learn. Whether committees use the information received as one might like, or whether the information they have is balanced or interpreted by them in an unbiased manner is not yet established, but committees clearly are well enmeshed in an impressive information network that many are in a position to exploit effectively.

That committee information networks are often well developed in the numbers of sources used or even in the effective use of the information made available seems to fit reasonably well with the "fire-alarm model" of congressional information gathering developed by Mathew McCubbins and Thomas Schwartz. They argue that, contrary to the conventional characterization of oversight as "Congress' neglected function,"[46] "what has appeared to scholars to be a neglect of oversight . . . really is a preference for one form of oversight [fire-alarm oversight] over another, less effective form [police-patrol oversight]."[47] In essence, "instead of sniffing for fires, Congress places fire alarm boxes on street corners, builds neighborhood fire houses, and sometimes dispatches its own hook-and-ladder in response to an alarm."[48] It structures the situation so that information can come its way. Then it chooses whether or not to respond. Congress, therefore, largely neglects the police-patrol approach—an active, direct search for information at "its own initiative"[49]—and instead follows the fire-alarm strategy in which "Congress establishes a system of rules, procedures, and informal practices that enable individual citizens and organized interest groups to examine administrative decisions (sometimes in prospect), to charge executive agencies with violating congressional goals, and to seek remedies from agencies, courts, and Congress itself.[50]

McCubbins and Schwartz argue that Congress prefers the fire-alarm to the police-patrol approach because it is cheaper (the costs are borne by others), brings more problems to Congress's attention than the alternative strategy, and is more profitable (yields more benefit per unit of time expended by congressional personnel).[51] Congress could go chasing after information, but it is easier and even, on balance, "more effective"[52] to use a fire-alarm policy for two reasons. First, Congress's legislative intent is usually vague. Therefore, it does best (and prefers) spelling out its goals in response to complaints. Second, while "a fire-alarm policy would almost certainly pick up any violation of legislative goals that seriously harmed an organized group, a police-patrol policy would doubtless miss many such violations, since only a sample of executive branch actions would be examined."[53]

There are numerous criticisms one can make of the fire-alarm approach to information gathering on normative grounds since this system obviously favors unusually articulate individuals and those represented by organized groups, but that is not the issue I want to emphasize here.[54] Rather I want to stress four points relevant to McCubbins and Schwartz's thesis:

—Contrary to McCubbins' and Schwartz's expectations, the police-patrol approach is prominent. It characterizes the information search styles of many congressional units, more than half if one combines the active and intermediate monitor categories on the active-reactive monitoring measure discussed in this chapter. McCubbins and Schwartz assert that the reactive, fire-alarm approach "predominate[s]", but this does not appear to be the case.[55]

—Given the rather elegant and generally convincing argument McCubbins and Schwartz make for the likely predominance of the fire-alarm approach, one must ask why active, police-patrol type approaches are so common and whether or not this represents a change in monitoring style.

—The data presented in this chapter indicate that an active, police-patrol type information seeking style coexists comfortably with a large number of information sources and a well-developed information network. Perhaps this active style is more rational than the pure fire-alarm approach, especially given the change in circumstances facing Congress since the early 1970s.

—Finally, the concept of police-patrol oversight may confuse two elements best left separate. One is an active or passive style of information seeking. The second is centralized versus decentralized mechanisms for information gathering. In their definition of the policepatrol and firealarm approaches, McCubbins and Schwartz identify the former as "comparatively centralized" and the latter as "less centralized."[56] If by comparatively centralized they mean simply that committee decisionmakers play an active role in information gathering, then there is no problem. If they mean to imply that information search and utilization is coordinated from the center of Congress or from the center of each committee or even of each subcommittee unit, then they are probably wrong. An active strategy does not require decisionmaking from the center other than the decision to permit or encourage staff and members to seek out information.

The first point has been developed at some length already. It therefore requires no elaboration. Assuming that I am correct and that the data indicating the prominence of active or intermediate congressional approaches to gathering information on executive branch activities accurately represent reality—and great care was taken to ensure that this is the case—one naturally wants to explore the second point. This means answering two related questions: Why is an active or intermediate type police-patrol approach to gathering information about programs and agencies so common among congressional committee units? Does the evidence of fairly widespread active or intermediate approaches represent a change in congressional monitoring style?

As McCubbins and Schwartz themselves point out, the explanations they develop for the asserted predominance of a firealarm approach to securing information on agencies and programs dovetail nicely with standard explanations given in the "Congress' neglected function" literature for the lack of oversight—greater opportunities in other areas. McCubbins and Schwartz argue, however, that it is not oversight that has been neglected, but rather one form of gathering information, that is, the police-patrol approach. The use of fire alarms, they say, was and is widespread, but ignored by most oversight analysts because these analysts define oversight in terms of an active, police-patrol approach.

The same incentives, indeed, that the literature says lead Congress to neglect oversight would cause it to neglect active, police-patrol approaches to securing information on agencies and programs. Let us assume an environment in which there is ample political payoff for approving new programs and in which resources are available to fund new programs and, through expansion, bring new constituencies under established programs. Further, if one assumes limited resources of time and staff, sitting back to wait for messages from the environment that things may be going wrong is a very rational, cost-effective strategy from Congress's perspective. To paraphrase the common saying, "If the people out there don't know it's broke, don't fix it."

If one assumes some changes in the environment and in congressional resources, however, the fire-alarm information strategy looks a little less attractive and the police-patrol approach more attractive. These changes will be familiar because they were described in chapters 2 and 3. In an environment in which it is harder to pass new programs or expand old ones because of a perceived budget scarcity and a skeptical public, where there are signs of public discontent with government, where the size and complexity of government concern citizens and elected officials alike, where Congress and its committees are struggling to protect their position after a period of intense conflict with the president and his appointees, where both congressional committee and support agency staff have been rapidly augmented (in part to help Congress address these changes), then it makes more sense for Congress and its committees actively to seek out information.

Why? First, when there is less opportunity to do new things, then fine tuning and correcting the old becomes more attractive. In and of itself, this makes a more active information search style more appealing. But there should be more to the argument than this point because sitting back and waiting for information to appear might still be an acceptable, if less appealing, strategy, even under the changed circumstances. And there are reinforcing factors. If Congress wants to stimulate information about the agencies because this information is now more valuable than before, then it makes sense to advertise its interest. Going out actively to seek information not only yields some increment of knowledge, it also stimulates others to come forth and, in the terms used by McCubbins and Schwartz, pull a fire alarm.

Second, in an era of executive-legislative confrontation, an active information-seeking strategy has greater appeal than in a quieter, more amicable period. Committees need to protect their power positions. They have greater incentive to seek information aggressively since the perceived costs of not knowing are greater.

Third, with the addition of committee, personal, and support agency staff, it is now cheaper for Congress to seek out information. Committee and personal staff have increased and the support organizations have been expanded. Once it may have been necessary to take staff away from some more desired activity in order to free up additional time for information search, but now there are more resources available and relatively fewer opportunities to do other things. Assuming the greater current value of information as just argued, the mere existence of this resource is a powerful incentive to use it actively. (In addition, the motivation to increase staff and support agency personnel was at least in part tied to an interest in securing more information.)

Finally, staff members have their own desires and needs that make them likely pursuers of information. This is not to argue that congressional staff are out of control in a fundamental sense (acting against members' interests or without their knowledge about basic goals or strategies), but simply that many have reason to be enthusiastic information seekers, along with the training or experience to make them knowledgeable seekers and fairly discriminating consumers of what they learn. For those who, either by training or experience, have some expertise in the area their committees oversee, seeking information actively is likely a source of personal pride and professional fulfillment. For those who want to make themselves known in the Washington community, and this includes more and more staffers as staff size grows, actively seeking information is one way to project one's presence.[57] This is especially true when, as now, conditions make it difficult for staff to make a mark by working on legislation creating new programs.

For these reasons, connected to changes in the congressional environment, it is possible that congressional information-seeking behavior related to the activities of executive agencies has changed over time. Once the fire-alarm style clearly predominated. Now it is important but not dominant.

At this juncture, the third general point relevant to the McCubbins and Schwartz thesis—that of the relative rationality of the two information-seeking styles—naturally arises.[58] The empirical evidence examined earlier shows that an active style of information seeking is strongly related to information network development. Those units reporting numerous information sources that they use well are also the most active information seekers. And units marked by an active information-seeking style are likely to report a larger number of information sources than those marked by a reactive style.[59] Many information sources, then, apparently coexist comfortably with an active information-seeking style. Active information seekers are almost certainly no less well informed on the activities of the executive branch than reactive monitors; if anything, they are probably better informed because they tend to have more sources and to use them better.

The conclusion I reach is that, at least in the contemporary period, an active style of information seeking has much to commend it and can be construed as quite rational in comparison with a more passive style. The argument in favor of waiting for information to reach congressional personnel is still a good one, but changed circumstances increase the attraction of vigorous information search activity. In the terms used by McCubbins and Schwartz, there are now greater benefits per unit of time spent by congressional personnel on an active police-patrol approach than before.

Even where search is active, it should be noted, congressional committees will not necessarily act on the information they secure. They can easily avoid, if they choose, acting on information exposing problems that do no harm to supporters or potential supporters and, therefore, may be of limited interest (that is, benefit) to them. Moreover, with a little effort, committees can use information turned up by active search and the process of the search to create new supporters, a difficult goal to achieve in Congress in the contemporary environment and, therefore, a stimulus to more active information search. Since an active style does not in any way preclude listening to complaints—indeed, it may even stimulate information sources— a congressional committee unit is not likely to miss much by using an active information-seeking strategy. In fact, by using the active strategy it is likely to gain useful information in addition to that forthcoming through a more passive approach. This is particularly likely when its information network is well developed, which the data show is empirically the case for active information seekers.

While a fire-alarm approach is usually cheaper than a police-patrol approach in some respects—most of the costs are borne by the alarm sounders, and Congress can try to dissociate itself from the apparent perpetrators of the acts stimulating the complaints—the relative costs do not stay the same over time.[60] Where before, staff resources were very limited, institutional rivalry somewhat muted, and opportunities for creating new programs greater, now staff resources are relatively plentiful, institutional rivalry more intense, and new programs harder to create, especially when one takes into account the proliferation of subcommittee units and, therefore, the small number of credits available per unit. Costs to Congress of active search are, therefore, lower and benefits higher. And I should emphasize that Congress is no less able to dissociate itself from the acts of the executive branch when it pursues an active information-seeking strategy as opposed to a more passive information-seeking strategy. It is as easy to say, "How terrible. We must try to do something about that," to someone contacted by committee personnel as to someone who contacts the committee. Finally, an active strategy does not require the immense costs associated with systematic, comprehensive sampling of the type McCubbins and Schwartz imply in their elaboration of the police-patrol approach.[61] Active information seekers can cultivate regular informants, make forays into the field to a fixed set of locations, or sample more or less at random. Most seem to do a bit of each. But they generally do not draw what a social scientist would regard as a systematic sample. They are more opportunistic than comprehensive.

In conclusion, an observer of the contemporary Congress can read Weber's classic essay "Bureaucracy," with minimum alarm. Weber's bureaucracy had an "overtowering" position relative to its nominal political masters because of its continuity, expertise, and ability to guard information.[62] U.S. congressional committees have now built a formidable counterorganization. Though the contemporary American bureaucracy is certainly marked by greater continuity (longer tenure) than committee staff, staffers are not mere "dilettantes" who stand opposite administrative "experts."[63] They have significant experience in the areas covered by the agencies they oversee and well-developed communication networks that give them significant opportunities to push aside any veil covering bureaucratic decisions and activities.

Most top committee staffers are well enmeshed in an extensive informal communications network with top administrative officials, and they supplement the information they receive from them through sources holding positions below the top levels. They are not confined to agency sources, however. Most report that they receive considerable information from outside of the executive branch. They have many information sources, well exploited. They also indicate a surprisingly active approach to keeping track of agency activities. Available evidence, therefore, indicates that lack of information is not Congress's major problem in regard to administration and policy.

Available evidence also suggests that Congress responds to changes in its environment. Research findings rooted in data of the 1960s show that Congress did not then engage in much formal oversight of policy and administration (using mechanisms such as hearings) or actively seek out information about government agencies.[64] This was explained, at least in large part, by a lack of incentives to engage in such activities and was clearly accurate for oversight hearings and almost certainly accurate for information seeking. But it is important to understand incentives in the context of the political and institutional environment facing members of Congress. When there is change in the relative payoffs of different types of behavior, and when resources change, people respond. Just as Congress is now more active in formal oversight activity, especially hearings, so it seems that it is now a more active seeker of information about policy and administration. The original passivity made sense in light of the greater returns, individual and institutional, available from other activities and modes of information seeking. The same logic can explain the more active stance now evident.

Chapter 5
Getting on the Oversight Agenda

CLEARLY, THE TYPICAL congressional committee unit has an extensive information network to help in tracking what goes on in the agencies. Many committees are also active in seeking out information. They are not content just to wait for information to come to them. Given that committee personnel seem to know a great deal about agency activities, what factors lead congressional committee members and staff to select the programs or agencies they oversee? Why, in other words, do some matters get on the active oversight agenda?[1]

With limited time and resources at their disposal, committee personnel must choose the matters they wish to pursue. Some factors are likely to be of greater importance than others. Of all the information coming to Congress's attention, some events or situations or predicaments are surely more likely than others to move a committee unit to place items on its oversight agenda. What these factors are, and especially their relative importance in setting the oversight agenda, are my central concerns in this chapter, along with an examination of who has the major influence in committee decisionmaking on oversight.

Selecting the Agenda

I focused on the 95th Congress (1977–78) and asked top staff members interviewed for my survey (see appendix A) to evaluate the importance of certain factors that might lead a congressional committee unit to select an agency or program for review. All the factors listed on the survey may have been important at some point during a staffer's tenure on a committee. But concentrating on the

95th Congress enabled me to gauge how important the respondents judged each factor to be in a two-year span (1977–78) typical of the period when oversight had become a prominent congressional activity. The importance of the factors could then be compared, by implication, to their importance in earlier periods. In addition, by narrowing the time frame, I could relate reports from respondents about the actual oversight behavior of their units in the recently completed 95th Congress to their assessments of the import of agenda-setting factors in the very same Congress, thereby getting a good sense of how the two are linked.

My list of factors was drawn up after I consulted the research literature on factors said to influence congressional decisions about whether to engage in oversight activity.[2] Staff members were asked to evaluate the importance of each factor to committee unit members (senators or representatives) and staff separately so that a rough estimate of the importance of the factors to actors in each of the roles could be obtained.[3]

The meanings of the factors (listed in table 5-1) are self-evident. Few of the top staffers interviewed had any difficulty with the list. But a few responses by representatives and senators to a broad, open-ended question they were asked in my interviews with committee members adds texture to the meaning of the stark terms on the list presented to the top staffers. The question asked members to identify the factors leading their committee units to select the agencies and programs they concentrated on in their oversight work during the 95th Congress.[4]

One senator on a Governmental Affairs subcommittee, for example, focused on a scandal in the General Services Administration (GSA), which was prominent at the time of the 95th Congress. The scandal led his unit to select the GSA as a program to oversee.

> We got into that [the Government Services Administration scandal] sort of early, before everybody knew that it was the problem that it turned out to be. . . . The committee did have GSA [in its jurisdiction] . . . and [Chairman] Ribicoff, when the first news came out, he said, "Maybe that's something that you should look at." And we began to. . . . It was announced that the FBI was looking at it, [the] Justice Department was looking at it. And we thought . . . maybe we need to send an investigator in and see

whether they're covering all of it now and that they're doing their investigation. We quickly found out that the extent of the Justice involvement at that time was in the Baltimore case . . . and . . . we began to figure that was the tip of the iceberg and that there were all kinds of other problems in GSA besides that. So, we decided that we would hold a hearing and . . . every hearing led to more.[5]

Scandals, of course, were only one of the many factors mentioned. Another senator, on the Finance Committee, talked about a severe crisis in social security as a major cause of program selection. "It was obvious," he said, "that the social security fund was being drained."[6]

And a representative on the Social Security Subcommittee of the House Ways and Means Committee mentioned a similar problem. "We did disability because that was the part of the system that was bankrupt and needed the most quick attention."[7]

Programs related to social security were not the only ones in crisis. A House member on the Postsecondary Education Subcommittee of the Education and Labor Committee began his answer to the question by saying, "Well, of course, we have to respond to crises. We had a crisis in the student, the default problem, and then some terrible problems for institutions that came out of the government's efforts to do something about the defaults. And . . . any kind of crisis like that produces a sort of a crash need for oversight."[8]

Sometimes there were sharp disagreements with agency policies. Take the case of the Communications Subcommittee of House Commerce: "We were interested in why the [Federal Communications] Commission . . . had either been indicating an apathy toward or even an antipathy toward the proposal for putting the Western hemisphere on the same . . . radio spectrum as all of Europe and Africa and the whole Eastern hemisphere. . . . There were suspicions that some of the Commissioners might be more interested in protecting . . . existing broadcasters in America rather than opening up every major market in the country to additional radio competitors."[9]

There are times when the reauthorization process forces a committee unit to select a program or agency for review. For example, a ranking minority member on a House Education and Labor subcommittee said, "I think the major factor in the 95th Congress was the reauthorization of legislation. I don't think there's any question that

that was the major purpose for oversight, to have some justification to go ahead with the program."[10]

And, finally, there are the obvious narrow political reasons, such as complaints from interest groups or the potential for publicity, that lead to the selection of agencies and programs for oversight.

A member of the House Ways and Means subcommittee said, "Probably there are some grave areas that you don't even provide any oversight for because the ones you are looking [at] are the ones that just leap out at you . . . or particular pressure groups lobby for you to look at."[11]

And a senator who served on the Senate Commerce Committee talked about the impact of publicity potential on his subcommittee's oversight selections.

> I think that too often the subject of oversight work may relate to political goals and objectives of the particular subcommittee chairman who . . . sees some publicity advantage perhaps in investigating in a particular area. It sort of depends on what's going on at the time, what would make news. . . . That isn't universally true; I don't mean to say that. But I think that in many instances those are the kinds of considerations that seem to predominate, rather than an orderly, . . . unbiased review.[12]

Research Questions

An elementary first question is whether or not the factors identified as leading to selection of program or agency for the oversight agenda occurred at all in the 95th Congress. A scandal in an agency, for example, might be very important in moving the agency onto the relevant committee's oversight agenda, but if there were no scandals in and around the period covered by the 95th Congress, the factor would almost certainly be irrelevant in setting the committee's agenda for oversight. Second, given the occurrence of a factor, how important was it in leading to the selection of agencies or programs for oversight? The importance of factors will be examined, with special attention to role and chamber comparisons. Third, how are the factors structured? Do particular factors cluster together along dimensions, so that knowledge of the relative importance of one factor in determining whether or not an agency or program is overseen by a congressional committee unit is a strong predictor of the relative importance of another factor? If the factors form dimensions, what are they and what do they imply?

A set of related, fundamental issues are broached along the way. What motivates congressional committees to put an agency or program on its oversight agenda? This is the basic question asked in much of the oversight literature. Whose interests are served best by the existing system? Is the agenda determined in a sensible way?

Choosing Agencies or Programs for Oversight

Table 5-1 gives the list of the agenda selection factors presented to top staffers and the percentages of those reporting that the factor was "not applicable; did not occur" in their committee units in the 95th Congress. The left column contains the percentages who said the factor did not occur for members (senators or representatives) of the respondent's committee unit. The right column contains the same estimates for staff.[13] Respondents were given the following instruction, "Now here is a list of factors people have identified as leading members and staff to select the agencies or programs they will oversee. Would you look at the list and check off how important you would say each factor was for this committee of the 95th Congress? There are separate sections for members and for staff and room at the bottom to add any factor that we might have left out."

Table 5-1 makes clear four important points. First, as expected, top staffers report that most of the factors identified in the list were of at least some significance (that is, they occurred) in leading members and staff to select agencies or programs for oversight. Second, top staffers also report a great correspondence between what occurred (led to selection decisions) for committee unit members and staff. Indeed, the rank order correlation (Spearman's rho) between the percentage entries is a very robust 0.868. Third, malfeasance (scandal), probably the most common trigger of oversight, occurred least.[14] Slightly over 25 percent of the staffers did not rate scandal in terms of importance (for themselves or members) because, so far as they knew, it did not occur in the agencies or programs under their committee units' jurisdiction. Fourth, the major staff-member differences were seen just where one would expect—staffers reported that casework and, to a lesser extent, publicity potential were more likely to occur as factors influencing what reached the oversight agenda for committee members than for staff. These findings help to validate

TABLE 5-1. *Selecting the Oversight Agenda: Percent for Whom Factor Did Not Occur or Was Not Applicable, Members and Staff*

Factor[a]	Members Percent	Members Rank	Staff Percent	Staff Rank	Number of cases
Evidence of malfeasance in administration: scandal	26.6	1	25.3	1	79
Crisis in a policy area	10.0	4	7.5	8	80
Low regard for agency administrators	9.2	6	9.2	6	76
Agency unresponsive to the committee	6.3	8	6.3	9	79
Belief that programs are not effectively or efficiently run	1.3	12	0	13	77
Complaints of clientele or interest groups	0	14	0	13	80
Commitment to review of ongoing programs and agencies	2.5	10.5	2.5	11	80
Termination of program authorizations; reauthorizations process[b]	16.9	2	15.4	2	65
Opportunity to gain public attention; publicity potential	5.1	9	12.8	4	78
General public concern about an agency or program	1.2	13	0	13	81
Concern in members' districts about an agency or program	2.5	10.5	5.0	10	80
Discoveries made when aiding a constituent; casework	10.0	4	18.8	3	80
Desire to assist an agency or program favored by the committee	10.0	4	11.3	5	80
Sharp disagreement with agency policies	8.9	7	7.6	7	79

$R_s = 0.888$

a. After each factor, respondents could check the following categories: major importance, 1; important, 2; some importance, 3; minor importance, 4; unimportant, 5; or not applicable, did not occur. Factors are listed in the order presented to the respondents.

b. Appropriations Committee respondents deleted because they were asked about the effects of a "request for a large budget increase for an agency."

the measurement instrument. Staff respondents distinguished the occurrence of factors affecting themselves from those affecting members in just the instances where such distinctions were most likely.[15]

Given the occurrence of the factors listed—and all were apparently relevant to the members or staff of at least three-fourths of the committee units studied—how important were they in leading to the selection of agencies or programs for oversight? Table 5-2 gives the mean scores for each of the factors. The table includes top staffers' assessments of the importance of each of the factors to the staff and to the members of their committee units. The scale presented to the respondents had five points ranging from "major importance" (1) to "unimportant" (5).[16]

Importance, the concept measured, means consequence, significance, influence.[17] My measure gauges top staffers' notions about how important each factor was in the selection of programs or agencies for oversight if the factor occurred at all, not how frequently each factor occurred. Measuring frequency would have been a useful addition to an understanding of oversight agenda setting. However, the decision to probe member and staff similarities and differences precluded that measurement, given the need to use an instrument respondents could complete in a reasonable time.

Table 5-2 demonstrates that, just as Morris Ogul's influential work on oversight would lead one to expect, when jarring stimuli like a "scandal" or a "crisis in a policy area" or a "sharp disagreement with agency policy" occur, they are immensely important determinants of the oversight agenda.[18]

But the picture is more complex. The results also suggest the substantial, and independent, importance of additional factors.[19] Some agencies and programs are chosen for oversight because the choice seems to promise members direct and immediate electoral payoffs—the basis of most congressional behavior according to some scholars.[20] "Concern in members' districts"—judged especially important for members (ranked sixth with a mean of 2.276), but also significant for staff (ranked eleventh with a mean of 2.882)—is an example.

Most of the factors in table 5-2 can certainly be tied, either directly or by clear implication, to members' electoral or legislative self-interest (incentives), the duo of motivating factors that contemporary studies commonly say underlie oversight behavior.[21] Yet one factor in the

TABLE 5-2. *Selecting the Oversight Agenda: Means of Importance Scores, Members and Staff*

Factor[a]	Members		Staff		Number of cases
	Score	Rank	Score	Rank	
Malfeasance (scandal)	1.411	1	1.411	1	56
Policy crisis	1.563	2	1.578	2	71
Low regard for administrators	3.147	14	3.015	12	68
Agency unresponsive to committee	2.459	10	2.311	7	74
Ineffectively run programs	2.013	4	1.934	4	76
Clientele complaints*	2.313	8	2.663	9	80
Commitment to review**	2.385	9	2.217	6	78
Reauthorizations process	1.907	3	1.889	3	54
Publicity potential*	2.721	11	3.338	14	68
General public concern	2.288	7	2.400	8	80
District concern*	2.276	6	2.882	11	76
Casework	3.016	13	3.188	13	64
Assist favored programs	2.786	12	2.843	10	70
Sharp disagreement**	2.028	5	2.183	5	71

$R_s = 0.864$

Significant differences:
*$p \le 0.05$.
**$p \le 0.10$.

a. After each factor, respondents could check the following categories on the importance scale: major importance, 1; important, 2; some importance, 3; minor importance, 4; or unimportant, 5. Scores are means. Factors are listed in the order presented to the respondents. See table 5-1 for complete item wording.

b. Appropriations respondents deleted. See table 5-1, note b.

table with a relatively high importance score, "commitment to review of ongoing programs and agencies," does not seem much affected by calculations of electoral or legislative payoff. It is rated as the sixth most important for staff (mean of 2.217) and the ninth most important for members (mean of 2.385), and it seems mainly to reflect a concern for disinterested review or even for promotion of the public interest. A very simple statement about the nature of the important factors underlying oversight behavior clearly will not do.

The top staffers rated most of the factors presented to them between important (scored 2) and some importance (scored 3) as determinants of the oversight agenda. Though there is a full range of scores on all items, no factor tends to be regarded as of minor importance (scored 4) or unimportant (scored 5) by the average respondent. Only three of the mean scores (one for members) fall below 3, and none below 3.5, on the importance rating scale. The big surprise is the relative downplaying, for both staff and staffers' reports about members, of "low regard for agency administrators," a factor long regarded as a key determinant of the attention Congress pays to the agencies.[22] The other two scores below 3, that is, toward the unimportant end of the scale, are for staffers' assessments of the import to them of casework findings and publicity potential when they choose the agencies and programs they oversee. In both instances their scores are lower than those they ascribe to members, a finding I will comment on when I discuss member-staff differences as staffers perceive them.

What is most striking about table 5-2 is the great similarity in the means of the importance scores that staffers ascribe to themselves and to members on factors leading to the selection of programs or agencies for the oversight agenda. The rank order correlation between the scores is (R_s) 0.864, and only five of the differences in means of member and staff scores on individual items are statistically significant at the 0.10 level.[23]

When differences do exist, they make eminent sense. Opportunities for public attention, and concern in the members' districts, the two largest differences, and casework findings and clientele or interest group complaints are areas where the connection to members' electoral fortunes are clear and the immediate press to action that factors like scandal or crises give is not obvious. Overall, though, staffers think that factors important to them and those important to members are the same in relative and absolute terms. I will argue later in this chapter ("Who Decides") that there is good reason for this perception of congruence, and that it is most likely a reflection of reality.

Given the very high correlation between the importance scores that staffers ascribe to themselves and to members, the balance of the analysis will focus on the staffers' scores for three reasons. First, seven respondents were willing to answer for staffers only. Therefore, the number of cases for staffers is higher, a more favorable condition for analysis.[24] Second, while I believe, for reasons just stated, that both sets of importance ratings are basically accurate, the obvious argument is that the staffers' self-ratings have at least somewhat greater validity. Concentrating on these data may thus yield results in which one may have marginally greater confidence. Finally, since all findings using the importance scores that staffers ascribe to members are similar to those using the scores that they give for themselves, the text is easier to follow by using just one set of scores. When important or even interesting differences exist, I indicate them in the text or in footnotes.

One of the most striking facts about the importance scores is that they do not differ very much by chamber. Table 5-3 presents means and ranks for both House and Senate top staffers. The rank correlation coefficient between the two sets of means indicates that they correspond almost perfectly ($R_s = 0.943$). The mean scores on each indicator also differ very little between chambers.[25] In fact, difference of means tests on each pair of scores show no significant differences for any of the variables, and a t-test for the chamber means also indicated no significant difference from 0.[26] In light of these facts, the dimensional analysis of the importance factors in the next section of the chapter pools House and Senate data, and I will give little additional attention to chamber differences in oversight agenda setting.[27]

The Dimensions of Oversight Agenda Setting

How are the individual factors (importance measures) leading to placement on the oversight agenda structured? Do particular measures cluster together along dimensions, so that knowledge of the relative importance of one variable in determining whether or not an agency or program is overseen is a strong predictor of the relative importance of another?

A method called factor analysis is well suited to help in answering these questions. Factor analysis is "a mathematical technique for reducing a large number of intercorrelated variables to a small number of distinct underlying variables."[28] Through it, one can better see the underlying structure of the influences leading congressional committees to choose the programs or agencies they oversee. The underlying common factors can be found in the welter of individual importance measures that are being examined.

Table 5-4 presents the results of the factor analysis. The malfeasance

TABLE 5-3. *Selecting the Oversight Agenda: Means of Importance Scores, Staff, by Chamber*

	Senate			House		
Factor[a]	Mean	Rank	Number of cases[b]	Mean	Rank	Number of cases[b]
Malfeasance (scandal)	1.656	2	32	1.628	1	35
Policy crisis	1.526	1	38	1.644	2	45
Low regard for administrators	3.058	14	34	3.181	12	44
Agency unresponsive to committee	2.486	8	37	2.302	6	43
Ineffectively run programs	1.948	3	39	1.958	3	48
Clientele complaints*	2.666	9	39	2.653	9	49
Commitment to review**	2.421	7	38	2.040	5	49
Reauthorizations process	2.067	5	30	2.000	4	31
Publicity potential*	3.151	14	33	3.595	14	42
General public concern	2.268	6	41	2.500	8	48
District concern*	2.810	11	37	2.956	10	46
Casework	3.111	13	36	3.343	13	32
Assist favored programs	2.756	10	37	3.025	11	40
Sharp disagreement**	1.972	4	36	2.333	7	45
$R_s = 0.943$						

Significant differences:
*$p \leq 0.05$.
**$p \leq 0.10$.
a. After each factor, respondents could check the following categories on the importance scale: major importance, 1; important, 2; some importance, 3; minor importance, 4; or unimportant, 5. Scores are means. Factors are listed in the order presented to the respondents. See table 5-1 for complete item wording.
b. Appropriations Committee respondents deleted. See table 5-1, note b.

(scandal) and reauthorization importance measures were omitted from the analysis. Malfeasance was omitted because of the relatively large number of committee units finding no scandal in their jurisdictions (see table 5-1) and because it is the most highly skewed of the variables (skewness = 1.738); reauthorization was omitted because of its low number of cases (N) (since Appropriations Committee re-

TABLE 5-4. *Factor Analysis (Varimax Rotation) of Agenda Importance Scores, Staff*[a]

Variable[b]	Clashes with adminis- trators (1)	Assisting favored programs (2)	Members' needs (3)	Policy crisis (4)	Duty (5)
Policy crisis	−.02539	.08739	.16389	**.85839**	.03354
Low regard for administrators	**.46283**	.31945	.17062	−.03110	−.03015
Agency unresponsive to committee	**.51592**	.13462	.18621	−.03812	.13433
Ineffectively run programs	**.62121**	−.08952	.30705	−.12880	.08143
Clientele complaints	.20582	−.11368	**.51698**	.05176	−.00353
Ongoing programs	.10073	−.10514	.04584	.02457	**.82772**
Publicity potential	.15102	**.54054**	.16092	−.02583	.01605
General public concern	−.09347	.10791	**.45000**	.02007	.23730
District concern	.30158	.20933	**.67405**	.15544	.03742
Casework	.21860	.10178	**.68256**	.03197	−.07676
Assist favored programs	.01975	**.87086**	−.06866	.17792	−.13496
Sharp disagreement	**.63587**	.09338	−.08889	.25389	−.07205

a. Factor loadings of .45 or above are boldfaced. The percent variance explained is 50.6. Kaiser's statistic is .62825.

b. See table 5-1 for complete item wording.

spondents were not asked this question).[29] A varimax rotation was employed, a method that seeks to simplify the structure of the factor matrix—the scores (loadings) indicate the correlation of each variable with the underlying factor—by maximizing the loadings of any variable (importance score) on one factor axis and minimizing them on all others. This method is meant to increase the substantive interpretability of the factor axes by yielding a simple structure (that is, a factor matrix in which loadings are as close to 0.000 or to 1.000 as possible).[30] Since the factors are at right angles to each other (orthogonal), they are uncorrelated and each, therefore, represents an independent, underlying factor. The analysis uncovered five underlying factors that cumulatively accounted for 51.5 percent of the variance of all variables.

The first underlying factor groups variables measuring congressional committee clashes with agency administrators over administrators' actions and committee disagreements with them about their policy choices. The high loading variables (that is, those above 0.45) all measure situations in which committee conflicts with administrators in the 95th Congress led the committee to place agencies or programs on the oversight agenda. When committee personnel believed that at least some programs in their jurisdictions were not effectively or efficiently run, and they rated this as important to them in selecting agencies or programs for oversight, then the following were also likely to be important determinants of the oversight agenda: low regard for agency administrators, beliefs that agencies were unresponsive to the committee, and sharp disagreements with agency policies.

We know from the means of the indicators (table 5-2) that beliefs that programs are not effectively or efficiently run and sharp disagreements with agency policies rank high relatively and absolutely on the list of determinants of oversight agenda selection. The other two variables loading on the first factor (low regard for administrators and unresponsiveness to the committee), while not ranked as high, are also part of the pattern. The underlying factor represents the efforts of congressional committees, sometimes unsuccessful, to get administrators to do a good job, with good seemingly defined as effective, efficient administration of programs as Congress would like to see them administered (thus, for example, the inclusion of the item measuring the importance of sharp disagreement with agency policies).

The second factor uncovered in the analysis has a rather blatant political quality to it of assisting favored programs and getting public credit for it. Two items load (correlate with the underlying factor) above 0.45: publicity potential and desire to assist an agency or program favored by the committee. The assist item has an especially high loading and seems to capture the essential meaning of the underlying factor.

The emphasis in the second factor on the assist variable may seem surprising at first, but it is common for congressional committees to develop a proprietary view of the programs in their jurisdictions. A particularly articulate explanation of this phenomenon was given by a House subcommittee chair during his interview:

> You will find that—and I'm not telling you anything you don't know—that people who go on the Agriculture Committee in the House generally come from agriculture districts. People gravitate here, normally, to the committees where they can be champions of the legislation that is written in those committees. . .
>
> So that you must not assume that you begin your analysis with a *tabula rasa*, with an empty blackboard. You've got to have a realistic description of the context within which oversight is carried out. Otherwise you're really not describing the real world. And you may well find—in fact, you will find—that there will develop relationships in which congressional committees will become champions of certain programs. They will work closely with an interest group that is the champion of those programs. And they will work closely with the subordinate, let's say the below-the-cabinet-level or below-the-subcabinet-level officials, of the executive branch, often career people who are champions of the particular interest involved—all over against the policy preferences of the president and his cabinet people.[31]

While one's first reaction to the word "oversight" is that Congress is at odds with the agency or program targeted,[32] committees sometimes use oversight because they want to defend "their" program or agency against others who would do it harm.[33] Indeed, in chapter 8 I will argue that most oversight takes place in a general advocacy context. The assist variable, which loads as high on the second underlying factor and ranks eleventh in overall importance with a mean of 2.896, suggests that, in addition to the general advocacy context of most oversight, a desire to protect an agency or program is a fairly important specific stimulus to oversight activity.[34]

Publicity potential, the other variable loading significantly on the second factor in table 5-4, has a surprisingly low mean (3.400) and rank (fourteenth) considering the emphasis it receives in the academic literature.[35] Two aspects should be noted. First, the variable is much more important for members than staff, but even for members, it ranks only eleventh. Second, it is, on average, a more important stimulus to oversight in the Senate than in the House.

That the opportunity to gain general public attention described in the item would be more important to members than to staff is not too surprising, but what about the relatively low rank for members and the chamber difference? Based on comments in the interviews, it is certainly not the case that members and staff place a low value on publicity, but publicity is hard to achieve. Members and staff almost always want publicity for their oversight activities, and there is almost always a possibility that they will get it, but mass media attention does not come easily, especially for House committee units.[36] As a result, while the opportunity to gain public attention is always lurking in the background, it is not as important a factor in setting the oversight agenda as one might expect. It is a possibility devoutly and constantly desired, but it does not dominate behavior in a complex environment because it is a possibility not often realized.

The greater import that the publicity factor has for the Senate is a reflection of reality. Senate activities get more press coverage, even in absolute terms.[37] Therefore, publicity potential is, on average, of greater import to senators in setting the oversight agenda because there is a greater chance that they will receive public attention for any action they take.

The third underlying factor is labeled "members' needs" in table 5-4. The emphasis in this factor is on agencies or programs selected for oversight because they meet the immediate needs of the members as representatives and elected politicians. The high loaders on the factor are casework; concern in members' districts about an agency; complaints of clientele or interest groups; and, at a somewhat lower level (0.45), the more global "general public concern about an agency or program." In absolute levels of importance, staffers state that general public concern is the most important of the four. However, all but casework have mean scores on the importance measure in the 2 range (between important and some importance on the scale), and even casework has a mean of 3.2. When the public has concerns about an agency or program, or interest groups complain, Congress listens and finds such reasons important in setting the oversight agenda. And there is a definite tendency for those who find one source of public or specialized group concern important to be especially sensitive to the concerns or complaints expressed by others.

The fourth and fifth factors identified in the analysis basically contain single indicators. The item loading high on the fourth, crisis in a policy area, indicates the singular importance of a policy crisis. When a committee unit has a program in crisis (social security, for example), it finds that situation an almost irresistible stimulus to oversight no matter what its other goals or concerns may be.

The fifth underlying factor is called "duty" in the table. Here, quite isolated from the other factors, is the item on commitment to review of ongoing programs and agencies. Analysis in chapter 7 will buttress the argument that this measure really does tap an underlying sense of duty (although, as always with Congress, tempered by the political context).[38] But for now it is enough to reiterate that commitment is a form of motivation for oversight agenda setting that so-called incentive theories do not emphasize. By definition, a member or staffer gets what he or she wants if he or she feels a need to review ongoing programs and acts on the need. However, the payoff generally assumed by an incentive theory (publicity, reelection, personal influence) is different from the sense of duty or fulfillment of institutional obligation implied by the commitment variable. When, as is the case here, the commitment variable forms its own dimension separate from the others, one should be especially careful about explanations of oversight behavior resting solely on crude notions of political payoffs.

Overview

The data indicate that committee oversight agendas are strongly influenced by jarring stimuli like scandals or policy crises when they occur, but the picture is much more complex. Other causes lead to selection of agencies or programs for oversight, and many are judged as important sources of agenda setting by the top staffers interviewed. Though there are some chamber differences and differences between top staffers' perceptions of what is important to them and what is important to members, the differences are minor.

The data break out fairly neatly into five dimensions of agenda setting. These dimensions buttress much of what the data on the congressional intelligence system analyzed in chapter 4 suggest. They indicate congressional committee units moved by crises when they occur, sensitive to input from constituencies and interest groups, alert to agency decisions and to the course of policy implementation, interested in assisting programs they favor, and even, it seems, moved at times by a sense of duty.

With the exception of the final factor (duty/commitment), the others are easily interpreted in terms of parochial interests. And even those carrying out the call of duty may do so using a narrow perspective. But even granting that most congressional review may occur within that context of parochialism, there are definite signs of a Congress on top of administrative actions. Crises and scandal move Congress to be sure, but so do constituent and clientele complaints and other signs that agencies are not performing as Congress would like.

Through their oversight, congressional committees try to cope with policy or administrative disasters, protect their constituents, keep administrators on their toes, and review ongoing programs. Some committees even ascribe great importance to oversight whose special aim is to boost favored programs. Much oversight behavior obviously furthers, or at least is meant to further, the electoral and policy interests of the committee members, especially of those members most influential in setting the oversight agenda. Oversight is clearly helpful at most times to the clientele and organized groups served by the programs, since group input is registered and clearly stimulates oversight activity. Oversight surely makes administrators anxious about the possible consequences of large failures and small problems, thereby controlling administrators' behavior to a great extent by making them more responsive to congressional committee units.[39] In that limited respect, congressional oversight surely serves the interests of Congress as an institution in relation to the president and his administration at least insofar as it implies that congressional committees are keeping abreast of administrative activity and are therefore in a better position to exert influence over agency behavior. What is still unclear is the extent to which other interests of Congress as a whole or of the polity are protected—good public policy in the broad sense—by the factors that apparently bring programs and agencies onto the committee oversight agenda. The duty (commitment) factor, as I mentioned, indicates at least some congressional attention to wider concerns. Chapter 8 examines just how these wider concerns fit with or transcend the narrower interests of the reviewing units.

Both the information on the congressional committee intelligence system developed in chapter 4 and the data on oversight agenda setting analyzed in this chapter indicate that three conditions hold. One, the agencies are watched by the committees. Two, Congress responds with oversight to signs of policy or administrative failure, or to signs of public concern about policy or administration, or when it clashes with administrators, or when it wants to assist favored programs, or even apparently when it feels some sense of duty to do so.[40] And three, many units of Congress are not merely passive recipients of information but active intelligence seekers. Far worse ways of gathering information and setting an oversight agenda are imaginable. In fact, within the possible limitations of a decentralized and advocacy-oriented system alluded to briefly here (and examined more intensively in chapters 8 and 9), Congress seems to have a sensible approach to monitoring the general flow of administrative behavior and policy outcomes and to selecting agencies and programs for more careful scrutiny.

Who Decides?

The discussion so far has covered factors influencing members and staff in setting the oversight agenda. But who actually makes the decisions about which agencies and program areas to oversee? How consensual are the decisions? And, most especially, what role do staffers—the major informants for this study—play in oversight decisionmaking? Are they in a position to know? How important are they? In fact, do they dominate?

The Major Influence in Decisionmaking

It is not immediately obvious whether members or staff have the major influence in committee decisionmaking on oversight. Oversight, after all, does not take up the major part of committee time, members have many duties other than those connected to committee work, and staff perform most of the tasks connected to oversight. Since committee staff usually perform most of the tasks in this area, perhaps they also have the major influence over oversight decisions.[41]

To ascertain who has the major influence in oversight decision-making, committee staffers and members were asked a very simple question: "Who has the major influence in deciding which agencies and program areas to oversee?" The question was meant to determine the single actor with the most influence, but respondents often felt that two or more actors shared major influence. As a result, the percentages in table 5-5 that indicate who, according to top committee staffers, has major influence in oversight decisions do not add to 100 across roles.

More than two-thirds (68 percent) of the top staffers interviewed believed that committee and subcommittee chairs have the major influence in oversight decisions.[42] Only a very few (5 percent) attributed similar influence to the ranking minority members. However, if one adds together those who nominated either a chairman or a ranking minority member, or attributed major influence to committee members (senators or representatives) without differentiating them by position in the committee hierarchy, one finds that nearly 75 percent thought that some member or combination of members was the most influential. An overwhelming majority of top staffers, then, mentioned members when asked who has the major influence in oversight decisions.

This contrasts with the 38 percent of top staffers interviewed who ascribed the major influence to themselves and their staff colleagues, with only 25 percent claiming the major influence exclusively for staffers. In the eyes of the typical top staffer, then, members are still very much in command, although a substantial minority of staffers certainly see themselves playing a most significant role.

There are some modest but important differences in answers to the question according to the chamber of the committee employing the top staffer. Top Senate staffers were less likely than top House staffers to say that unit chairmen have the major influence (60 percent of Senate staffers versus 75 percent of House staffers), a bit more likely to mention ranking minority members (7 percent in the Senate versus 4 percent in the House), and more likely to mention staff in answer to the major influence question (48 percent in the Senate versus 31 percent in the House). In essence, the Senate staffers portrayed a chamber that fits the common image of it in contrast to the House—a relatively more important role for staffers and ranking minority members as opposed to unit chairs—but even in the Senate top staffers typically nominated unit chairs as the most influential individuals in oversight decisionmaking.

Results from the interviews with members of the committees (see appendix A for a description of the interviews) are reassuringly

TABLE 5-5. *Top Staffers' Assessments of Who Has the Major Influence in Committee Oversight Decisions, Total and by Chamber*[a]
Percent[a]

Who has the major influence	Assessed by top staffers of		
	All units	Senate units	House units
Chairs	68	60	75
Ranking minority members	5	7	4
Any type of member (chair, ranking minority, other)	75	64	83
Staff	38	48	31
N	(94)	(42)	(52)

a. Totals do not add to 100 across roles because of multiple mentions.

similar to those with staffers, although the question used was modified for committee and subcommittee chairs.[43] For the representatives and senators who were not chairs, 88 percent mentioned unit chairs as most influential in deciding which agencies or program areas to oversee.[44] This is more than the figure for the staff (68 percent), but that is hardly surprising given the inclination some members would have to emphasize member influence, and that of some staff to deemphasize member influence, and the fact that much member interaction with committee unit staff would be via the unit chair. (In other words, staff could sometimes be the most influential in making decisions, although members of the committee units who were not chairs would not know it.) As to staff influence, 28 percent of the representatives and senators interviewed said that staff had the major influence in deciding on oversight targets, a lower level than the figure from the staff interviews (38 percent), but not much lower, especially if staff tends slightly to overestimate its import and members slightly to underestimate it. In brief, a majority of both staffers and members agreed that members are in control of selecting agencies and programs for oversight, and a minority of both groups—although a sizable minority in each case—ascribed major influence to staff.

The interviews with senators and representatives also reinforce conclusions drawn from the staff data on differences between the chambers in member and staff influence. The number of senators interviewed is too small to have any faith in precise statistics, but it is suggestive that 42 percent of the senators answering the question (five of twelve) said that committee staffers have a major influence in selecting agencies and programs for oversight of their units as contrasted to 24 percent (thirteen of fifty-three) of the representatives who ascribed comparable influence over House committee decisions to House staff.[45] The slightly hyperbolic statement of one representative captures the way many House members and some senators see the contrast between the chambers and also speaks volumes about staff influence in general. "In the House the members run the House heavily assisted by the professional staff, and the professional staff runs the Senate sometimes assisted by the Senators. And the role of the professional staff [in both chambers] in anything—oversight activity, writing legislation—is very significant. Quite often staff will suggest, 'We need to look into this or that,' just as staff will play a heavy role in legislation."[46]

No matter who has the major influence over oversight agenda setting, virtually all agreed that staffers are important in decision-making. Virtually everyone agreed, for example, that committee unit staff professionals play a significant role in choosing oversight topics.[47] Only 9 percent of top staffers interviewed described the role of unit staff professionals as unimportant or insignificant in this endeavor.[48] More important, when senators and representatives were asked the same question fewer than 7 percent (6.6 percent to be exact), described the role of staffers as unimportant or insignificant in choosing oversight topics, with no chamber differences.

One chair, who was very much in command, described the role staff played in his former subcommittee as follows: "I gave them a great deal of responsibility. They always were listened to. I felt the staff had to be fully backed, with a clear understanding with me as to the nature of their duties and the authority they could exercise, and in the exercise of it [the authority] fully backed. If there was to be criticism of the staff, I would finally take care of it; if had to get rid of them, I'd get rid of them. But I never let anyone else jump them or embarrass them."[49]

In short, staffers may not dominate, but their importance is just about unquestioned in the Senate and the House. This importance simply confirms what most observers of the contemporary Congress would have predicted. It should, moreover, be reassuring about the viability of the approach employed in this study, that is, using top staffers as major informants on the oversight process.

How Consensual Are Decisions?

Do ranking minority-party legislators typically share the major influence in selecting the agencies and programs that committee units oversee? Not surprisingly, in the vast majority of cases, ranking minority members do not have (or even tend to share) major influence (table 5-1). That was not just the claim of the majority members and staffers. Staffers appointed by the minority agreed that minority representatives and senators do not share major influence.[50]

At the same time, according to both majority and minority staffers, the minority typically agrees with the decisions the majority makes about what to oversee. Table 5-6 presents relevant data from the "matched samples" of majority and minority staffers. (See appendix A for a description of the matched samples.) When asked, "Is there generally agreement within the [committee unit] concerning what the [committee unit] should oversee?" majority staffers were certainly more likely than minority staffers to give a positive answer (yes or qualified yes) to the question. But even most of the minority staffers (64 percent) answered in the yes range. Considering the fact that the minority staffers did not have an inflated view of minority influence in making decisions—almost all agree that the majority clearly have the major influence in selecting oversight targets—the consensus reported by the minority on what should be overseen was quite high, and the similarities between the perceptions of the majority and minority striking.[51] While the minority staff and members are not the key to decisions on the oversight agenda in congressional committees, they do not seem to feel overridden or even ignored.[52]

Other indicators fill out the picture and give a portrait of considerable minority consultation. When asked as part of a series of questions about minority member influence, "Is the minority consulted on what ought to be overseen?" 79 percent of the top committee staffers (majority) said yes. Another 8 percent reported that although the minority members on their unit were not consulted, they could get items on the oversight agenda if they wanted to. Senate majority staffers reported more minority consultation than House staffers reported (86 percent versus 74 percent), a finding in line with the

TABLE 5-6. *Agreement in Committee Units about Oversight Decisions as Reported by Majority and Minority Staffers*
Percent[a]

Agreement within unit	Majority	Minority
Yes	68	52
Depends, leans toward yes	18	12
Depends	3	6
Depends, leans toward no	3	3
No	3	21
Chair decides, others not consulted	6	0
Other	0	6
Total[a]	101	100
N	(34)	(33)

a. Totals may not add to 100 because of rounding.

more consensual images of Senate committees, but the differences are not great. And the minority did not dissent from the view of the majority. Minority staffers believed either that minority members were consulted on what ought to be overseen (66 percent) or that, even though not consulted, they could get items on the oversight agenda if they wanted to (21 percent).[53]

In sum, committee consensus on oversight decisions is apparently the norm. Even the minority, though to a lesser degree than the majority, agrees that there is consensus. Virtually all, including the minority, agree that the minority is consulted, with the Senate showing evidence of slightly greater minority consultation than the House. Therefore, while the minority is definitely less influential than the majority, it is hardly left out in the cold.

The Role of Staff

In *Unelected Representatives: Congressional Staff and the Future of Representative Government*, Michael Malbin documents the burgeoning of committee staffs and of the tasks they perform, and notes that "some members [of Congress] publicly ask whether they or their staffs are in charge."[54] Malbin is also concerned because increased staff contributes to the "frenetic pace of congressional life that pulls members in different directions, reduces the time available for joint deliberation, and makes concentration all but impossible,"[55] important issues indeed but probably not as important as the issue of staff influence and its limits. For if an appointed congressional staff is in control of the bureaucracy, but out of the control of the elected members of Congress, then the problem of democratic control has simply been shifted from one bureaucracy to another.

As already mentioned, staffers apparently have or share the major influence in setting the oversight agenda for only a minority of congressional committee units, but that minority is substantial, especially in the Senate. The judgment that staffers play a significant role in oversight decisions, however, is virtually unanimous. These are not just the judgments of staffers but also of senators and representatives.

With this kind of influence, are substantial numbers of staff out of control? A precise answer to this question is impossible, but there are some data that will enrich our understanding of the issue.

Not surprisingly, the overwhelming majority of top staffers were certain that they could and did convince members to pursue oversight efforts they (staffers) thought important. No one among the top staffers thought that he or she was unable to convince members, and only 4 percent claimed that they actually refrained from doing so.[56] However, even the comments of staffers who ascribe the major influence in oversight decisions exclusively to themselves or their staff colleagues (25 percent of the total top staffers sample) usually give evidence of underlying respect and attention to member interests.

A Senate subcommittee staff director, for example, said the following in his answer to the question about who has the major influence. "Well, it's clear that the staff plays the major role in suggesting courses of action along the lines. But, on the other hand, it's done with the full knowledge of members' interests and [of their] previous interests and activities in these areas, and with the expectation that they will be agreeable."[57]

Another Senate subcommittee staff director, who ascribed the major influence in oversight decisionmaking exclusively to staffers, said of his recently retired chair, "He pretty much left it to the staff [in deciding on oversight] as to what they wanted to do."

But he then added quickly,

You get into discussions about how powerful staff is and all that hogwash. My feeling is, from a staff standpoint, if you're a good staff person, you reflect what your member wants. . . . Given parameters, you can make or break different things. But I think . . . you have the tremendous turnover of staff on the Hill because [basically] you lose your autonomy. When [name of senator] gave me the job of staff director, [he] never said, 'you are my staff director.' He said, 'from now on you are going to have a lot more friends than you thought you would ever have.' And it's true. It was his way of telling me, watch your ass. You recognize that and you deal with that. But that was a good way for him to tell me.[58]

Sometimes, of course, staffers are somewhat contemptuous in private conversation of the members who employ them. They indicate that, left to themselves, members would be incapable of accomplishing much, because members either lack the time or the ability or both. But staffers recognize that members are there by dint of election, a source of legitimacy with deep symbolic meaning in our culture and even deeper meaning in Congress. Beyond the legitimacy, however, lies the brutal, central fact of the congressional personnel system— staffers can be dismissed by members without cause. Unlike the typical bureaucracy, committee staff personnel have no job protection. They serve at the pleasure of members. Members may give them immense leeway to make decisions, may not even check what they do, but in the end they will form an opinion about whether and how much the actions of their committee units have helped or hurt them. Staffers do not want to be on the negative side of that judgment because they have both jobs and reputations to protect. (A reputation for effectiveness and influence in the policy area, after all, is what the staffer generally sells to his next employer.) Even though it may not be difficult to convince the relevant members that a committee should undertake some oversight effort, it is a legitimate and safe thing for staffers to take some care to do so.

If this line of argument is basically correct, then in the end oversight decisions are made either by committee members, especially by unit chairs, or by staffers acting in good faith as their agents.[59] The decisions may not always be wise or the oversight systematic or well executed, but that is another matter.

Chapter 6

Types of Oversight
Activity

I HAVE ALREADY examined at some length longitudinal data
on congressional hearings whose primary purpose is oversight. But there is more to oversight than such hearings, important
though they may be. In this chapter I look at other types of hearings
used for oversight and at additional (nonhearings) forms of oversight
behavior. The focus in chapter 5 is on why agencies or programs are
selected for oversight and who makes the decisions to oversee; in
this chapter I turn to what committees do when they oversee. I look
at the techniques that committee units use for overseeing, especially
at the frequency and effectiveness of their use, and at the general
dimensions of oversight activity.

Oversight Techniques

Congressional committees use a variety of techniques for oversight.
Some techniques involve the use of formal procedures or processes,
such as committee hearings or program evaluations done by congressional support agencies. Other oversight is more informal, such as
communication with agency personnel by staff or committee members. In some cases, to use the distinction employed by Morris Ogul,
the oversight may be quite manifest, such as in the primary-purpose
oversight hearings that are discussed earlier. And in some cases
oversight may be a latent function of some activity ostensibly performed for another purpose, such as the oversight done as part of
legislative hearings or in casework.[1]

Frequency of Use

To measure the full panoply of committee oversight activity, top
staffers were given a list of fourteen commonly used oversight

techniques. The activities listed in table 6-1 cover the range of oversight techniques—formal and informal, manifest and latent. In each case the respondent rated how frequently the technique was used by his or her committee unit in the 95th Congress, with the understanding that frequency of use for *oversight* was the proper focus of the response.[2] It is possible therefore although empirically not the case, that a committee could have held numerous program reauthorization hearings, for example, but not used reauthorization hearings very frequently for oversight. In this circumstance, the frequency score on the scale for use of program reauthorization hearings for oversight would be low, even though many reauthorization hearings were held.[3]

Categories on the frequency scale ranged from "very frequently" (scored 1) to "never" (scored 5). The entries in table 6-1 are means of the scores reported by top staffers. (See appendix D for an analysis of the validity of the measuring instrument. The evidence indicates that the reports given by top staffers are accurate.)

The data in table 6-1 indicate a high overall frequency of use for oversight of most of the techniques listed (eleven of fourteen average above 3) and, in particular, show that staff communication with agency personnel is by far the most frequently used oversight technique. The mean for staff communication (1.274) is more than one unit greater than the mean of the next most frequently used technique (program evaluations done by congressional support agencies—mean of 2.382) and it is the only technique with a truncated distribution.[4] Whatever else a committee unit may do in conducting oversight, its staff communicates with agency personnel.[5]

Table 6-1 also makes clear that congressional committees rely more frequently on themselves and their allied support agencies than on others in reviewing the programs and agencies of the executive branch. Evaluations done by the various congressional support agencies (General Accounting Office, Congressional Research Service, Congressional Budget Office, and the Office of Technology Assessment) are the second most frequently used oversight technique,[6] followed by program reauthorization hearings, primary-purpose oversight hearings, and hearings on bills to amend ongoing programs. It is true that two committee actions are at the bottom of the list— the legislative veto and review of casework—but the veto is a special case, and casework is a technique more heavily centered in senators'

TABLE 6-1. *Frequency of Use of Oversight Techniques, 95th Congress*

Technique[a]	Mean	Number of cases[b]	Rank
Staff communication with agency personnel	1.274	91	1
Member communication with agency personnel	2.802	86	9
Oversight hearings	2.561	89	3
Program reauthorization hearings[c]	2.685	73	5
Hearings on bills to amend ongoing programs[c]	2.756	70	7
Review of casework	3.551	87	13
Staff investigations and field studies (other than for preparation of hearings)	2.644	90	4
Analysis of proposed agency rules and regulations	2.800	90	8
Agency reports required by Congress	2.813	91	10
Program evaluations done by congressional support agencies	2.382	89	2
Program evaluations done by the agencies	2.954	87	11
Program evaluations done by "outsiders" (nongovernmental personnel)	3.227	88	12
Program evaluations done by committee staff personnel	2.696	89	6
Legislative veto	4.304	82	14

a. After each technique, respondents could check the following categories: very frequently, 1; frequently, 2; occasionally, 3; rarely, 4; or never, 5. Techniques are listed in the order presented to the respondents.

b. The number of cases is inconsistent for two reasons: some respondents did not rate a technique or wrote in an "other" response; and Appropriations Committee staffers were not asked about reauthorization hearings and hearings on bills to amend ongoing programs and are therefore excluded from the table in these instances. They were asked instead about hearings on appropriations bills and hearings on supplementary appropriations bills.

c. Ascertained only of non-Appropriations respondents. See note b.

and representatives' personal offices. In tenth, eleventh, and twelfth places are reports and evaluations done by agency people and nongovernmental personnel. Though these are used occasionally, committees are definitely more likely to rely on evaluations done by their staffs or the staffs of congressionally sponsored support agencies than on agency or nongovernmental evaluations.

The relatively frequent use for oversight of so many types of formal hearings stands out. Hearings are usually not "models of efficiency or objectivity," a leading textbook on the legislative process notes, but the authors also say, "it is not unfair to characterize Congress as preoccupied with the hearing process."[7] Hearings are usually significant events when they occur. "Hearings focus the member's attention," as one member told Morris Ogul.[8] People go on record in this forum—stating their views, establishing facts, affirming commitments—and they do it in public, thus giving members and staff a forum to demonstrate their central role to interest and clientele groups and, with a little luck and some well-crafted press releases, to the general public. According to Herbert Kaufman's study of federal bureau chiefs, administrators also regard what they say and do in hearings as of the utmost importance.[9] My own Brookings roundtable discussions with federal executives confirm this view (see appendix A).[10] Whatever their views of Congress, administrators are at risk (and have opportunities for gain) when they appear before Congress, and most either know it well or soon learn.[11]

Although a single survey cannot prove that there has been an increase over time in the use for oversight of the three types of hearings included in table 6-1, it is reasonable to infer that there has been. The increase in primary-purpose oversight hearings through time is well documented in chapter 2, and appendix D documents the close association between the measure of oversight hearings used in chapter 2 (that is, the *Daily Digest* measure) and the survey item used in this chapter to measure the frequency of oversight hearings. Most reauthorization hearings have a heavy oversight component,[12] and clearly the number of programs reauthorized on a short-term basis has increased through time.[13] If one makes the not unreasonable assumption that the increase over time in the number of pages of legislation enacted each year occurs partly because of more amendments to ongoing programs, then chances are that oversight done by all three types of hearings has gone up through the years.[14]

The infrequent use of the legislative veto as an oversight technique in the 95th Congress occurred partly because of its inaccessibility to many committee units.[15] Even though the number of statutes with legislative veto provisions had increased dramatically since the veto's introduction in 1932, there were still relatively few statutes even in the late 1970s whose terms allowed a committee to veto, or participate in the veto, of agency regulations.[16] Of the few top staffers reporting that their committee units made some use of veto provisions (and this does not necessarily imply an actual veto but rather some aspect of it), most say that they employed it rarely.[17] In light of this finding, the fact that the Supreme Court took a strong stand against the constitutionality of the legislative veto in the 1983 *Immigration and Naturalization Service* v. *Chadha* case[18] does not seem quite so significant for oversight as one might have guessed, even if the decision in the case eventually results in many fewer veto provisions in legislation (as it apparently has not done to date).[19] However, before reaching this conclusion, I should examine the data on the effectiveness of oversight techniques. Perhaps the veto, though infrequently used, was considered a very effective technique by those who had the opportunity to use it.

Effectiveness

After each top staffer indicated how frequently a given technique was used for oversight in the 95th Congress, he or she then rated its effectiveness. Ratings ranged from "very effective" (scored 1) to "ineffective" (scored 4).[20] Mean scores for the effectiveness of each technique appear in table 6-2, along with the number of staff responding and the ranks for each of the means—ranked from high (very effective on average, with scores closest to 1) to low (very ineffective on average, with scores closest to 4). The numbers used in the analysis (Ns) are lower than those in table 6-1 mainly because those staffers who reported that a committee never used a technique were not then asked to rate its effectiveness.

Most techniques are, on average, rated between very effective and moderately effective (between 1 and 2), but a few (review of casework, agency evaluations, agency reports required by Congress, and evaluations by nongovernmental personnel) are below 2.5, that is, closer to the not very effective (3) than to the moderately effective (2) level.

TABLE 6-2. *Effectiveness of Oversight Techniques, 95th Congress*

Technique[a]	Mean	Number of cases	Rank
Staff communication	1.430	86	1
Member communication	1.626	83	2
Oversight hearings	1.714	84	4
Program reauthorization hearings[b]	1.688	61	3
Amendment hearings[b]	1.750	60	5
Review of casework	2.694	72	14
Staff investigations and field studies	1.780	82	6
Analysis of proposed regulations	2.279	86	10
Agency reports	2.534	86	12
Congressional support agency program evaluations	2.000	88	8
Agency program evaluations	2.541	85	13
"Outsiders" program evaluations	2.523	84	11
Committee staff program evaluations	1.891	83	7
Legislative veto	2.085	35	9

a. After each technique, respondents whose units used it could check the following effectiveness categories: very effective, 1; moderately effective, 2; not very effective, 3; or ineffective, 4. Techniques are listed in the order presented to the respondents. See table 6-1 for complete item wording.

b. Ascertained only of non-Appropriations staff. See table 6-1, note b.

If one compares the ranks of the means for effectiveness in table 6-2 to the ranks for use found in table 6-1, it is clear that they are highly correlated.[21]

Despite a generally high correlation between the two, there are three major discrepancies in ranks between the frequency and effectiveness scores. Member communication with agency personnel presents the greatest discrepancy in ranks. This technique is, on average, used relatively infrequently according to top staffers, but when it is used, it is rated second most effective of all the techniques listed. Members' direct intervention is clearly a valuable resource for the committees—one used somewhat sparingly but, top staffers believe, to great effect.

Almost as great a discrepancy in ranks is found for congressional support agency program evaluations. This is the second most frequently used oversight technique, yet it is rated only the eighth most effective. (It has an average score of 2.0, moderately effective.) In essence, when doing oversight, congressional committees use evaluations produced by their "own" evaluators (the support agencies) much more frequently than they use evaluations produced by other sources. They also clearly rate support agency evaluations as more effective than those produced by noncongressional sources. However, they downplay the relative effectiveness of support agency evaluations so that support agency evaluations are closer in rank to the effectiveness ratings of others' evaluations. Even the most frequently used program evaluations, then, are not seen as having the same effectiveness as other frequently used oversight techniques that do not involve the systematic approaches implied by the term "program evaluation."

Finally, the legislative veto is regarded as moderately effective (mean of 2.085, ranked ninth) by staffers reporting on the small number of committee units employing it in any way. For proponents of the legislative veto, this is probably a disappointing figure since it indicates that even users do not tend to rate the veto at the top of the effectiveness scale. However, the rating also backs up case studies indicating that the veto has some utility, at least as seen from the perspective of congressional committees.[22] While the veto was used by some committees in the 95th Congress who tended to regard it as moderately effective, the data suggest that its loss (despite the *Chadha* case just cited, the veto is still written into statutes) would probably not be a great blow to congressional oversight activity or potential.[23]

Even in the cases of discrepancies in rank order, two out of three of the individual frequency and effectiveness measures are strongly correlated. The measure for frequency of use and effectiveness of agency program evaluations are correlated (Pearson r) at the 0.59 level and the legislative veto measures at 0.70, placing them above the very high average level of correlation of the frequency and effectiveness items (0.55).[24] The one exception is the member communication measure where the correlation is actually slightly negative (-0.11), although the level is not statistically significant. In this case, top staffers on committees using member communication least frequently had a tendency to rate it slightly higher in effectiveness as an oversight technique than those who reported using it more frequently. The slightly inverse relationship is probably a good reflection of reality, since agencies would probably be jolted by personal inquiries from representatives or senators who do not ordinarily contact their personnel.

This exception aside, however, the overall pattern is one of great congruence in one-to-one relationships (correlations) and in the rank order of the means for the frequency and effectiveness measures. As a result, in the rest of this chapter I will concentrate on analysis of the frequency measures since these have higher Ns. Future work may turn up some differences in the antecedents or consequences of the two sets of measures, but these differences should not be great.[25]

Differences by Chamber and Type of Unit

House and Senate committee units showed great similarities in the pattern of factors that led them to choose programs and agencies for their oversight agendas (chapter 5). Thus one might expect the same similarity to occur for the frequency of use of oversight techniques by the two chambers. On first look, this expectation is disappointed, but further analysis indicates that much of the difference occurs because of the heavier concentration of oversight units in the House.

Table 6-3 presents means for the House and Senate on the frequency of use of the oversight techniques staffers were asked to report on. The rank order correlation (Spearman's rho) is a strong 0.543, but not anywhere near the 0.943 reported in chapter 5 (table 5-3) between the two chambers on the importance of factors that lead to selection for the oversight agenda.

As a Spearman's rho (R_s) of 0.543 would indicate, most of the differences in rank between the chambers are small ($\leq$ 3 ranks). Two of the three exceptions occur mainly because of the following facts. The Senate Governmental Affairs Committee has a larger legislative jurisdiction than the House Government Operations Committee. Therefore, it has greater opportunities for reauthorization and amendment activities than the House Government Operations Committee. Overall, there is a heavier concentration of specialized oversight units in the House sample. Again this limits the amount of oversight through reauthorization and amendment hearings that House committees are likely to engage in when compared with Senate units. To test the import of the first fact for the chamber differences reported, the two techniques whose use by a committee unit is most dependent on the unit having a significant legislative jurisdiction were dropped

TABLE 6-3. *Frequency of Use of Oversight Techniques, 95th Congress, by Chamber*

Technique[a]	House			Senate		
	Mean	Number of cases	Rank	Mean	Number of cases	Rank
Staff communication*	1.163	49	1	1.404	42	1
Member communication	2.723	47	6	2.897	39	9
Oversight hearings	2.250	48	4	2.609	41	5
Program reauthorization hearings[b]	2.821	39	10	2.529	34	3
Amendment hearings[b]	3.027	36	11	2.470	34	2
Review of casework	3.543	46	13	3.561	41	13
Staff investigations and field studies*	2.408	49	3	2.926	41	10
Analysis of proposed regulations	2.734	49	7	2.878	41	8
Agency reports	2.795	49	9	2.833	42	7
Congressional support agency program evaluations**	2.229	48	2	2.561	41	4
Agency program evaluations*	2.766	47	8	3.175	40	11
"Outsiders" program evaluations	3.145	48	12	3.325	40	12
Committee staff program evaluations	2.604	48	5	2.804	41	6
Legislative veto	4.219	41	14	4.390	41	14

$R_s = 0.543$

Significant differences:
  * $p \leq 0.05$.
  ** $p \leq 0.10$.

a. After each technique, respondents could check the following categories: very frequently, 1; frequently, 2; occasionally, 3; rarely, 4; or never, 5. Factors are listed in the order presented to the respondents. See table 6-1 for complete item wording.

b. Ascertained only of non-Appropriations staff. See table 6-1, note b.

from the calculation of Spearman's rho (R_s). With program reauthorization and amendment hearings removed, the rank-order coefficient (R_s) between scores for the two chambers jumps to a very robust 0.839. As to the second, when the committee units are grouped into those whose named purpose is oversight and all others, the Spearman's rho between the means for the frequency of use of all techniques for the two subsamples (oversight and nonoversight) is only 0.426.[26] However, dropping the reauthorization and amendment hearing techniques from the calculations and comparing rank orders for use of the remaining oversight techniques by the oversight and nonoversight subsamples raises the rho to 0.923.[27]

At first glance, it is surprising that the chamber difference in the frequency of use of primary-purpose oversight hearings is so slight since there are more oversight units in the House than in the Senate. However, when we recall the findings in chapter 2 on the diffusion of primary-purpose oversight hearings throughout Congress in the 1970s, the small chamber difference is understandable. Oversight units do report significantly greater use of primary-purpose oversight hearings than nonoversight units (the mean difference is 0.840; $p < 0.001$—oversight units reporting greater use), but this difference is not nearly so great as the difference in the frequency of use for oversight of reauthorization or amendment hearings reported by these same units (the differences are 1.604 and 1.412, respectively; $p < 0.001$—oversight units reporting less frequent use). Oversight can be done in a variety of hearings settings. Primary-purpose oversight hearings are within the province of all committees, but the use of reauthorization and amendment hearings for oversight is available only when committees have the authority to consider reauthorizing or amending programs. Because congressional structures are not governed by inflexible definitions, the authority to consider reauthorizations and amendments is sometimes given to the oversight units, but their opportunities in this regard are limited. Therefore, oversight units are much less likely to use reauthorization or amendment hearings for oversight. But authorization units are quite free to hold primary-purpose oversight hearings, and by the late 1970s they did so with great regularity. As a result, data collected from top committee staffers in 1978 and 1979 show raw committee type (and chamber) differences in the use of primary-purpose oversight hearings to be relatively moderate.

The third major difference in rank between the chambers is in the frequency of use for oversight of staff investigations and field studies. House committees use them more frequently. The difference holds with oversight units included or excluded, although excluding oversight units and recalculating the data reduces the chamber differences in rank and in mean slightly.[28] The greater House use of staff investigations is most likely a function of the greater number of staff available to House committees, which gives them more resources to use. Also, the greater decentralization of House committees offers House units more autonomy to use the available resources.[29]

Another statistically significant difference in mean, but not in rank, between the two chambers is also compatible with this line of explanation. Top House committee staff report greater frequency of staff communication with agency personnel, although, to reiterate, both chambers use this communication technique for oversight the most of all those listed.[30] The greater staff resources and more intense specialization of the House committees, and the concentration in the House of more specialized oversight units, are the most likely explanations for the staff communications finding and, indeed, for the tendency of House units to use most oversight techniques a bit more frequently than Senate units.

Overall, then, one is most struck by the similarities between the chambers and between the types of committee units (oversight versus nonoversight units). Consequently, the next section of this chapter looks at the dimensionality of oversight behavior for the total sample. The significance of the chamber and unit differences that do exist will be considered in chapter 7, which analyzes the sources of the various types of oversight activity.

Dimensions of Oversight Activity

Congressional committees have numerous oversight techniques available to them. Table 6-1 demonstrated clearly that, with the exception of staff communication and the legislative veto, the techniques rated in the study were, on average, used somewhere between the frequently (2) and rarely (4) points on the frequency scale, and most between frequently (2) and occasionally (3). It still remains to be seen how the techniques used cluster together—what common attributes, if any, underlie the many oversight techniques used.

To determine this, I employ the same factor analytic approach utilized in chapter 5.[31] I omit certain variables, however, from the factor analysis. The staff communication with agency personnel and the legislative veto measures are omitted because they are so highly skewed. In the former case (staff communication), nearly everyone does it frequently ($\bar{x}$ = 1.274, skewness = 1.322), and in the latter case (the legislative veto), almost no one does it ($\bar{x}$ = 4.304, skewness = − 1.172). The three hearings variables— primary-purpose oversight hearings, program reauthorization hearings, and amendment hearings—are also omitted from the factor analysis. This is done for two reasons. Two of the three hearings variables (reauthorizations and amendments) are relevant only for the non-Appropriations committees. Omitting them allows one to analyze data with a significantly higher number of cases. Hearings are also the most visible and "official" of the formal congressional techniques. They define what some people mean by oversight, and many of the other techniques are often input to them. Keeping the various types of hearings separate therefore allows me to analyze a more complete data set and then to consider other techniques as inputs to hearings. (For example, do committees typically consult program evaluations when reviewing agencies prior to reauthorization decisions?)

I am not going to divide oversight techniques into the formal and informal or the manifest and latent, useful as this might be for some purposes.[32] Instead, I will simply divide the techniques items into those involving hearings and those involving other approaches to oversight.

Hearings, as table 6-1 shows, are among the most frequently employed oversight techniques. However, the use of one type of hearing for oversight is not very strongly correlated (either positively or negatively) with the use for oversight of others. The coefficients are all modest, ranging from a high of 0.21 between the items for reauthorizations and amendment hearings to a low of − 0.14 between the use of primary-purpose oversight hearings and amendment hearings.[33] Treating each type of hearing separately for purposes of analysis is clearly a safe (and also a substantively more interesting) approach, and the one I will follow in chapter 7.

Table 6-4 reveals three underlying dimensions of nonhearings oversight activity. I shall call them oversight approaches. Each of the

TABLE 6-4. *Factor Analysis (Varimax Rotation) of the Frequency of Employment of Nonhearings Approaches to Oversight*[a]

Variable[b]	Comprehensive review (1)	Staff review (2)	Piecemeal review (3)
Member communication	.00590	−.09720	**.66040**
Review of casework	.19122	.01232	**.59934**
Staff investigations	.12072	**.79823**	−.00526
Analysis of proposed regulations	.04686	.01089	**.78442**
Agency reports	**.83308**	−.29947	−.11879
Congressional support agency program evaluations	**.63206**	.24544	.10594
Agency program evaluations	**.59773**	.42119	.27386
"Outsiders" program evaluations	**.62574**	.32240	.23888
Committee staff program evaluations	.09739	**.76067**	−.14114

a. Factor loadings above .45 are in boldface. Percent variance explained is 57.2. Kaiser's statistic is .68374.
b. See table 6-1 for complete item wording.

factors (dimensions) groups a set of related activities sharing a common attribute. The common attribute, which is not directly observed and is, therefore, hypothetical, distinguishes the activities prominently clustered in one factor from those prominently clustered in the other factors.

The first factor is labeled comprehensive review. With the significant absence of program evaluations done by a committee unit's own staff, the factor includes each of the variables measuring the frequency of use of program evaluations for oversight, plus the item measuring use of agency reports required by Congress. The reviews included in this factor are ostensibly objective and inclusive (broadly based on available information sources), most are the product of a systematic method, and all are done by experts outside of the unit's direct control. Note that congressional support agency program evaluations, which rank very high (second) in frequency of use (see table 6-1), cluster with the other evaluation indicators that rank much lower. This is in line with the fact that support agency evaluations have an effectiveness score much like the other program evaluation indicators.[34]

The second factor is labeled staff review. The two techniques most prominent on this factor involve committee staff, either through their conduct of investigations and field studies or more formal (and, by implication, systematic) program evaluations. More intensive analysis of the data indicates that the distinction between investigations and field studies and program evaluations is empirically meaningful, with the staff program evaluation variable behaving more like the other evaluation indicators than the investigations measure.[35] However, this distinction pales before the fact that the clearest and most generally applicable underlying dimension is the one indicated by the "staff review" label.

The third factor is labeled piecemeal review. It is dominated by three component oversight techniques. All imply turning up, scanning, or checking a lot of information piece by piece to see if all is okay, but without a clear target or procedure guiding the search or analysis. This description is most obviously apt for the two items loading highest on the factor—member communication and review of casework—but even the other major item, analysis of proposed agency rules and regulations, suggests a superficial review of the mass of rules and explanatory material churned out by the agencies in a committee unit's jurisdiction. All these techniques involve activities done by committee personnel themselves—talking, checking, reviewing. Like the staff review techniques, the committees have direct control over their use.

Overview

In sum, the nonhearings techniques employed by congressional committees in their approaches to oversight are arranged along three dimensions. One groups the use of program evaluations and reports prepared by noncommittee personnel. This comprehensive review dimension is generally downplayed in studies of congressional oversight. Indeed, with the exception of program evaluations done by congressional support agencies, its components are among the least frequently employed oversight techniques, but, according to committee staff, they are used. The second dimension is committee staff review and involves efforts (investigations and program analyses) conducted by the staffs of committee units to review agency programs and policies. These staff reviews are, on average, used much more frequently by committees than comprehensive review techniques (staff reviews rank fourth and sixth respectively in frequency use, with a mean use score of 2.67, see table 6-1). This is not a surprising finding since staff reviews are totally within the control of the committees, thereby ensuring the "right" results if necessary (that is, results the committee wants or can accommodate). They also give committees maximum control over the timing of the studies (getting them done in the time frame desired by the committee and released or leaked to the committee's advantage).

Finally, piecemeal review techniques fit the stereotype of congressional approaches to oversight—a piece by piece, generally unsystematic, and superficial search for or scanning of information about the agencies. Top staffers report that piecemeal techniques are used with middling frequency (on average, occasionally), close to the same amount as they say they use comprehensive approaches.[36] This similarity in frequency of use raises questions about the ways in which Congress approaches oversight, questions I will address in the next two chapters.

Of the other oversight techniques examined, but not included in the dimensional analysis, staff communication with agency personnel is by far the most used technique and the legislative veto by far the least used technique. Neither of these facts is very startling. The frequency with which all types of hearings are used for oversight, and especially their perceived high effectiveness, is more noteworthy. Since these formal vehicles for conducting committee business (hearings) take up so much of Congress's total work time, it is not surprising that they are frequently used for oversight, but their high effectiveness ratings raise questions for the observer skeptical about what committees aim for in the oversight process.[37]

To help in interpreting the purposes served by hearings and other oversight techniques, I will first examine models linking each of the techniques to congressional structures and oversight motivations (chapter 7) and then in chapter 8 place them in a broader political context.

Chapter 7

Linkages

MY GOAL IN THIS chapter is to understand better the linkages between oversight behavior and its sources. An underlying objective is to probe the coherence of the oversight system Congress uses. What are the effects, if any, of motivations for setting the oversight agenda and of congressional structures on types of oversight activity? Are oversight motivations linked to oversight behavior in a coherent manner? Do the linkages make sense? Are they well meshed?

Indicators and Approach

I use regression models to help answer the questions raised. The various oversight activities identified in chapter 6 serve as dependent variables in the analyses. For the three types of hearings used for oversight—primary-purpose oversight hearings, reauthorization hearings, and amendment hearings—scores on the single-item indicators were reversed so that a high number equals high utilization.[1] For the three nonhearings approaches identified—comprehensive analysis, staff analysis, and piecemeal analysis—the individual indicators were also reversed and average scores calculated.

The independent variables fall into two groups. One consists of objective characteristics of Congress, its committees, and its environment. Two of the variables in this group measure characteristics of Congress and its committees (chamber and committee unit type), one variable indicates policy jurisdiction type (the distributive variable from the Lowi policy scheme employed in the analysis of oversight hearings in chapter 3), one records a characteristic of the committee's legislative workload (whether or not it has a heavy concentration of programs on short-term authorizations), and one is a dummy variable for the Appropriations Committees (House and Senate combined), whose behavior is sometimes unique.[2] The variables overlap substantially those included in the regression analysis of oversight hearing frequency in chapter 3—in particular, chamber, committee unit type, policy type—and results can be compared to those discussed there.[3] The underlying hypothesis is that objective characteristics of Congress, its committees, and its environment strongly influence which oversight techniques committee units use most frequently. In other words, committee units behave as they do in oversight activity because of their chamber, mission, policy jurisdiction, or characteristics of their legislative workloads.

When relevant, I coded the variables the same way as in chapter 3 for ease of comparison. For the chamber variable, the House is coded 1 and the Senate 0. On the oversight unit variable, those units whose primary function is oversight are coded 1, the others 0.[4] For the redistributive policy issues variable, units with a heavy concentration of redistributive policy issues in their jurisdictions are coded 1, the rest 0.[5] For the variable measuring whether or not a unit has a heavy concentration of programs on short-term authorizations in its jurisdiction, called reauthorization or reauthorization frequency in the text, units reporting that they had many, most, or all of their programs on annual or periodic reauthorization cycles were coded 1, the rest 0.[6] Finally, all Appropriations units in the sample were coded 1, the others 0. For each of the regression analyses, then, a positive coefficient indicates that, controlling for the other variables in the equation, the element represented by the 1 code on the dummy variable engages more frequently in the type of oversight behavior measured by the dependent variable than the element represented by the 0 code. For example, if the coefficient for the chamber variable is positive, then in the 95th Congress the House used the oversight technique being examined more frequently than the Senate.

The second group of independent variables was selected from the analysis in chapter 5 of member and staff motivations for selecting the programs and agencies that committee units oversee. Five dimensions of oversight agenda setting were identified using factor analysis (table 5-4). A measure from each list was selected for the analysis in this chapter on the basis of its high relationship to the underlying factor (factor loading) and the number of respondents evaluating the measurement item. The number of respondents was a criterion in order to keep the N in the analysis as high as possible. The dimensions and the items selected to represent them are as follows:

Dimension	Item
Policy crisis	Crisis in a policy area
Clashes with administrators	Belief that programs are not effectively or efficiently run
Duty	Commitment to review of ongoing programs and agencies
Members' needs	Concern in members' districts about an agency or program
Assisting favored programs	Desire to assist an agency or program favored by the committee

The items were rescored from the original so that the numerically highest score now indicates "major importance" and the lowest score "unimportant."[7] Therefore, a positive sign on a regression coefficient indicates the positive impact of a given importance factor on the frequency of occurrence of the oversight technique used as a dependent variable in the analysis. The goal is to specify the situations in which, controlling for the objective characteristics specified and for the other motivations, a given motivation for selecting a program or agency for oversight leads to the use of each oversight technique. For example, one might reasonably hypothesize that those who score high on the duty factor (that is, those who give great importance to their commitment to review ongoing programs and agencies when they select oversight targets) are more likely than others to report that their committee units use the program evaluation techniques grouped under comprehensive approaches to oversight. However, when an immediate policy crisis or members' needs (concern in their districts) are very important, piecemeal approaches may well dominate. Such at least are the hypotheses underlying the analyses.

The variables used in the regressions were standardized[8] and analyzed for the models detailed in tables 7-1 and 7-2.[9] By standardizing the variables and using data from the same samples, the regression coefficients can be compared across the equations and within the equations.[10] The regression coefficients (called standardized coefficients or beta weights) indicate the amount of change in the standard deviation of the dependent variable (Y) produced by a change of one standard deviation in the independent variable (X).

When one uses this method and looks across the equations (across the rows of tables 7-1 and 7-2), one can compare the coefficients for a given predictor variable and see which are greater and which smaller as predictors of change in the dependent variables. And within a given equation (down the columns of the tables), the magnitudes of predictors can be compared and their relative importance discussed. For the purposes of this chapter, this is a concise and powerful way to examine the data. I can compare and contrast the relative impact of the structural characteristics and agenda motivations on the different types of oversight behavior and then use the knowledge of linkages derived from the analyses to draw some implications about the logic of the congressional oversight system.[11]

The Linkages

Table 7-1 displays the most relevant results from the regression analyses. For presentation purposes, the entries consist only of standardized regression coefficients statistically significant at the 0.10 level or better. This facilitates reading the table and finding the coefficients I want to emphasize.[12] Independent variables are labeled with X and a subscript, dependent variables with Y and a subscript. The equations for reauthorization (Y_5) and program amendment (Y_6) hearings are based on smaller samples than the other four equations because Appropriations Committees do not engage in these activities.[13] This makes the two final equations (Y_5 and Y_6) not strictly comparable to the others. However, because the conclusions would not be appreciably modified using the smaller subsamples for all of the equations, and the effects of the Appropriations variable are presented where significant (equation Y_1) and adjusted for elsewhere (in the second through fourth equations), I use the equations in table 7-1 in place of a more elaborate presentation.[14]

The results in table 7-1 contain a rich set of implications. I want to concentrate on two here.

First, while the objective characteristics of Congress, its committees, and its environment have some import in explaining how frequently the different approaches to oversight are used, they really come into

TABLE 7-1. *Estimated Effects (Standardized Regression Coefficients) of Objective Characteristics and Agenda-Setting Motivations on the Frequency of Use of Various Oversight Techniques (Approaches and Hearings), 95th Congress*[a]

| | Dependent variables | | | | | |
| | Approaches to oversight | | | Use of hearings for oversight | | |
Independent variables	Piece-meal (Y_1)	Staff (Y_2)	Compre-hensive (Y_3)	Primary-purpose oversight (Y_4)	Reauthor-ization (Y_5)	Amend-ment (Y_6)
Objective characteristics						
Chamber (X_1)	n.s.	n.s.	n.s.	n.s.	n.s.	−0.21**
Oversight unit (X_2)	n.s.	0.28*	n.s.	0.36*	−0.37*	−0.41*
Redistributive policy issue (X_3)	n.s.	n.s.	n.s.	n.s.	n.s.	0.25**
Reauthorization frequency (X_4)	n.s.	41*	n.s.	0.32**	0.42*	−0.29*
Appropriations unit (X_5)	−0.41*	n.s.	n.s.	n.s.	. . .	. . .
Agenda-Setting motives						
Policy crisis (X_6)	0.24*	−0.21**	n.s.	n.s.	n.s.	n.s.
Clashes with administrators (X_7)	0.43*	n.s.	n.s.	n.s.	n.s.	0.26**
Duty (X_8)	n.s.	0.26*	0.28*	n.s.	n.s.	n.s.
Members' needs (X_9)	0.24*	n.s.	0.25**	n.s.	n.s.	n.s.
Assisting favored programs (X_{10})	n.s.	n.s.	n.s.	0.28*	n.s.	0.22**
R^2 Total variable equations	0.54	0.33	0.28	0.26	0.50	0.46
Significance tests for total variable equations						
$p \leq$	(0.01)	(0.02)	(0.05)	(0.07)	(0.01)	(0.01)
N	(63)	(63)	(63)	(63)	(50)	(50)
R^2 Objective characteristics only	0.19	0.22	0.07	0.20	0.45	0.34
R^2 Agenda-Setting motivations only	0.34	0.16	0.24	0.11	0.08	0.12

n.s. Not significant at $p = 0.10$.

* $p \leq 0.05$.

** $p \leq 0.10$.

a. Equations: $Y_{1 \ldots 6} = B_1 X + B_2 X_2 + B_3 X_3 + B_4 X_4 \ldots + B_{10} X_{10} + u$. The text contains operational definitions of the variables.

their own in explaining the use of hearings for oversight. Conversely, motivations for setting the oversight agenda are most important in the approaches equations and play a much smaller role in explaining the frequency of hearings used for oversight. For example, there are only three significant coefficients (out of a possible fifteen) for the objective characteristics in the equations explaining the frequency with which the approaches to oversight were employed by committee units in the 95th Congress. However, there are eight significant coefficients (out of a possible thirteen) for the objective characteristics when the use of hearings is being estimated. On the other side of the coin, there are seven significant coefficients (out of a possible fifteen) for agenda-setting motivations in the equations that explain the frequency with which the various approaches to oversight were used. But there are only three of a possible fifteen significant coefficients for the agenda-setting motivations when the use of various types of hearings for oversight are the dependent variables.

If one looks at this in another way and examines the amount of variance explained by equations for the objective characteristics and agenda-setting motives separately, one can see clear signs of the relatively strong influence of objective characteristics on the use of hearings and of the strong influence of motivations on the frequency with which the various approaches are employed. (Look at the R_2 entries for "objective characteristics only" and "agenda-setting motivations only" in table 7-1.)[15] And a more precise but controversial way of measuring this phenomenon yields similar results. When one estimates the "unique contribution" of each independent variable to the variance explained by the regression equation,[16] the average unique contribution of the sum of the objective characteristics is only 37 percent for the three approaches to oversight (piecemeal, staff, and comprehensive), and it is almost twice as much, 70 percent, when the three types of hearings are the dependent variables.[17]

As a first general statement, then, there is little doubt that the objective characteristics of Congress, its committees, and its environment are much more important in explaining the frequency of use of the three types of hearings for oversight than in explaining the frequency with which the piecemeal, staff, or comprehensive approaches are employed.[18] Conversely, motives for setting the oversight agenda are more important in explaining the approaches that committee units take to oversight than in explaining the types of hearings they employ.

Turning to the second set of implications from table 7-1, one finds that the coefficients fit a nice pattern. The independent variables are connected in a logical way to the particular oversight techniques whose use they predict.

Piecemeal approaches to oversight (equation Y_1), it seems, are chosen in response to policy crises, members' needs defined in the narrow electoral sense, and especially clashes with administrators about administrative and program problems. When things are clearly going wrong or are perceived by constituents and clientele groups as going wrong, then committee units look more closely at regulations, review casework complaints from members' offices, and employ what is generally their most scarce resource—the time of committee members—to communicate with administrators.[19] Piecemeal approaches are most common, then, when there is a pressing problem to which committee members are likely to want a rapid, and probably a visible, response.

Comprehensive approaches to oversight (equation Y_3), on the other hand, are most commonly used when the committee units score high on the duty measure—when they have a strong commitment to review ongoing programs and agencies. To a somewhat lesser (and less statistically significant) extent, committee units also use comprehensive approaches more frequently when there is concern about programs or agencies in members' districts. The use of comprehensive techniques, then, reflects most strongly a commitment to review ongoing programs, but it is also a response to members' political needs. Note also that none of the coefficients for objective characteristics is a significant predictor of the use of comprehensive approaches. The use of comprehensive approaches to oversight, it seems, is a response solely to the motives of committee personnel, uninfluenced by objective characteristics of the committees and their environment.

The equation estimating committee use for oversight of staff investigations and field studies and of staff-conducted evaluations (Y_2) at first glance presents something of a riddle. There is a marked resemblance to the equation estimating the use of comprehensive techniques (Y_3) in that duty—a commitment to review ongoing programs (X_8)—is a significant predictor. This buttresses the conclusion that the duty factor isolated in the factor analysis in chapter 5 is a key to understanding approaches to oversight emphasizing program evaluation techniques. The fact that the policy crisis indicator (X_6) is significant (although at a lower level) with a negative sign merely reinforces this interpretation, especially when one remembers that the policy crisis variable has a significantly positive effect for the piecemeal techniques (Y_1) equation. In essence, in a crisis, piecemeal approaches to oversight get the emphasis, not evaluations or investigations, not even evaluations or investigation done by the committee unit's own staff. This is all quite consistent, but the coefficients in table 7-1 also show a marked influence of objective characteristics uncharacteristic of the other oversight approaches—the coefficients indicate that oversight units (X_2) and committee units with frequently reauthorized programs on their agendas (X_4) use staff evaluations and investigations more frequently than others. Why should this be so?

Breaking the staff index into its component parts helps to clarify the findings. While the signs of the key coefficients that are presented in table 7-1 remain the same—the measures for staff investigations and staff program evaluations fall on the same dimension in the factor analysis, after all—there are substantively and statistically important differences in magnitude, and one suggestive addition to the list of statistically significant coefficients, when equations estimating the use by committee units of staff investigations and of staff-conducted program evaluations are calculated separately.[20]

The results of the separate equations presented in table 7-2 dovetail nicely with the conclusions drawn based on analysis of the index measuring comprehensive approaches to oversight (Y_3). For the program evaluation component of the staff index (Y_2), the duty—commitment to review—item (X_8) is a significant positive predictor (the standardized regression coefficient is 0.39, $p \leq 0.05$). And, consistent with the equation for the combined-item staff index (Y_2), the policy crisis variable remains a smaller, marginally significant negative predictor (the standardized regression coefficient is -0.23, $p \leq .10$). The only significant objective characteristic in this equation is reauthorization frequency (X_4), indicating that staff program evaluations are employed more frequently when units have programs coming up for periodic review prior to reauthorization. Committee units probably like to use their staffs for program evaluations in such

TABLE 7-2. *Estimated Effects (Standardized Regression Coefficients) of Objective Characteristics and Agenda-Setting Motivations on the Frequency of Use of Staff Program Evaluations ($Y_{2.1}$) and Staff Investigations ($Y_{2.2}$) for Oversight*[a]

	Dependent variables	
Independent variables	Staff program evaluations ($Y_{2.1}$)	Staff investigations ($Y_{2.2}$)
Objective characteristics		
Chamber (X_1)	−0.04	0.34*
Oversight unit (X_2)	0.11	0.34*
Redistributive policy issue (X_3)	0.02	−0.09
Reauthorization frequency (X_4)	0.43*	0.21
Appropriations unit (X_5)	0.18	0.18
Agenda-Setting motives		
Policy crisis (X_6)	−0.23**	−0.10
Clashes with administrators (X_7)	0.05	−0.07
Duty (X_8)	0.39*	0.01
Members' needs (X_9)	−0.11	0.04
Assisting favored programs (X_{10})	0.12	−0.17
R^2 Total variable equations	0.30	0.33
Significance tests for total variable equations		
$p \leq$	(0.02)	(0.01)
R^2 Objective characteristics only	0.06	0.22
R^2 Agenda-Setting motivations only	0.19	0.10

* $p \leq 0.05$.
** $p \leq 0.10$.
a. Signs are reversed for correspondence to table 7-1 models.

situations because they can then pinpoint the questions they want asked and control the timing of the answers to fit the process at hand. The overall picture is one in which the use of staff program evaluation is linked to a commitment to review programs in a context of regular (noncrisis) reconsideration of program merits.

The other component of the staff index, staff investigations, naturally shares much in common with the staff evaluations measure, but the emphasis is different. When an equation for it is estimated separately (Y_{22}), the coefficients for the commitment to review agenda-setting motive (duty— X_8) and policy crisis (X_6) are not statistically significant, although both have the right signs. In fact, none of the agenda-setting motives has significant coefficients for this component of the staff index. The same is true of the reauthorization frequency variable. However, two of the other objective characteristics are statistically significant—chamber (X_2) and oversight unit (X_2). As you may recall from chapter 6, House committee units (which have more staff resources) do more staff investigations—a difference that holds up in the equation even with other factors controlled. Oversight units, which also tend to have large staffs, use staff investigations more frequently, and this holds independent of staff size. Recalling that the staff investigations addressed in the survey are employed "other than for preparation of hearings" (table 7-1), their frequent use by oversight units makes great sense. Oversight units are the most free-wheeling investigative units of the congressional committee system, relatively free of the need, and opportunity, to hold hearings for reauthorization of programs or for amendments to existing statutes. Furthermore, because they are least tied into subgovernmental relations (relations with the agencies and interest groups), they are most in need of information. Their information sources may not be particularly well developed or utilized, but one of the things that oversight unit staff have time to do more frequently than the staff of other types of committee units is to conduct an investigation when a lead presents itself.

The overall pattern of findings on approaches to oversight is clear. Though certain objective characteristics of committee units are linked to particular approaches to oversight—and these links can be readily explained—in general, objective characteristics do not explain the frequency of use of the approaches examined here. What does explain their use are the agenda-setting motives that unit staffers identify as important. And there is a nice pattern in the relationships of these motives to oversight approaches. Piecemeal approaches are most commonly used when there is a pressing problem to which committee members are likely to want a rapid, and, probably, a visible response. What I have labeled comprehensive approaches and also staff program evaluations, but not investigations, are used most frequently by units whose staffers report a strong commitment to review ongoing programs and agencies. (To a lesser extent, the comprehensive approach reflects members' political needs, such as the concern in their districts about a program or agency.) And frequent use of staff evaluations, not surprisingly, occurs when a crisis in the relevant policy area is not pressing. Program evaluations, after all, are usually time-consuming to do, and committee staff time would not generally be used for evaluation when a crisis is pressing.

When one turns from approaches to oversight to the use of particular types of hearings for oversight, one finds that use of the different types of hearings is linked most significantly to objective characteristics of Congress, its committees, and its environment but not to agenda-setting motives. However, some exceptions merit discussion. And, as noted, the individual coefficients in the oversight hearings models equations (Y_4, Y_5, Y_6) present a nice pattern that clarifies understanding of the decisions to use each type of hearing and, incidentally, increases confidence in the data.

A close look again at table 7-1 shows that committee units tend to specialize in the types of hearings they use for oversight. This pattern holds most strongly for the use of reauthorization and amendment hearings. As expected from the analysis in chapter 3, it holds least strongly for primary-purpose oversight hearings.

There are two variables in the equations that give us the best insights here. Not surprisingly, reauthorization frequency (X_4), a dummy variable indicating whether or not a unit has a heavy concentration of programs on short-term authorizations, is most potent in explaining the frequency of use of reauthorization hearings for oversight. The sign of the standardized regression coefficient is in the right direction (a positive coefficient indicates that units with numerous programs to reauthorize use reauthorization hearings for oversight more frequently than others; a negative coefficient indicates the opposite), and the absolute magnitude of the coefficient is much higher for the reauthorization equation (Y_5) than for either of the other two hearings equations (Y_4 and Y_6). The sign of the reauthorization frequency coefficient is negative for the amendment hearings equation (Y_6), I would suspect, because committee units with programs on short-term authorizations do not often need to hold hearings focused on amendments to statutes. They can easily review programs and amend statutes through the reauthorization process, a viable option when reauthorizations occur fairly frequently. In contrast, the use of primary-purpose oversight hearings (Y_4) is positively associated with reauthorization frequency, although the coefficient is at the margin of statistical significance. This fits with the analysis presented in chapter 4. Oversight through primary-purpose oversight hearings was so pervasive in Congress by the late 1970s that even committees with many programs on short-term authorizations appeared to use primary-purpose oversight hearings as one way to prepare for program reauthorizations.[21]

That common (widely diffused) quality of oversight hearings is also suggested in a comparison of the coefficients for the oversight unit variable (X_2), the second variable I want to highlight, for each of the three hearings equations. Whereas the reauthorization frequency (X_4) variable—an objective characteristic that one would expect to have an exceptionally strong influence—was clearly most potent as an explanation of frequent use of reauthorization hearings (Y_5), the absolute value of the oversight unit variable (X_4) coefficient is larger in both the reauthorization (Y_5) and amendment (Y_6) equations than in the primary-purpose oversight (Y_4) equation.[22] Oversight units do indeed conduct primary-purpose oversight hearings more frequently than other units, a consequence of their specialized function, but the oversight unit variable is an even better predictor of what they tend not to do—oversee through reauthorization and amendment hearings.

Still, unlike the result in the equations in chapter 3, the coefficient for the oversight unit variable is here a significant predictor of the frequency use of primary-purpose oversight hearings. However, it is important to note that the oversight unit variable used in this chapter separates committee subunits into those primarily dedicated to oversight and those with other primary missions. In chapter 3, the analysis was on the committee level. Committees were separated into those having a specialized oversight unit and those lacking such a unit. That analysis demonstrated conclusively the emergence by the late 1970s of relatively equal levels of oversight activity for committees with and without specialized oversight units, and the fact that by then a decided majority of almost all units engaged in some primary-purpose oversight activity. But on committees with designated oversight units, one would expect the oversight units to do a disproportionate share of the committee oversight, especially where primary-purpose oversight is involved. Oversight units clearly do hold primary-purpose oversight hearings more frequently than fellow units of their own committees, yet even as the predictor variable is configured in this chapter, it is not so potent as one might expect. Just compare its effect to the stronger impact of a comparable objective variable like reauthorization frequency on the use of reauthorization hearings for oversight and the larger coefficients of the oversight unit variable in equations predicting the use of reauthorization and amendment hearings for oversight. As I see it, therefore, the results in this chapter are fully compatible with the results in chapter 3.

Aside from the oversight unit and reauthorization frequency effects already discussed, two other objective characteristics show somewhat significant effects. Units with redistributive policy issues in their jurisdictions (X_3)[23] and Senate units (X_1) use amendment hearings more frequently for oversight than others. The Senate finding is a function of minor differences in committee jurisdiction in the two chambers—more Senate units (in the Finance Committee, especially) have a preponderance of permanently authorized programs and, therefore, are more likely to hold hearings on amendments. The redistributive policy issue finding reflects the fact that redistributive programs such as social welfare and labor tend to have permanent authorizations to insulate the programs from effective challenges by passionate opponents or to give beneficiaries certainty about benefit levels. Therefore, because amendment hearings as a generic category are used most frequently by committees with redistributive programs in their jurisdictions and because more Senate units are more likely to have the permanently authorized redistributive programs, hearings on amendments to statutes are more often used by them for oversight than by others.[24]

Finally, I should look briefly at the few significant agenda-setting motives coefficients predicting use of hearings for oversight. The positive coefficient of the variable clashes with administrators—programs ineffectively run (X_7) in the amendment hearings equation (Y_6) can be "explained" easily enough, but why it should be present is not clear. One can easily make the case that when staff and members of committee units are unhappy with the way administrators are conducting a program and when this is an important motivation for their decision to undertake oversight—the case for high scorers on X_7—they would be likely to propose amendments to statutes and use amendment hearings as an oversight mechanism. However, the same case can be made for many of the other agenda-setting motives and for their linkage to any of the types of oversight hearings. My guess is that the finding, which is barely significant in a statistical sense, is a chance occurrence.

More intriguing are the coefficients in table 7-1 for the assisting favored programs (X_{10}) indicator. Those who report that a desire to assist favored programs or agencies is an important motive in their decisions to oversee are also likely to report that their units frequently employ primary-purpose oversight hearings and that they frequently oversee through amendment hearings. One's initial guess, and a prominent view in the academic literature, is that oversight is a decidedly adversarial act by Congress—aimed at opposing some policy or righting some wrong.[25] Criticism certainly is common in oversight endeavors, but the critic may aim to strengthen or protect a program, not to undermine it. A Senate subcommittee chair, for example, addressed this issue as follows: "In most all the hearings I conduct, well, we ask tough questions, but . . . I wouldn't say they're adversary. After all, we're trying to find out from them how could the program be improved, and if we've got criticism we raise it and see what answers they've got. . . . We're working together on programs. We want them to execute efficiently, and I assume most of them want to execute efficiently."[26]

The coefficients for assisting favored programs (X_{10}) in table 7-1, then, indicate that oversight hearings, especially primary-purpose oversight hearings, are often linked to desires to assist programs in some way. Readers who recall the quotation from the subcommittee chair in chapter 5 will not be totally shocked by this finding, but the inference that oversight hearings may well be, more often than not, linked to a desire to assist programs or agencies is important enough to follow up in detail. This will be done in chapter 8.[27]

Approaches and Hearings: More Comprehensive Models?

To this point, the three approaches to oversight (piecemeal, staff, and comprehensive) and the three types of hearings in which oversight commonly takes place (primary-purpose oversight, reauthorization of programs, and amendment to statutes) have been treated separately. A measure of each served as a dependent variable in a regression analysis, and the effects on each of the same set of independent variables was compared and contrasted. In chapter 6 the relationships among the various approaches to oversight and types of oversight hearings were examined. Now I want to look briefly at the question of linkages between the approaches and types of hearings, and at the possibility that more comprehensive models can be built. Is it worthwhile to build models linking the objective characteristics of Congress, its committees, and its environment, committee oversight agenda-setting motives, the approaches to oversight that committees employ, and the frequency of use of various types of oversight hearings?

Linkages between approaches to oversight and types of hearings, where they exist at all, are weak. The average absolute value of the correlations between the two sets of indicators (N = 9) is 0.15 (s = 0.10). No coefficient is above the midtwenties. Though it is certainly interesting to note that those committee units using piecemeal approaches to oversight (Y_1) are also somewhat more likely to hold primary-purpose oversight hearings (Y_4) more frequently ($r = 0.24$), or that use of reauthorization hearings for oversight (Y_5) is slightly associated ($r = 0.19$) with use of comprehensive approaches (Y_3), there is no major story to tell here.

Nor, as the low correlations would suggest, is there much to be gained in modeling paths from objective conditions and oversight agenda-setting motives, through approaches, to types of hearings.[28] The most revealing model, and the only one with statistically significant ($p \leq 0.10$) path coefficients (and these are at the 0.2 level only) through any of the approaches, is one explaining primary-purpose oversight hearings. And what makes it of interest, given the earlier discussion of the impact of oversight units and desire to assist favored programs on the frequent use of oversight hearings, is that the direct path from the oversight unit variable is quite weak (0.19), while the direct path from the assist variable is relatively robust (0.31).[29]

The overall conclusion, however, must be that use of the various approaches and types of hearings are not linked in any significant way. More comprehensive models than those discussed here do not seem necessary.

Overview

Based on the analysis in this chapter, the following generalizations apparently hold. One, agenda-setting motives determine the approaches that committee units take to oversight. Two, objective characteristics of Congress, its committees, and its environment determine the types of hearings that committee units use most frequently in their oversight work.

When one looks at the linkages between motivations to oversee and approaches to oversight, one sees that piecemeal approaches to oversight are most commonly used when there is a pressing problem to which committee members want a rapid and probably visible response. The frequent use of comprehensive approaches is most strongly associated with units whose staffers report a strong commitment to review ongoing programs and agencies.[30] To answer one of the questions posed in the introduction, all of this seems quite rational. Motivations and types of approaches selected are basically well meshed.

In addition, committee units tend to specialize in sensible ways in the types of hearings they use for oversight. Units with a heavy concentration of programs on short-term authorizations tend to use reauthorization hearings for oversight. Those with numerous redistributive programs in their jurisdictions more frequently use amendment hearings for oversight, presumably because redistributive programs tend to be permanently authorized, which makes amendments to the basic statutes an attractive way to consider improvements. Frequent use of primary-purpose oversight hearings is significantly associated with units specialized to perform oversight although, as the analysis presented in chapter 3 also indicated, the use of primary-purpose oversight hearings is now very widespread.

Use of the various approaches to oversight (piecemeal, staff, and comprehensive) and of the different types of hearings (primary-purpose oversight, reauthorization, and amendment) are not linked in any significant way. As should now be clear, they basically have different sources and, therefore, there is no logical reason why they should be linked in a systematic manner.

Naturally, in a complex world, there are exceptions to these generalizations. The most interesting is the existence of a positive link between the desire of a committee unit to assist programs or agencies and its frequent use for oversight both of primary-purpose oversight hearings and of amendment hearings. The implication is that many oversight hearings, no matter what surface appearances might imply, are done in a fundamentally nonhostile, indeed a supportive, context. The context of oversight activity is the subject of the next chapter.

Chapter 8

Oversight in an Advocacy Context

THOSE SERVING ON congressional committees in the 1978–
80 period showed a marked tendency to regard themselves as advocates for "their" programs and thus to oversee within
this context. This chapter examines the nature of advocacy in Congress—who are advocates and why, how advocacy affects oversight,
and when advocacy breaks down.

Webster's New World dictionary defines an advocate as a person
who pleads . . . speaks or writes in support of . . . another's cause.
I use the expression advocacy context in this chapter not because I
think members or staff always speak in positive terms about the
programs in their jurisdictions or support everything done in the
name of these programs, but because the context within which they
operate most often is one of support. The nature, causes, limitations,
and implications of the advocacy context are my subjects here.

Oversight in an Advocacy Context

Politics is rarely, if ever, a neutral endeavor. As a consequence,
whatever the long-run tendencies toward advocacy or opposition,
oversight of agencies and programs by congressional politicians
almost always takes place in a nonneutral context.

The point just made about nonneutrality is well grounded in the
literature on politicians as a genus and, with some caveats, on
congressional politicians as a species. In my work on politicians and
bureaucrats in Western democracies, for example, politicians the
world over were found to "define problems chiefly in terms of political
principle and political advantage. Strong commitments, even at the
risk of intense conflict, marked the contributions of most politicians

162

to the discussion."[1] Both their "greater awareness of technical considerations in policymaking" and their tendency "to see their political advantage as lying with the interests that are intimately connected with the legislative functions performed through their committees"[2] set American congressional politicians off from other parliamentarians in the West. It is this somewhat contradictory combination of technical awareness, ties to the interests served by their committees, and strong commitments that I want to examine as I look broadly at the context of oversight behavior.

As part of the follow-up to the survey of top committee staffers (done mainly in 1980, see appendix A), respondents were asked a straightforward question, "Would you describe your [sub]committee as basically an advocate of the programs under its jurisdiction—advocating their continued growth and development—or as an opponent of them?" Because the respondents were educated, articulate members of the elite, and since the interview was conversational in format, I had little concern that the advocacy/opposition question would be a straightjacket for the respondents, unnecessarily confining their views. This assumption proved correct. However, I did use a separate, independent measure to supplement and confirm the conclusions reached on the basis of the advocacy/opposition item.

The advocacy/opposition question was not a very difficult one for the respondents to handle. Many, in fact, answered before the full sentence could be uttered. For example, one respondent simply interrupted after the word advocate to say enthusiastically, "Yes, yes, yes."[3] Or another said, "Oh, definitely advocate. Strong advocate."[4] And another: "Clearly an advocate."[5]

A less precipitous, but almost equally positive response from another top staffer, was as follows: "I think any subcommittee that has its subject, whatever its subject is, they're advocates. I mean, the Aging Subcommittee is advocating for aging programs, the Arts for arts, you know, Education for education, Health for health. They wouldn't be doing their work if they weren't interested."[6]

And, as a final answer of this type, one that avid readers of the academic literature on Congress will not find too surprising,[7] a respondent from one of the Public Works committees said, "Sure. [We're advocates.] You know, the trouble of it is we get in bed with agency people in some respects. We're hoping that they'll distribute good projects in our state, you know, and it's a kind of a working with them so that, you know, there'll be more, more and better of everything for everybody."[8]

Not all responses were so easy to categorize, but most respondents were comfortable with the question and, in addition, willing and able to express their views on the positions of their units in a nuanced manner. As a result, their answers were coded along a scale, rather than into a simple advocate-opponent dichotomy. But the scale was truncated because there were *no* reported opponents, or even descriptions of units that, on balance, showed a tendency to act as opponents. Instead, respondents' attitudes ranged from strong advocacy to neutrality.

While the committee units of the top staffers just quoted were coded as advocates, some responses indicating advocacy were more tempered. Qualified advocates, as I label them in table 8-1, were categorized from answers like the following: "I guess I want to quibble with the question. Growth isn't what we're looking for; strengthening, certainly; refinement, yes; and continuation, yes."[9] And "I would characterize it as a critical advocate; critical in the sense that we weren't blindly trying to promote programs without an eye to quality of the kind of program developed. Frequently our oversight hearings did dwell on problems that we saw in the management of the program, but we were still clearly advocates of a strong program in that area."[10]

Or, in an area where deregulation was an active issue but typically not the only one before the subcommittee, the respondent broke in after the advocacy part of the question to say, "Yeah [We're advocates], except for [industry] deregulation. I don't know how you would characterize that."[11]

Not all respondents reported that their committees were advocates or qualified (modified) advocates, although I emphasize again that none of the top staffers characterized their units as opponents or even modified opponents. Those who did not describe their units as advocates of some type fell into two broad categories. One group stressed balance, emphasizing that its unit's stance on programs depended on the agency or the issue. Typical of the depends group was the following: "I don't think it's possible to say either way. I think it simply depends on, you know, the effectiveness of the programs. If the programs are effective, we generally tend to be proponents; if they're ineffective, we tend to be opponents of those programs."[12]

Other top staffers insisted that their units were neutral, neither advocates nor opponents. Those coded into the neutral group gave answers such as, "No, I would say neither. I would say as an objective judge of the activities."[13]

Or, as a top staffer on an Appropriations subcommittee said, "Well, we're not advocates. We're more neutral in being an appropriations committee. You know, the authorizing committees tend to be more advocates. The Appropriations Committee has to be the hard decision-makers to keep the dollars within the limited resources available. So we are—we're not advocates, but we're not the opponents either. . . . It's a neutral stance."[14]

Close to two-thirds of top staffers characterized their units as advocates of some type (table 8-1). In fact, more than 40 percent did not hesitate to call their committees advocates plain and simple—embellishing their remarks, sometimes, but with no significant qualifications. Another 21 percent gave qualified indications of advocacy, for a total of 63 percent of the committee units described as advocates. The balance of the responses consisted of 11 percent who said of their units "it depends" on the agency or the issue and 26 percent who described their units as neutral, neither advocates nor opponents.

The bias toward advocacy is especially pronounced among nonoversight units. As table 8-1 shows, over 70 percent (72 percent, to be exact) of nonoversight top staffers classified their units as advocates or qualified advocates, while the same was true of only 19 percent of the top staffers who work for oversight units. Some form of advocacy, then, was the common stance of most nonoversight committee units in the 1978–80 period.

The nature of the oversight and nonoversight unit breakdown gives us more confidence in the measure—units with less significant (or no) legislative jurisdiction are most likely to have a neutral stance proclaimed by their top staffers, while those with significant legislative responsibility are said to be either wholehearted or qualified advocates of the programs that are their bread and butter. Still, it is possible that the conclusion implied by the distribution on the measure misleads us. The dichotomous nature of the options given in the question, the stark choice between advocacy and opposition, may

TABLE 8-1. *Committee Unit Advocacy/Opposition Posture, Total and by Type of Unit*
Percent[a]

Advocacy/opposition	All committees units	Type of unit[b]	
		Nonoversight	Oversight
Advocate	42	49	6
Advocate, qualified	21	23	13
Depends	11	10	19
Neutral	26	18	63
Opponent, qualified	0	0	0
Opponent	0	0	0
Total	100	100	101
N	(89)	(73)	(16)

a. Totals may not add to 100 because of rounding.

b. The oversight units in the study consist of all House Government Operations and Senate Governmental affairs units, and the specialized oversight subcommittees of House Commerce, House Public Works, and House Ways and Means.

downplay the true level of unit opposition or neutrality. Even if the latter fear is not justified—something strongly indicated by the nature of the discussion accompanying the answers and the sophistication of the respondents—oversight might still tend to take place in a less supportive atmosphere than answers to such a general question suggest.

Consequently, I constructed two additional measures. These measures are independent of the advocacy/opposition item, and, unlike that item, focus exclusively on oversight behavior. They were constructed from the answers to a set of questions asking top staffers first to identify the most successful oversight case conducted by their units in the 95th Congress and then to describe the case fully by explaining such things as why it was most successful, why it was undertaken, what those in the unit hoped to accomplish, and what was accomplished.

On the basis of detailed discussion in the interviews about the unit's most successful oversight case, two assessments were made about the relationship of the staffer's committee unit to the program or agency that was the focus of discussion (table 8-2).[15] The first

TABLE 8-2. *Orientation to Agency or Program in Committee Unit's Most Successful Oversight Case, Total and by Type of Unit*
Percent[a]

Orientation	All committee units	Type of unit[b]	
		Nonoversight	Oversight
Sympathy/hostility toward the agency or program's basic charter or purpose			
Sympathetic; supportive of; likes; agrees with	75	78	55
Hostile; disapproving of; dislikes; disagrees with	6	3	18
Other	20	18	27
Total	101	101	100
N	(71)	(60)	(11)
Can't tell from discussion of case, N	(16)	(11)	(5)
Approval/disapproval of conduct in carrying out the charter or purpose (implementation)			
Approves; supports; sympathizes with	8	9	0
Disapproves; disagrees; is hostile toward	63	58	81
Other	30	33	19
Total	101	100	100
N	(80)	(65)	(16)
Can't tell from discussion of case, N	(7)	(7)	(0)

a. Totals may not add to 100 because of rounding.
b. See table 8-1 for definition of oversight unit.

assessment was one of sympathy to or hostility toward the agency or program's basic charter or purpose. The second assessment was one of approval or disapproval of agency conduct in carrying out the program under discussion, that is, implementation. In both cases, I encouraged use of the "other" or "can't tell" categories if the coding dimensions did not fit the top staffer's discussion.

Top staffers' case accounts present a picture of committee units overwhelmingly sympathetic (75 percent) to the basic charter or purpose of the agency or program overseen. In fact, if the "other" category in the table is removed from the base used in the calculation, the percentage of those in the sympathetic category rises to 93 percent. The fact that this assessment of sympathy was based on discussions by top staffers of their units' most successful oversight cases, cases that should bring out any latent tendencies of opposition to the charter or purposes of programs or agencies, increases my confidence that committee units do indeed take a basic advocacy posture toward programs in their jurisdictions. And it supports the implication that the advocacy stance measured by the general advocacy-opposition item includes committee oversight behavior.[16]

Table 8-2 also shows, however, that close to two-thirds of the unit top staffers (63 percent) indicate disapproval of the way the program is being carried out. If the "other" category is removed from the base used to calculate the percentage, the percentage disapproving rises to 89 percent.

In short, for these oversight endeavors, the overwhelming majority support the basic purpose of the government activity in question *and* are critical of some aspect of its implementation.[17]

This finding helps to explain what may have appeared as a bit of a paradox in the discussion so far–the advocacy posture that seems to mark most congressional units, combined with the fact that their oversight is often (though certainly not always) motivated by discontent about program operation. The two postures coexist quite comfortably, even when the same case is analyzed. Two implications already drawn are thereby reinforced: first, basic advocacy does not preclude oversight; and second, oversight only rarely involves a reach for the program or agency jugular. The advocacy posture obviously fits with the overt desire to assist a favored agency or program identified in chapter 5 as an important motivation for many to undertake oversight, but it also coexists with critical views about agency or program operation.

The differences between oversight units and other units shown in table 8-2 reinforce the findings in table 8-1. First, top staffers of oversight units are the least likely to indicate a sympathetic or supportive stance toward the agency or program's basic charter or purpose, although they are apparently much more sympathetic when an actual case is the basis for the evaluation (55 percent are sympathetic in table 8-2) than in the abstract where they indicate a more evenhanded, neutral stance (only 19 percent reported that their units were advocates or qualified advocates in table 8-1). And oversight staffers are the most likely to describe cases in which their units disapprove of the way the program overseen is being implemented by the agency. Therefore, while an unambiguously neutral setting for oversight is hard to find in any congressional committee unit, the most likely setting for a neutral perspective is a committee unit whose primary function is to oversee the executive.

Second, both parts of table 8-2 have large entries in the "other" category (20 percent for the sympathy/hostility measure and 30 percent for the approval/disapproval measure). The entries in "other," of course, represent diverse case accounts,[18] but an important reason for the discrepancy between the size of the "other" categories reinforces the general interpretation in this section. There are more "other" responses on the approval/disapproval measure than the sympathy/hostility measure in good part because many top staffers report strong support for the basic charter or purpose of the agency or program being overseen combined with revealing criticisms of program administration. According to the accounts of top staffers, committees often disapprove of attempts by political higher-ups (the department secretary or the president) to influence program administration or policy interpretation in ways the committee does not like. Oversight in these cases is aimed at the presidential administration and its goals in carrying out the program in question, not at the agency's actions or interpretation of its mandate. The committee is trying to help "its" program keep on the right track, often with surreptitious aid from agency program administrators. For example, one case selected by a top staffer as his unit's most successful oversight endeavor was concluded by transferring an agency from one organizational hierarchy to another. The goal was to enhance the agency's ability to maintain the integrity of its major program by preventing the Office of Management and Budget from imposing presidential priorities. Committee (and agency) views on proper program conduct were thus reinforced in practice.

In sum, all available evidence indicates that the most common context for oversight is an advocacy context. This does not mean that committee units are uncritical. Indeed, they are often critical of programs and their administration. Nonetheless, the context is generally one of basic support and underlying sympathy.

The Consequences of Advocacy

So far, I have established that oversight behavior for most committee units takes place in a basic context of advocacy. However, not all units are out and out advocates. Some committee units are qualified advocates and others apparently take a more neutral stance.

Committee units that are set up primarily to do oversight (those I have labeled oversight units, that is, units whose primary function is oversight) are most likely to proclaim a neutral stance and least likely to take a position of advocacy or qualified advocacy.[19] Analysis based on the "most successful oversight" questions buttresses this finding. Committee role is important in determining which units are most likely to be advocacy oriented.

The academic literature goes beyond this finding to make the somewhat more subtle point that constituency committees are the most likely to be advocacy oriented. Steven S. Smith and Christopher J. Deering in their recent book *Committees in Congress* speculate about committee type and advocacy. Smith and Deering expect constituency committees (those that "attract members primarily for constituency-oriented reasons")[20] to be the most advocacy oriented because members tend to join them to protect established programs benefiting their districts, with "policy committees" less advocacy oriented and, by implication, "prestige committees" and "mixed policy/constituency committees" less advocacy oriented also.[21]

A first look at my interview data seems to confirm this notion but not strongly. The correlation (r) between a variable classifying committee units into those identified by Smith and Deering as constituency oriented and those not is 0.26.[22] However, simply cutting the two main oversight committees—House Government Operations and Senate Governmental Affairs—from the sample reduces the correlation to 0.11. If the other oversight units—the oversight subcommittees of House Commerce, Public Works, and Ways and Means—are eliminated, the correlation drops to only 0.06. In other words, almost all of the positive relationship between the constituency committees and advocacy posture is because most oversight units are in the nonconstituency category. Drop the oversight units from the calculation and most committee units are about equally advocacy oriented.[23]

In fact, the only committee units even approaching the level of "nonadvocacy" of the specially designated oversight units are the subcommittees of the House Appropriations Committee. But even here, the proper word is approach and not equal. As the literature would lead one to expect, Senate Appropriations Committee units look much like other units (63 percent of the Senate respondents report a strong or qualified advocacy stance),[24] while House Appropriations units are less advocacy oriented with only 25 percent of their top staffers reporting a strong or qualified advocacy stance—a low figure, certainly, but still above the 19 percent reported by top oversight unit staffers.[25]

In sum, with the clear exception of specially designated oversight units and the weaker exception of House Appropriations subcommittees, the top staffers on congressional committee units uniformly describe their employers as strong or qualified advocates of the programs in their jurisdictions. House Appropriations staffers, like the typical top staffers on oversight units, claim their units take a more neutral position or one that depends on the issue, but their overall stance never places them on the opposition end of the scale.[26]

This finding, which is based on an item measuring committee units' overall stance, is buttressed by data on units' relationships to programs or agencies during a specific instance of oversight behavior. These data show overwhelming support for the basic charter or purposes of the program or agency being overseen, even though there may well be disagreement with agency implementation efforts. All indicators, then, are that most oversight, other than perhaps that done by specialized oversight units, takes place within an advocacy context—often critical of particulars but almost always supportive of basic goals. Even the work of the specialized oversight units takes place in a neutral, not a hostile, context and is generally supportive of basic program or agency goals in actual cases.

The data on support posture in specific oversight cases are so invariant (table 8-2) that statistical analysis is not practical. However, as table 8-1 shows, on the more subtly calibrated general advocacy measure, some units can be classified as strong advocates, some as qualified advocates, and others, according to the accounts of their top staffers, are best scored as neutral or evenhanded. This measure, therefore, at least provides a vehicle for exploring the consequences of a unit's advocacy position for its oversight motivations, approaches, and hearings behavior. Perhaps where one stands on the advocacy measure has important effects on behavior. For example, intuition might lead one to expect those who are neutral on the advocacy scale to exhibit an unusually strong commitment to review ongoing programs or agencies (that is, to review even when review is not forced or stimulated by the end of a program or agency's authorization) and, in their oversight work, to use the more objective, comprehensive (evaluation) techniques with greater frequency than others. And the underlying logic of this expectation leads one to expect that those who qualify their advocacy posture would have weaker commitments to review and a weaker preference for the use of comprehensive techniques than those who are neutral on the advocacy scale. Strong advocates, one might think, would be the least open to objective evidence about program operation and the least likely to exhibit a commitment to review the work of ongoing programs or agencies.

To examine these issues, the advocacy measure (table 8-1) was grouped into three categories—advocates, qualified advocates, and a category combining those taking either a neutral or depends stance. Tests to determine whether or not collapsing the neutral and depends categories made a difference in the results of analysis uncovered no significant differences, and thus the categories were collapsed.[27] (I refer to the combined neutral-depends category as neutral because the neutral category is the predominant one.) Test runs including and excluding the House Appropriations Committee cases also indicated that including the House Appropriations units in the analysis does not distort results. Accordingly, the House units are included. However, including the oversight units does affect some results in misleading ways.[28] Therefore, this group was excluded from the analysis of the consequences of a committee unit's position on the general advocacy measure.

Initially, the advocacy measure was correlated with the indicators of oversight motivations, approaches, and hearings behavior analyzed in chapters 5, 6, and 7. Most of the results are substantively and statistically insignificant. Units said to be advocates, qualified advocates, or neutral show remarkably similar motivational and behavioral patterns in most respects.[29] Advocates, for example, are about as likely as others to undertake oversight when scandal is an important stimulus, and they use piecemeal approaches no more frequently than others.[30] What I will emphasize, therefore, are the situations most likely to show a relationship between advocacy and oversight motivations or behavior, particularly the relationship of advocacy to a unit's commitment to review ongoing programs and to how frequently it uses comprehensive oversight techniques (mainly evaluations of programs and agencies).

One might expect strong relationships in these cases. Units that are advocates should be much less likely than neutral units to score high on the duty measure (that is, to have a strong commitment to review ongoing programs or agencies) because advocates are already convinced of the basic merit of a program or an agency. Whatever gains in program operation or design that advocates might achieve by review must be weighed against the possibility of publicizing a program's faults. Advocates might well review ongoing programs for political reasons of one sort or another, but they are not likely to review out of a sense of commitment. And the same should hold true, perhaps more so, for the use of comprehensive techniques.[31] Advocates should be much less interested than neutrals (or even qualified advocates) in the elaborate and more objective information available through comprehensive techniques. Advocates as well as others may want and use information, but it is less likely to be information of the type produced by comprehensive techniques, especially the types of program evaluations included in my comprehensive approaches measure since these evaluations are almost always conducted by personnel not directly under the congressional committee's control.

Results of the analysis disappoint these expectations quite a bit, but they are very revealing about the overall advocacy climate of congressional committee oversight behavior. The correlation (r) of advocacy with the duty (commitment) indicator is 0.15, and it is 0.23 with the comprehensive approaches index. Both are positive, indicating that my expectations about the direction of the relationship are confirmed, but the magnitudes are low.[32] What these correlations reflect is that neutral units are, indeed, more committed to review and more likely to use comprehensive approaches than others but not by much. Or, to put it another way, those committed to review and those who use comprehensive approaches most frequently are less likely to be advocates but not very much less likely.

Advocates predominate at all levels of the two measures. Eighty-eight percent of those low on the commitment to review (duty) measure or on the use of comprehensive techniques are advocates, for example, but so are 67 percent and 60 percent of those at the high end of each measure.[33] The relationships represented by the percentage differences are not trivial, but the reality they represent must be understood in the proper environmental context. The environment is best characterized as an advocacy environment, and most oversight takes place within the context of this environment.

Of the many other relationships examined between the advocacy measure and indicators of oversight agenda-setting motivations or oversight behavior the only two that are statistically significant do nothing to modify this conclusion. Units rated high on the advocacy measure use committee staff investigations of agency activities less frequently than others ($r = -0.26$, $p = 0.031$), but even here the differences are not that great, and even those who use staff investigations least frequently are self-professed advocates.[34] The only other significant relationship buttresses a point made in chapter 7. Those who make frequent use of oversight hearings are *most likely* to be advocates ($r = 0.27$, $p = 0.027$).[35]

In sum, the dominant ethos of the nonoversight units of Congress has a clear advocacy component. Even those who undertake oversight because they are committed to review ongoing programs and agencies generally share an advocacy posture and, to a slightly lesser extent, so do those most likely to use comprehensive approaches to oversight. In addition, those congressional committee units using oversight hearings most frequently are the most likely to be advocates. This does not necessarily mean that these committee units are uncritical or uninterested in knowing about what is going on in agencies or programs. It just means that their quest for knowledge takes place within a general context of advocacy and, by implication, says something about how they are likely to interpret and use the information they get. In an advocacy context, people are likely to want to fix or adjust what is broken, not to discard it.

The data based on specific ("most successful") oversight cases reinforce these conclusions. In these cases, support for the basic charter or purpose of the agencies overseen is even stronger than the more general advocacy item might imply, yet at the same time units conducting oversight clearly are most often stimulated by some dissatisfaction with the way programs are being carried out. This posture of critical support also characterizes the specially designated oversight units, although to a lesser extent than the nonoversight units. Even those on specially designated oversight units evidently are more affected by the feeling of commitment to government programs typical of members of other committees than one might suppose from an examination of their responses to the general advocacy measure alone. (The general advocacy measure probably plays up their sense of neutrality since it is detached from a behavioral reference. When one gets away from the abstract to actual cases of oversight, the advocacy posture of those on oversight units is quite prevalent.) The implications for congressional reform are worth noting: though oversight units apparently present the most impartial setting for oversight, they are probably more often impartial in the abstract than in actual operation.

Advocacy Forever?

The overall findings discussed so far fit reasonably well with the notion put forward at the beginning of the chapter that politicians (and, by implication, the institutions they inhabit) are marked by strong commitments. Except for specialized oversight units, the great majority (72 percent) of top staffers describe their committee units as advocates or qualified advocates of the programs under their jurisdiction, while less than one-fifth (18 percent) use the term neutral to describe their units. And information on actual oversight cases—the most successful oversight case of the unit as selected by the top staffers interviewed—leads one to conclude that the advocacy item, if anything, overstates the level of neutrality, including the level of neutrality for oversight units. When Congress oversees, it is often skeptical about the implementation of policy or about particular aspects of policy, but this skepticism is mainly sympathetic. Congressional reviewers are predisposed to preserving the core of any enterprise, even when they aim to modify some aspect of policy or of agency behavior.[36] And though, as earlier chapters suggest, congressional committees are avid users of information, even technical information, it seems that this information is considered in an advocacy context where it is used mainly to modify existing programs.[37]

It is natural to ask why committee units tend to be advocates and not opponents, and whether it will always be so. Politicians may tend to be committed individuals, but commitment could as easily be associated with opposition as with advocacy. And indeed we know from the literature that committee units do at times oppose basic program goals, even when Democrats control both Congress and the presidency.[38] Yet advocacy clearly marks most of the committee units studied. So why, first, the predominance of basic advocacy?

The answer is fairly easy to spell out. Most aspects of the congressional committee system are biased toward advocacy. When seeking membership on committees, people elected to Congress look to committees with jurisdiction over programs that benefit (or might benefit) their constituencies, or have jurisdiction over policies that members may find appealing or interesting, or have great power in Congress. The first aim obviously predisposes committee members toward support of the basic purpose of programs in the committee unit's jurisdiction. Members with the second aim are biased toward advocacy if a constituency benefit is also at stake, if the policy is personally appealing, or more subtly (and certainly less powerfully) because of the tendency to develop an affinity for those things that one finds interesting. The last aim in seeking committee membership, building power in the chamber, once fit with a degree of disinterested decisionmaking, at least on the House Appropriations Committee. Members of that committee were once chosen from safe districts and were expected to act as guardians of the federal treasury. However, with the greater opportunities now available for the House rank and file to secure an appointment to the Appropriations Committee, and the relative ease with which committee members may choose appointments to subcommittees important to their districts, the members of the Appropriations Committee more and more resemble the advocates on other committees.[39] Since the reforms of the 1970s, subcommittee assignments, which are keys to oversight, are now mainly a matter of self-selection. This situation tends to promote (or reinforce) the basic advocacy posture of committee units.

Whatever their predispositions before membership, members of committees, once they take their seats, are drawn to support at least the basic aims of programs and the continuation of agencies over which they have jurisdiction, that is, to take an advocacy position of some sort. First, if there were no programs or agencies, or even severely reduced programs, the value of membership on the committee with jurisdiction would decline. This reality leads to identification with the basic missions of the programs or agencies, especially for those with the longest service on the committees who also tend to be the most influential and to have the greatest stake in committee membership. Second, members of committees with jurisdiction in a given area are not only likely to start with a positive predisposition, but their contacts with clientele groups or other program beneficiaries tend to reinforce or stimulate a basically supportive posture. Such groups may complain about particulars, but in the end they usually want their agency, the source of their benefits, to prosper. They therefore provide support for key politicians like committee members who can and, as a result of the support, usually do help them. Third, according to some influential literature, many in Congress who look like opponents to the naive observer because they denounce programs and the officials who implement them are actually program advocates. They gain credit from unhappy constituents through rectifying problems connected to the programs but need the programs in operation to gain the credit. They therefore work to preserve and even enhance programs while sounding the alarm about an agency's faults.[40] Fourth, the relative weakness of political parties contributes to the patterns just described. Finally, the most senior members, those who are generally most influential in making oversight decisions, often develop a special bias in favor of programs they have helped to shape. They want these programs to continue, indeed to grow and prosper, as monuments to themselves.

Research shows that government organizations, once established, enjoy a tenacious hold on life.[41] The advocacy posture of congressional committees, which play a very important role in the birth and nurturance of government organizations, is obviously important in this tendency toward "immortality" of government organizations. However, in rare instances, government organizations do die and, probably somewhat more often than the death of government organizations, the basic purposes of programs or agencies are called into question by congressional committees. The conditions under which agencies are threatened with extinction or their basic purposes called into question tell us much about basic advocacy biases in the system.

In the latter years of the Carter administration (when the interview data for this study were collected) deregulation was the principal issue relevant to a discussion of the opposition end of the advocacy/ opposition spectrum. Congressional committees played an important, although clearly subordinate, role in deregulation. Deregulation represented a significant reversal of basic policy in all cases, and even included the phasing out of an agency in the case of the Civil Aeronautics Board.[42] A very thorough study of *The Politics of Deregulation* by Martha Derthick and Paul Quirk is instructive on the conditions under which committee advocacy breaks down.

In their explanation of the success of deregulation, Derthick and Quirk stress several factors. They mention the convergence of elite opinion in support of deregulatory reform, the initiatives taken by officeholders in positions of leadership, and the limited ability of affected industries to protect themselves through political action. But the explanatory element of most interest for my purposes is the fact that "Congress did not have to act for deregulation to occur."[43] As Derthick and Quirk say in a revealing passage,

It is hard to overstate the importance of this fact for our cases. It is crucial. An instrument was available—the independent regulatory commission—that had broad powers to act and was driven to do so by a combination of external sanctions and criticism and entrepreneurial leadership committed to reform. Action by the commissions promptly elicited the desired economic responses from industry, since removing anticompetitive restraints compelled firms to compete whether they wanted to or not. And action by the commissions precipitated legislation (in the transportation cases) or adequately substituted for it (for terminal equipment in telecommunications). Moreover, insofar as the commissions failed to institute reforms, courts were available as an alternative instrument; it was a court, not the legislature or a commission, that in effect dictated that long distance telephone service should become competitive.

Had Congress alone been able to take effective, authoritative action, far-reaching reform would have been much less likely to occur. In the absence of action by the commissions, Congress would not have felt that its prerogatives were being challenged; it would not have come under pressure from the regulated industries to take action as a way of restoring stability; and, insofar as it might have preferred to preserve the old regimes, it would not have borne the considerable political burden of reversing reform measures already instituted.

Had the independent regulatory commissions not been both

very vulnerable to external influence and exceptionally endowed by statute with authority to act, they would have been less capable of forcing Congress's hand.[44]

These, then, were very special circumstances. And, indeed, when they did not hold, when control did not rest outside of Congress to the same degree, that is, when conditions "forcing Congress's hand" were weaker, deregulation was much less successful.[45]

Committee units may also tend toward opposition under another special set of circumstances: when there is a massive turnover in unit membership and the new members have basic policy preferences that are very much at variance with the policies the agencies in their jurisdictions are currently following.[46] It is possible that forces outside of Congress could push members on a committee unit to reverse their previously held basic policy preferences—preferences refined and reinforced over time in relations with an agency and its clientele—but large membership turnover is probably a necessary condition for most basic shifts in unit preferences. Large membership turnover is, however, not a likely occurrence because of the nature of the congressional committee system.[47] Therefore, it is unlikely that committee unit preferences will shift radically against the fundamental goals of agency policy, especially if there is no shift in party control of Congress.

In sum, exceptions to the advocacy posture typical of congressional committees clearly do occur, but it seems that they are best characterized as exceptions, at least when the architects of the relevant programs and agencies (in this case the Democrats) control Congress.

But even Democratic control of Congress is not eternal. In the 1980 election Ronald Reagan carried a Republican Senate into power along the tide of his success. He then launched a frontal attack on many of the domestic agencies and programs of government. The reactions of Congress, especially of the Republican Senate, help to shed more light on the conditions of congressional advocacy.

This is not the place for a complete account of the complex struggles over policy in the Reagan administration; indeed, even the complexities of the administration's relations with Congress and its committees is beyond what I can do. But enough exists in accounts by participants and by scholars to provide a basis for some preliminary conclusions about the advocacy posture of committees when the Democrats do not control Congress.

To summarize briefly, drawing on experience gained in 1980 by a relatively minor but innovative use by the Carter administration of the reconciliation provision of the Budget and Impoundment Control Act, the Reagan administration (in particular, budget chief David Stockman) proposed significant changes to be adopted in 1981 through reconciliation. The key precedent, established almost by accident in 1980, was the use of cuts in spending levels contained in authorizations to make program cuts.[48] In the end, the 1981 bill "altered the course of more than 250 programs worth $36 billion,"[49] and "virtually all of the program changes enacted in the 1981 reconciliation bill were initially recommended by the President."[50] What happened to congressional committee advocacy during this process and afterward?

The "success" of the 1981 reconciliation process in the House rested in large measure on the fact that the influence of the authorizing committees was effectively eliminated. Even the influence of the House Budget Committee was minor. In both the initial budget resolution (which established the instructions for reconciliation) and the final bill (the actual reconciliation cuts), substitutes adopted on the floor (so-called Gramm-Latta I and II) carried the day. Gramm-Latta II substituted the Reagan administration agenda for those of the House committees, most of which had "reported their recommendations with bipartisan support."[51]

The cuts, then, say relatively little about changes in the basic advocacy/opposition posture of the standing committees of the House committees, but much about the conditions under which the committees can be bypassed. The 1980 election resulted in a reduced Democratic majority in the House and a sense, through Republican success in carrying the Senate, that the public was strongly behind Reagan. Those conditions and the existence of an extraordinary mechanism like reconciliation combined to reduce significantly the committees' power to protect their programs.

In the Senate, the results of the 1980 election unsettled the institution profoundly. Unexpectedly, Republicans gained a majority. Suddenly, the committees and subcommittees had new chairs, staffs had to be built and organized, new majority members (now often chairs of committee units) integrated, and relationships with the agencies established on a new basis. And, of course, the political leaning of the Senate had shifted to the right. When faced almost immediately with an administration plan for cuts in domestic programs drafted under the direction of the OMB's David Stockman, the Senate fell into line. It passed the reconciliation act quickly and followed the administration's lead to a remarkable degree.[52]

By 1982, the Senate was not so pliable. Committee and subcommittee chairmen were more experienced and generally more protective of "their" severely cut programs. Interest groups, often confused by the process in 1981, were now better prepared. Resentment and fear of the growing power of the Budget Committee emerged.[53] Problems with the economy and the upcoming election made the administration's position less powerful.

Steven Smith describes the rapid reemergence of centrifugal politics in congressional (both House and Senate) decisionmaking as follows:

In 1981 the Reagan administration's supporters in Congress used the reconciliation procedure after the first budget resolution to prevent committees from pigeonholing administration proposals. Republican leaders in Congress served as "point men" for the president, and much of the administration's success was due to their efforts.

The subsequent years . . . demonstrate that 1981 was very unusual and that the centrifugal forces in Congress are still powerful. Both House and Senate committees exercised great independence from Reagan and party leaders after 1981. And many members, including Senate majority party Republicans, expressed concern that congressional decisionmaking processes not be "subverted" in the fashion of 1981 again.[54]

Tied to the notion of centrifugal forces in Congress are more basic notions about the biases of American politics. David Stockman, the major architect of the Reagan budget cuts, admits defeat of the "Reagan Revolution," a revolution Reagan evidently only vaguely comprehended, aimed at a "minimalist government–a spare and stingy creature, which offered even-handed public justice, but no more." Stockman wrote, "The true Reagan Revolution never had a chance. It defied all of the overwhelming forces, interests and impulses of American democracy. Our Madisonian government of checks and balances, three branches, two legislative houses, and infinitely splintered power is conservative, not radical. It hugs powerfully to the history behind it. It shuffles into the future one step at a time. It cannot leap into revolutions without falling flat on its face."[55]

Even by March of 1981, Stockman says, "Resistance began to crop up everywhere, both within the cabinet and on the Hill. In its totality, it amounted to a counter-revolution—a broad range of political signals that the free market and antiwelfare state premises of the Reagan Revolution were not going to take root."[56]

And, overall, Stockman concludes, based on his experiences, that Republicans like Democrats are tied to most established programs, especially those that serve their constituencies–and these, of course, are the programs in the jurisdictions of their committee units. "The Reagan Revolution as I have described it is really a radical, anti-welfare-state view of how society is best served. And, essentially, that view is not shared by elected Republican politicians. They adhere to the Tip O'Neill maxim: 'All politics is local.' And so, therefore, all policy is local. If you're from the wheat belt, you are for wheat subsidies. If you're from Detroit, you're for the Chrysler bailout."[57]

In the end, then, it seems reasonable to conclude that the basic advocacy posture of the substantive committees of Congress continued in the Reagan era. This was surely true in the House, and it did not take most Senate committee units too long to find the same position. Once control over programs began to shift from the floor back to committees, the days of hostile congressional action on programs were largely over.

To reiterate several important points, I do not mean to imply that congressional committee units are uncritical of programs or agencies or that they are unaffected by events or by the related tides of public opinion. Indeed, there is ample evidence to suggest that the amount of formal oversight activity changes over time in response to these factors, among others. But it seems that oversight most often takes place in what I call an advocacy context—an environment of support for the basic goals of programs and agencies. When David Stockman talks about the conservatism of the American political system, he touches a fundamental point in understanding congressional oversight: once programs are established, there are built-in biases in favor of program maintenance and, when conditions are at all favorable, their growth and development. The current committee system greatly reinforces these biases and, since committees are the locus of congressional oversight activity, oversight therefore tends to take place in an advocacy environment.

Periodically, special circumstances remove major leverage over programs from the congressional committees. At these junctures, the evaluations of others count for more. And, of course, there are idiosyncratic factors that affect individual cases. But the more "natural" condition—certainly given the current system of committee authority, assignments mechanisms, and relative insulation from the influence of central party leaders—is one where congressional committees adopt an advocacy posture toward agencies and programs, and most oversight occurs in an advocacy context. So the safest answer to the query "Advocacy forever?" is, "Maybe not forever and certainly not always, but probably for the foreseeable future."

Part Three
Conclusion

Chapter 9

Oversight and the American Political System

THE PREVENTION OF tyranny was a major goal of those who designed U.S. governmental institutions. Based on their assumption that human beings naturally act in their own self-interest, the Founders devised a system in which ambition would counteract ambition. Through a system of different constituency bases and overlapping functions, officeholders would check one another in "a harmonious system of mutual frustration."[1]

The bureaucracy was not an overt part of this system because the Founders did not foresee a substantial administrative component for the new government. However, a large administrative state developed in the twentieth century, with special impetus from the New Deal, World War II, and the postwar period of world power and a maturing welfare state. As the administrative state grew in size and importance, the question of its control also loomed larger.

The president was given major new responsibilities for coordinating and controlling the growing bureaucracies of the government, and his influence increased accordingly. However, this development led to concern that Congress was losing influence, especially in relation to policy and its administration (increasingly seen as intertwined). Part of this concern is reflected in the complaint that oversight of the now large bureaucracy is "Congress's neglected function," that is, oversight is not done, or when done that it is uncoordinated, unsystematic, sporadic, and usually informal, with members of Congress (or groups of members on narrowly based committee units) seeking particularistic influence or publicity for purposes of reelection. Members of Congress neglect oversight, say such scholars as John Bibby, Seymour Scher, and Morris Ogul, because they have few incentives to do it.[2] There are more payoffs from other activities. And when members of Congress do oversee, they do it sporadically, for the quick payoff, usually with little long-term significance.

In this incentives-based view, any stirrings of more intensive oversight behavior will be transitory. As Morris Ogul said in describing the surge of oversight activity in the early 1970s during the Nixon administration, "These stirrings . . . should be viewed more as a transitory phenomenon than as the first step toward an enduring pattern of vigorous legislative oversight."[3]

A closely related, recently elaborated perspective on congressional oversight behavior, although one portraying Congress in a much stronger position in relation to the executive, sees Congress as mainly responding to "fires" (complaints or scandals).[4] Rather than actively seeking evidence of how programs are working, let alone evidence about program effectiveness or about the role of programs in the broader context of government, Congress sits back and waits for information to come to it. Proponents of this fire-alarm strategy say that it is rational and effective, using easy and efficient means of gathering information and checking on the bureaucracy. Congress receives information on administration and policy from the environment and acts on it in a manner that serves the interest of certain members (committee members or individuals doing casework for their constituents). Hence its emphasis on solving constituents' problems, reacting to scandals and seeking publicity; its preference for informal contacts with administrators; and its very limited use of formal oversight mechanisms like hearings except in unusual cases such as scandals when a great deal of publicity can be secured.

The explanations scholars like Mathew McCubbins and Thomas Schwartz put forth for the dominance of these types of behaviors, like those put forth by Bibby, Scher, and Ogul, stress congressional incentives in the American system—representatives as reelection- and influence-seeking entrepreneurs operating in a weak party, independent institution. Time is spent more effectively and efficiently in responding to complaints brought to Congress's attention by constituents and interest groups than in formal oversight procedures such as hearings or in an active search for information about programs and policies. This accounts for the sporadic formal oversight activity and the intensive, usually informal, and overwhelmingly reactive particularistic oversight activity said to typify congressional oversight behavior.

In essence, both those who feel that oversight has been a sadly neglected function of Congress in the era of the administrative state and those who argue that oversight, if properly understood and recognized, is common and effective seem to agree on certain facts. First, formal oversight activities are very uncommon. Second, informal activities that help monitor administrative behavior are more common (although Ogul firmly believes that even adding what he calls "latent" oversight to the "manifest" oversight that most scholars consider still leaves unaltered the intermittent and noncomprehensive character of oversight.)[5] Third, congressional behavior in the oversight area, as in others, is best explained by the incentives experienced by members of Congress. Reelection-seeking political entrepreneurs spend their time and resources on activities yielding the most payoff, and the cost-benefit ratio of much of what one thinks of as oversight behavior is low relative to the alternatives. Therefore, formal activities, such as oversight hearings, that typically involve an active orientation to review of administration and policy, have a low priority, and much of what is learned about administration and policy is a result of passive (reactive) information gathering by Congress or a by-product of endeavors undertaken for other purposes (oversight that is "latent" in other activities, to use Morris Ogul's term).[6]

These scholars disagree about the effectiveness of the congressional oversight behavior observed. And even those who believe that the oversight done is effective in monitoring and influencing administration and policy disagree about whether it is rational for the system as a whole.[7] Nevertheless, there is agreement that the pattern of oversight behavior is individually rational. Most legislators respond to the incentives presented to them by their environment. No amount of wishing or pontificating about what ought to be done can significantly change this.[8] From this basic notion comes Ogul's conclusion, just cited, that the oversight stirrings of the early 1970s would surely be "a transitory phenomenon."[9]

The data collected for this book, however, give strong evidence of behavioral change. In the early 1970s, the incidence of a major type of formal oversight activity (primary-purpose oversight hearings) started to increase. Contrary to expectations in the oversight literature, that increase has been sustained in absolute and relative terms (that is, as a percentage of total hearings activity). Furthermore, there is significant evidence in the survey to suggest that Congress became much more active than previously in seeking out information about the executive branch.

In light of these facts, I believe the incentive-based, self-interest perspective on congressional oversight behavior needs to be refined. Even though incentives are very important in determining behavior, incentives are not static.[10] The literature tends to neglect the fact that behavior offering little payoff in one period may well be much more attractive in another.

The Madisonian system of separate institutions sharing powers gives Congress great influence and independence. Because of such features as different constituency bases, terms of office based on fixed time periods, and overlapping functions protected by constitutional mandate, the interests of members of Congress and of the president can be, and often are, different. And Congress has the means to act on these differences. This does not mean that Congress and the president always disagree. However, the Constitution provides for a system in which the "tone," "terms," and "balance between the combatants change constantly," and "the conflict is unending."[11] Since the roles of the president and Congress in relation to the administrative agencies is one of the most ambiguous areas in an already ambiguous system, the possibility always exists that those in Congress will choose to assert themselves in this area. Indeed, the Madisonism system means to set ambition against ambition; permanent quiescence would be a warning sign of failure.

The possibility that Congress will assert itself is strengthened by features of the party system. Not only is it possible for Congress (or one chamber of Congress) and the presidency to be dominated by different parties, it has become commonplace. Add to that the strong local basis of the parties, a nominating system dominated by primaries, the weak discipline in the chambers, and the familiar trappings of a committee system in which members often secure positions on the basis of their constituency interests, and one has many more reasons for Congress to differ with the president about administration and policy and to keep a watchful eye in these areas to protect its interests.

By constitutional design, then, supplemented by related features of the party system, Congress can protect and pursue its own interests. Members have the means as well as strong incentives to guard institutional and individual prerogatives. This system does not guarantee a high level of congressional hearings activity or informal assertiveness in oversight or in any other area. But it does mean that Congress has the potential for increased and assertive oversight, and if the system works as described, that is, if it harnesses and directs self-interest, Congress should behave in this manner when conditions are favorable.

Chapters 2 and 3 suggest that in increasing oversight activity in the 1970s, Congress was responding to the demands of a citizenry frustrated by government growth and complexity, to conditions of relative resource scarcity, to heightened rivalry with the president, and to internal change (that is, to increasing decentralization and increased staff resources within Congress). These changes, and changes connected to them, worked together to increase the payoffs of oversight relative to other activities in several ways.

First, when congressional elites believed that the public was highly receptive to government solutions to problems and to a larger and larger government role, they naturally saw a much bigger payoff in creating new programs than in overseeing those already in existence. For the obvious reasons, creating new programs would have the greater appeal. The accomplishment would almost always look more substantial (perhaps it would actually be more substantial), the chances to increase one's constituency base or help one's established constituency would be greater, the benefits of the new programs could be advertised more easily, and the costs fairly easily masked. When those in Congress began to believe that the citizenry was increasingly burdened by government size and complexity, or even disenchanted with government per se, then there was a shift in the relative payoffs of endeavors such as creating new programs compared with overseeing those already established. Oversight, especially visible manifestations such as oversight hearings, now looked more attractive than before. Obviously the new attractiveness was not so great that it made oversight a dominant activity, but oversight was now attractive enough to be pursued more often. The citizenry certainly seemed more receptive to it, and the complexity of government provided a wealth of topics.

Second, supplementing this new balance in the relative payoffs of congressional activities brought about by disillusionment with government was the related pressure caused by a growing scarcity of resources. The problem was not one of declining resources but of high demand for resources relative to supply and to the willingness of decisionmakers to increase supply. In such a situation, there were fewer opportunities to create new programs. Members of Congress then had greater incentive to oversee programs already in existence. They wanted (1) to protect favored programs against pressure to limit their scope, decrease their budget shares, or eliminate them; (2) to maintain a full agenda of committee unit activities; and even (3) to get more output for the dollars spent in a tight budget situation, that is, to increase program efficiency.

Third, part of Congress's struggle with President Richard M. Nixon was centered on spending control, but of course the struggle went well beyond that. The Vietnam War had already exacerbated executive-legislative tensions in the Johnson administration. However, Nixon's gradual development of an "administrative presidency" strategy brought struggle with Congress over policy and administration to a fever pitch.[12] Using budget impoundments, creative regulation writing, reorganization, and a personnel policy designed to place individuals wholly loyal to the White House in top agency positions, Nixon's aim was to bypass Congress and seize effective control of the government. With its institutional position as well as many of its favored programs threatened, Congress fought back vigorously, using oversight as one of its tools. Restrictive legislation was a favored means, but oversight was a mechanism totally under Congress's control and therefore easy to employ.

Nixon pushed the normal tensions of legislative-executive relations in the American system of separate institutions sharing powers to a high point. He chose an administrative strategy to pursue his agenda, and Congress reacted in kind. Congress was motivated by institutional and policy reasons of substantial import to behave as it did, but narrower desires to protect individual power were also consonant with the actions taken. After all, the value of a seat in a greatly subordinated Congress is of much reduced value to a reelection-seeking entrepreneur. Assertiveness against presidential abuses helped to establish a more active and aggressive oversight posture by Congress, and, once in place, institutional routine combined with lingering suspicion helped to carry it forward.

Finally, during this period Congress also made a major internal change that, the analysis in chapter 3 indicates, increased the relative attractiveness of oversight. In the early 1970s, Congress altered the locus of committee decisionmaking, making subcommittees more autonomous than they had been previously. With many more decisionmakers effectively in place, fortified by greatly increased staff resources (personal, committee, and support agency staff), and confronted with the environmental changes just outlined, the incentives to undertake oversight increased. Even without the changed environmental factors, decentralization of decisionmaking encourages oversight. Subcommittee chairs and staff have greater time, opportunity, and incentive to build expertise—and, therefore, to seek out information aggressively—in their narrow areas of jurisdiction than full committee personnel do. And since subcommittees are almost always more limited than full committees in what they can do legislatively, their personnel are more likely to want to spend time on oversight in order to gain maximum visibility from their positions.

In short, the conditions just elaborated gave members greater incentives than they had previously to oversee policy and administration more actively. As a consequence, formal oversight proceedings (such as oversight hearings) became common activities in the 1970s, and it seems that aggressive information search also became more common. The institutional design features of American government encourage the growth of oversight under the circumstances outlined.

Congress is a peculiarly independent entity in the American system of government. It yields great power over policy and administration to the president from time to time as it did, on balance, in initial reaction to the growth of the administrative state, but it is jealous of the power it gives away. When there is a pressing institutional interest or narrow political advantage to members of Congress if they become involved in the administrative side of government, they do so with relative ease. To keep the logic of the incentive theorists in place, but turn the outcome they so comfortably explain on its head, Congress has great incentive to pursue a more vigorous and variegated oversight strategy under the conditions outlined, and it does. As the political situation shifts, Congress responds—not necessarily immediately or even well, but noticeably and apparently with significant effect.

The Nature and Effects of Oversight

Chapters 4 through 8 demonstrate the nature of the active and rather aggressive oversight of policy and administration pursued by the contemporary Congress. Congress has a well-developed information network. It is a significantly more aggressive seeker of information than the "fire-alarm" conceptions suggest. Its committee oversight agendas are, to be sure, strongly influenced by jarring stimuli like scandals or policy crises when they occur, but other (nonscandal, noncrisis) causes are also important sources of agenda setting. Most committee units are sensitive to constituency and interest group concerns about policy or administration, alert to agency decisions during the course of policy implementation, interested in assisting programs they favor, and even moved at times by a sense of duty to review programs and agencies with an ongoing life. Committee units have active staffs, which seem not to be running amok but rather doing what their employers want. And committees use an impressive array of oversight techniques, many of them quite frequently, and employ them in a logical pattern related to the reasons they choose for placing items on the oversight agenda.

Chapter 6 provides ample detail on the frequency of use, perceived effectiveness, and dimensional characteristics of the oversight techniques used. Top staffers report that Congress employs a wide variety of techniques for oversight, with the frequency of their use closely related to their perceived effectiveness. Staff contacts with the agencies and the three types of hearings studied (primary-purpose oversight hearings, hearings on the reauthorization of programs, and hearings on the amendment of existing statutes) are four of the seven most frequently used oversight techniques. Of the nonhearings approaches to oversight, staff reviews (investigations and program analyses done by committee staffers) are also used frequently on average, while piecemeal review techniques (piece by piece, generally unsystematic, and superficial checking or scanning of information about the agencies) as well as comprehensive review techniques (mainly program evaluations prepared by noncommittee personnel) are used with middling frequency, that is, occasionally, by the committee units studied. Though the use of program evaluations is not at a stunningly high level (except for program analyses done by the congressional support agencies, a special case), they are used about as frequently as the stereotypical piecemeal techniques. The fact that piecemeal approaches are used less than staff reviews buttresses the notions suggested in chapter 4 about the contemporary Congress's often active information search mode. And the relative parity of piecemeal and comprehensive approaches is another indicator that Congress does not confine itself to one easily categorized approach.

The linkage analysis presented in chapter 7 documents the logical pattern of committee use of oversight techniques. The factors of importance in motivating units to undertake oversight mesh well with the approaches they take. Piecemeal approaches to oversight are used most commonly when there are pressing problems to which committee members want a rapid response. The frequent use of what I labeled comprehensive approaches is associated with units whose staff report a strong commitment to the review of ongoing programs and agencies. And committee units tend to specialize in sensible ways in the types of hearings they use for oversight. Units with heavy concentrations of programs authorized for only a few years tend to use reauthorization hearings for oversight. Those with numerous redistributive programs in their jurisdictions more frequently use amendment hearings for oversight (most likely because redistributive programs tend to be permanently authorized). Specialized oversight units tend to concentrate on primary-purpose oversight hearings. Again, this represents a basically sensible and efficient pattern, a good matching of motivations and structural and environmental factors to oversight techniques used.

And congressional oversight has a significant effect on agency behavior. Although I cannot assess these effects with any precision, the existing literature and indications in the interview study and in the roundtable held with federal executives at Brookings suggest that this is so. I have already cited Herbert Kaufman's study showing the emphasis federal bureau chiefs place on their relationships with Congress, including great concern about their performance in congressional hearings.[13] Classics such as Richard Fenno's *The Power of the Purse* and Aaron Wildavsky's *The Politics of the Budgetary Process* confirm these same facts in the appropriations area.[14] And small wonder. Congress plays an active role both in writing the laws that establish the skeleton and muscle and in setting the budgets that give the lifeblood to administrative agencies. When Congress shows an interest, agencies ignore it at their peril.

The interviews with members of Congress give some sense of the potent position Congress enjoys in its relationship with the agencies. Said the chair of one House Ways and Means subcommittee about the posture of agency personnel toward his unit during oversight,

"I find them to be duly respectful and prompt, and [they] try to—you can tell we've got them in a sensitive place because they begin to squirm."[15]

A senator chairing a Commerce Committee unit made the following comment about his relationship to the agencies overseen by his subcommittee, a comment demonstrating the close ties of the typical unit to "its" agencies: "I just know that the ones I oversee are on the phone and in the office all the time. I think the hearings do it. You just have to demonstrate some serious interest . . . serious thoughtful interest, and make suggestions. On the whole they welcome them. . . . They know that they need you to go to bat for them at OMB. So it can become a very mutually supportive and pretty constructive relationship."[16]

Clearly, oversight activity must be taken as a sign of interest, although agency personnel obviously try to judge in each case just how serious the interest is. When the oversight is done in connection with a legislative undertaking, the potential effects on the agency are often plain enough so that the agency must react as if the committee's interest is serious. As the quotations above should suggest, even threats of action only implicit in legislative hearings are probably quickly perceived and frequently acted on by agency personnel.

The place where the seriousness of Congress may be hardest for administrators to gauge is in primary-purpose oversight hearings, those where oversight and not legislation is the focus of congressional activity. However, the data from my survey study indicate that committees do a variety of things to signal the agencies, with sizable proportions doing things to signal that their concern is genuine. Seventy-seven percent "usually" follow up primary-purpose oversight hearings by communicating with the agency involved (only 4 percent report that they never or usually do not do this). Fifty percent "usually" issue reports, and almost 50 percent (47.9 to be exact) "usually" follow up oversight hearings with legislation (a figure that goes above 50 percent if oversight units are not included in the calculations).[17] Even assuming some overreporting of activity, the results indicate the extent to which oversight hearings are followed up and the effects they may have.

The chair of one particularly active and feared specialized oversight unit had no doubt about the impact his unit had on the Department of Health, Education, and Welfare in an oversight case he described:

"Oh, I think it [the investigation and hearing] had a fair amount. I know, for example, that Secretary Califano put in some new rules and regulations in the Department of Health, Education, and Welfare that had quite an impact."[18]

Another oversight subcommittee chair said simply, "I think the mere fact that [our] oversight subcommittee is looking at something all of a sudden will make the agency pay a little more attention to that [concern] every day. . . . . I think it's that constant visibility, potential visibility, that you want to keep holding as the stick on an agency to make sure that [they are] implementing the program as that might have been intended by the Congress."[19]

Moreover, the Brookings roundtable discussion with federal executives was alive with indications of the effects of oversight. Executives, for example, often focused their complaints about oversight on what is often called micro-management, the intrusion of Congress into the details of administrative decisionmaking. To quote one experienced hand,

> For whatever reason, the oversight, in my view at least, tends to get distorted into an arena in which it [Congress] becomes really a participant in the carrying out of policy, which I think is potentially a pretty serious problem. . . . I think it really weakens [the true mission of] congressional oversight. I think it compromises their objectivity. I think it tends to divert attention to details which perhaps seem fairly significant individually but at least seem to me . . . not nearly as significant as some of the overall policies and issues.[20]

Whatever its faults, however, this attention to details by Congress often yields results from administrators. For instance, at the roundtable an executive told a story about a senator who took a deep interest in an agency's delinquent accounts. In fact, he had them listed each year in the *Congressional Record*. The agency responded to the senator, who though in the minority party was a member of a committee important to the agency, by working each year to give a better "report card" to the senator. The belief of the executive was that this response took the agency's attention away from more important things and thereby "distorted and biased the efforts of the executive branch,"[21] but the agency responded because "the political realities of the bureaucracy are that they respond to that sort of thing."[22] For the moment, that is the point.

The bureaucracy does tend to respond. And not just on micro issues, although one can argue that they are the real stuff of policy. A recent report entitled the *Presidential Management of Rulemaking in Regulation Agencies*, for example, talks about "incentives for agency officials to respond at *every stage* to the concerns of their congressional overseers."[23] Administrators, naturally enough, do not often find it one of the pleasures of the job to respond to those who intrude too deeply into what they regard as their space, but they do respond. The source of their disquiet is worth consideration, especially as it reflects a lack of coherent policy direction, but the disquiet is part of the evidence that oversight has telling effects.

Overall, the portrait of oversight drawn to this point in the chapter can be interpreted positively. At the macro level, Congress responds to environmental changes in seemingly appropriate ways. Though oversight may well not be Congress's top priority in terms of what its members would prefer to do in the best of all worlds, Congress operates in a real world where calculations based on individual interest, policy needs, opportunities within institutional structures, and institutional interests are made in a dynamic environment. Beginning in the 1970s, all four factors tended to push Congress in the same direction—toward more oversight.

And the nature of congressional oversight is rather impressive. Oversight is not only more frequent than it was before, it is based on a widespread and often aggressively operated intelligence system. It involves a variety of motivations and techniques, sensibly joined. It seems to have an effect on administrators, so much so that it often makes them uncomfortable. It seems fair to say that oversight addresses problems and checks, and even corrects, many errors affecting at least the more organized and articulate members of the polity. As a result, congressional oversight probably improves policy at the margins. Not bad for a maligned system. In fact, not bad for any system.

Criticisms and Shortcomings

Yet all of this activity will probably not satisfy many critics of congressional oversight because part of the reason for their dissatisfaction is qualitative, not quantitative. The nature of the advocacy context within which Congress oversees is the basis for one criticism. Congress may indeed now keep a more watchful eye on policy and administration, but it looks at them through a narrow myopic lens. A related criticism concerns the uncoordinated nature of much congressional oversight activity. This lack of coordination inhibits continuity in oversight and reinforces what critics see as the inadequate accountability resulting from it.

The first criticism, that Congress's oversight is neither comprehensive nor systematic enough, that it takes neither a broad nor objective enough view, has two closely related components. One component concerns the approaches Congress uses to gather information and the other how information is interpreted.

Congress, like any organization or person, does not operate the way a textbook scientist (or even a textbook social scientist) would want.[24] Though it uses a large number of information sources and casts its net more widely and aggressively than many believe, it does not gather information from all possible sources or even from a random sample of sources. Some people and groups (interest groups and professional groups, especially) are clearly advantaged in the process, as the data in chapters 4 and 5 suggest. Their views receive greater attention. Congress learns much, but more from some than others.

And what Congress learns, it learns in a value-laden context. Those on congressional committees represent constituencies with interests, have frequent contacts with administrators with interests, and often themselves have strong interests, even if for some members of Congress the interest is mainly in reelection. Moreover, as chapter 8 demonstrates, oversight most often takes place in an advocacy environment—an environment of support for the basic goals of programs and agencies. Once programs are established there are built-in biases in favor of program maintenance. Further, the current committee system, particularly the system for selecting members and the lack of party discipline, significantly reinforces this bias. This is most emphatically not to say that congressional committees are uncritical of programs or agencies, or that they are unaffected by events or by the related tides of public opinion, but that oversight does take place in an advocacy context that shapes how criticisms and events are interpreted.

The analysis in chapter 8 also shows that even those most likely to use comprehensive approaches to oversight generally share the advocacy posture common in Congress. This helps to explain the otherwise surprising finding that while comprehensive approaches to oversight are quite widely used, critics nevertheless typically do not regard Congress as a comprehensive overseer. For in their view no matter what techniques Congress might be using, it still does not take a broad or objective enough view of the typical program or policy.

So, what we have is a clash between the rather impressive real and the often yearned for ideal in congressional oversight of policy and administration. The contemporary Congress learns a lot from many sources, but it does not learn enough or with the proper balance to satisfy some critics. It does use (on average, "occasionally," the midpoint of my use measure) the results of studies employing what pass for scientific techniques in the world of program analysts, but it tends to consume (and by implication interpret) the results of those studies in an advocacy context. Congress, in other words, is a political body filled with people who have preferences and who are given license to pursue those preferences through their committee assignments. The political nature of the body and its members' preferences do not inhibit, or even much limit, the occurrence of oversight in its many manifestations, but they do tend to shape what occurs. Members of Congress, it seems, want to know and do know more than one might naively suspect, but naturally enough they want to know more about some things than about others. And the information they get is viewed through their politically ground lenses and used for their own purposes.

All in all, then, this is a pretty good system—flexible, responsive to large environmental changes and to many policy problems, open to a variety of approaches and sources, and evidently with impact on administrators. The system can probably be improved, but its good points are readily apparent.

However, some of the unease about oversight and the broader issue of control of bureaucracy in the United States becomes apparent when one tries to answer the following question: how effective is congressional oversight and control of the bureaucracy in the United States? There are at least two quick and easy answers to the question. At the level of checking and even correcting errors directly affecting the (most organized or articulate) citizenry and of improving policy at the margins, oversight is quite effective. But at the level of coordinated review and control of policy and administration, oversight is relatively ineffective. There is an irony here: the weaknesses of the American system in regard to coordinated, centrally directed policymaking and administrative control make it highly responsive to groups and vociferous individuals in the society. As a result, many irritants are responded to, but the response is uncoordinated, and the system can career along without coordinated direction. That situation is in tune with the institutional design features of a governmental system that was not set up with a large state role and, therefore, with a large administrative apparatus in mind. The administrative system is at once highly responsive and accountable in the narrow sense, and not well coordinated or centrally controlled in the broad sense. An easily identified set of central political authorities cannot reasonably be held accountable for its operation.

Reforming the System

The evidence indicates that in its oversight behavior (as presumably in other areas), Congress responds to changes in its environment. When there are changes in the relative payoffs of different types of behavior, and when resources change, Congress reacts. The U.S. system brings together the self-interest of congressional politicians and the performance of oversight. And if one accepts the basic assumptions of a sloppy governmental system like our own, a system designed with the prevention of tyranny as its foremost goal rather than the promotion of efficiency or centralized accountability, then one can say that it works remarkably well when it comes to oversight. It is open; information flows freely (certainly in the domestic policy area); elected politicians have a staff system that gives them access to information; and Congress has the means to express itself relatively free from executive dominance. Evaluations of programs and policies are produced not only by executive branch agencies but by committee staff and by support agencies linked directly to Congress. There are obvious problems of coordination, inconsistent messages to the bureaucracy (and the possibilities for manipulation inherent in such a situation), and errors that go uncorrected in this system, but the benefits may well outweigh the costs.

The fact that the system may have a positive balance is no reason to ignore possible improvements, although one should always be aware that reforms of highly complex systems can unintentionally make things worse rather than better. In this section I look at some issues that have been raised about oversight and at some reforms offered to address these issues. The discussion emphasizes the overall effects of reforms, not the details.

In a leading work published in 1976 but based on case studies done a decade earlier, Morris Ogul summarized the reigning critiques of congressional oversight behavior and evaluated some suggested reforms. Ogul was skeptical that either the quantity or the quality of oversight could be sharply increased, primarily because reelection incentives pushed members of Congress to give priority to other (nonoversight) things, but also because congressional structures inhibited substantial change.[25] We have already seen that the quantity of oversight has increased sharply since the 1960s and I have, I hope, provided a good perspective on the reasons for the increase. The qualitative issues are more difficult because conceptually they are more elusive. I will turn to them shortly, but first I will look at a way to influence the quantitative level of oversight.

If one's goal is simply to put a floor under the level of oversight in times less favorable than those existing now, then the establishment of committees and subcommittees whose main function is oversight (that is, specialized oversight units) is a good step.[26] The analysis in chapter 3 clearly indicates that oversight units do significant amounts of oversight in years when the overall level of oversight behavior by other units is low. Other (nonoversight) units adjust their behavior to meet changing conditions, but oversight units are more steadfast in doing oversight. As circumstances change, it is possible that nonoversight units will once again shift away from oversight (although one would expect lags owing to habit, built-up expertise, and so on). However, oversight units are limited in what they can do. Therefore, on the assumption that the chairs of specialized oversight units will continue to prefer oversight activity to the alternative, which is mainly inactivity, the maintenance of existing oversight units and the establishment of new ones is a simple and straightforward course to recommend.

Issues related to the qualitative aspects of oversight are more complex. In his concluding chapter, which covers qualitative issues as well as reform, Ogul talks about congressional failure to do comprehensive and systematic oversight, continuous rather than sporadic and intermittent oversight, and about problems in coordinating oversight activity.[27] Precisely what comprehensive and systematic mean is not entirely clear—these are attractive but very elusive terms. Let us assume, however, that what Ogul (and others) have in mind when it comes to the qualitative side of oversight, is oversight that has the following characteristics: it is more objective than what seems to typify oversight now (that is, it uses what passes for scientific approaches to gathering and interpreting evidence and is relatively unbiased); it is done on a scheduled basis and not merely in response to signals that a problem exists or on whims of decisionmakers; and it is coordinated within Congress and perhaps even with the executive branch. Reforms to produce quality oversight defined in these ways are a tall order, especially if one limits oneself to reforms that do not change the system too fundamentally, my self-imposed mandate for the early part of this section.

The goal of producing greater objectivity in oversight as just defined is challenging. As shown in chapter 7, the best predictor of frequent use of program evaluations is the motivation labeled duty— a commitment to review ongoing programs. The simple injunction to recruit staff and members to congressional committees who are so motivated is easy but obviously futile.

It is not futile, however, to maintain and even expand the current analytic capacities of congressional staff agencies and of other sources of program evaluations. The data show that the overall use of program evaluation is modest, not low, and that evaluations are also used more frequently when there is concern in a member's district about an agency or program. A reasonable interpretation of these data is that the mere existence of available program evaluations probably has an impact on use, particularly when constituency concerns or clientele complaints give members a need for information about programs and anything readily available that might possibly be of help is likely to be consulted.

That point, along with the "advocacy context" analysis of chapter 8, should give one the proper caution in interpreting what use may often mean. Even making the heroic assumption that program evaluations are always objective, there is probably a fair amount of selective use and selective interpretation by congressional personnel.

One would expect little else in the real world of politics; in fact, most voters would be less than happy with politicians who were devoted too much to judging evidence rather than to representing interests.[28]

Still, there are some ways suggested by the data or by logic to increase the likelihood of greater objectivity in the oversight Congress does. One is to encourage more specialized oversight units that, as chapter 8 shows, tend to be self-professed neutrals on the advocacy-opposition measure. That should help but may not be an especially strong means for achieving the end, however. Recall that the evidence in chapter 9 also suggests that when oversight units get down to actual cases, they tend to show quite a bit of support for the basic charter or purpose of the agencies or programs they are overseeing. Even they, after all, often have set jurisdictions and the leeway to select topics for oversight, factors that encourage basically supportive relationships between committees and agencies.

However, the reasons why basic advocacy tends to predominate on congressional committees suggests a second, and likely more effective, approach. As discussed in chapter 8, the way committee members are selected (better, self-selected) also contributes to the committee's advocacy posture. Once on committees, members are drawn to support at least the basic aims of programs and agencies over which their committees have jurisdiction. Basically, members need the programs to give their committee assignments value. Even shifts in party control do not seem to shake this tendency.

Rotating committee assignments, however, might significantly affect the advocacy posture. If committee members served limited terms on committees, they would not form the same political and emotional attachments to programs and constituent groups; they could not easily link their committee assignments and their constituency interests in the manner the current system not only permits but encourages; and they would develop a broader perspective.[29] The obvious question is why members would choose to alter the committee system in the manner suggested. The brief answer is that there is no obvious reason for them to do so other than to redirect their behavior in ways that will not benefit them politically or even institutionally.

It is important to note that the institutional benefits of rotating committee assignments would be mixed. In exchange for a better balancing of the interests represented on committees, a diminishing of the tendency toward an advocacy posture by members, and consequently a greater willingness to take an objective look at programs, one would expect a decided diminution in members' expertise and interest. With the prospect that tomorrow's assignment would not be today's, members would have less incentive and time to develop expertise. This would lessen their interest in the future of programs and in oversight. It would increase the power of committee staff and of the congressional support agencies. These outcomes are good neither for oversight nor for democratic influence over policy and administration (at least as expressed through Congress). So, on balance, the costs of this reform probably outweigh the benefits if congressional oversight is a major concern.

A proposed reform that has been much more prominent on the congressional agenda, and that aims to produce systematic, comprehensive, and continuous oversight of the type Ogul and others seem to hope for, is commonly labeled Sunset.[30] A version of Sunset actually passed the Senate in 1978, although late enough in the session so that passage was primarily symbolic.[31] The heavily symbolic nature and failure of Sunset says much about the problems inherent in much oversight reform.

The basic aim of Sunset is to place a termination date on statutes so that Congress is forced to reconsider (review) them periodically, thereby ensuring continuous oversight of programs. The most prominent version of Sunset, sponsored by former senator Edmund S. Muskie, is the one I will focus on. I chose the Muskie version not only because it aimed to produce systematic and comprehensive oversight but because the threat it represented to committee autonomy reveals much about Congress's reactions to centralizing reforms.[32]

Periodic review by itself would mainly affect the workload of Congress. Numerous programs are already on a limited-term authorization/reauthorization cycle.[33] From that narrow perspective (workload), therefore, the problem is difficult but not insurmountable. Reviews would surely be superficial in most cases, but all items would at least make a nominal appearance on the agenda for review. At this primitive level, Sunset is another scheme that would increase— or at least put a floor under—the quantity of oversight, and it would ensure more continuous though often rather nominal reviews.[34]

On the quality side, some Sunset proposals would require that each committee target a subset of its programs for thorough evaluation.[35] Such targeting would almost surely increase the use of systematic studies, at least to the extent that more studies would be produced in certain areas, and there would be a greater likelihood that studies would at least be considered, although not necessarily consulted more carefully or with a more neutral perspective than now prevails. As with cases in which systematic studies are now used by Congress, the basic advocacy context would still prevail.

An element of the original Muskie proposal, one that went well beyond Sunset in the narrow sense of a forced review for each program brought on by a fixed termination date, might produce a far more significant change. It even went beyond proposals requiring committees to target a subset of programs for systematic evaluation. Indeed, it addressed an issue often latent in the call for continuous, systematic, and comprehensive oversight, namely, centralized control.

Muskie's proposal was quite radical in its political implications. Besides the relatively straightforward goal of forcing reconsideration of programs and tax expenditures through limited-term authorizations of five years (certain entitlements and payments of interest on the public debt would have been excepted), Muskie proposed to

> establish a schedule for the reauthorizations of program and activities on the basis of groupings by budget functions and subfunctions. Programs within the same function would terminate simultaneously. This would give Congress an opportunity to examine and compare federal programs in an entire functional area rather than to do so in bits and pieces. The schedule would be set up so that all of the functional areas would be dealt with within one five-year cycle.[36]

This meant that Muskie, and the Budget Committee he chaired, would have gained significant power because all programs in a budget function or subfunction would have been vulnerable in the same year. Programs in a given area would have been subject to comparative examination. Sunset reviews for an entire functional area would have provided input to the Budget Committees, which could then have acted more effectively as central arms to coordinate programs and policy. This prospect did not please many members of Congress.

Congressional personnel were also uneasy about Sunset in its many versions for other reasons. They were, for example, concerned about workload problems and problems with inflexible scheduling provisions in many of the proposals. They were troubled about the exemption of some programs (entitlements) and the inclusion of others (controversial programs in the labor and civil rights areas that might be severely threatened if a mechanism for automatic termination was in place).

Sunset eventually faded away because of a lack of enthusiasm for imposing cumbersome requirements that offered little benefit to most committees while threatening their autonomy. Many of the objections were arguably quite well founded, but the more a reform opens the possibility of centralized control of the oversight agenda and the more comprehensive the reviews it encourages—reviews cutting across committee jurisdictions and increasing the vulnerability of programs to actions by those outside the committees—the more resistance it is likely to meet in Congress. Members of Congress want the institution to be powerful, especially when Congress faces threats to its power from outside, but members want to surrender as little of their power as possible. The more comprehensive that reviews of policy and administration are in scope, and the better they fit into a centralized system of control, the less attractive they are likely to be to most in Congress. This is not surprising in a system of separation of powers with an independent legislature, especially one that lacks a strong, disciplined party system and is organized around relatively autonomous committee and subcommittee units.

Before turning to some of the implications for oversight of systems where the legislature is not independent or where party systems are strong, I want to look briefly at congressional experience with a modest reform designed to foster greater coordination in oversight. The House of Representatives adopted a set of committee reforms in 1974. The version they adopted was watered down from reforms originally proposed by the Select Committee on Committees, commonly known as the Bolling Committee.[37] The Bolling Committee proposed that the Government Operations Committee, after consultation with the leadership and representatives of the standing committees, issue a report within sixty days of the convening of a new Congress. The report was to outline the review plans of each committee, recommend steps to coordinate oversight activities among authorizing, appropriating, and Government Operations committees, and suggest oversight priorities.[38] Most of this proposal, a pale version of the Bolling Committee's more aggressive earlier ideas for an oversight agenda coordinated by the leadership, eventually found its way into the reforms the House adopted (known as the Hansen substitute).[39]

Even this attempt at coordination was a failure. The Government Operations Committee was clearly reluctant to risk the ire of other committees by actively carrying out its new mandate, contained in clause 25(c) of House rule X, "to assist in coordinating all of the oversight activities of the House" during each Congress. It noted in its first report that it was compiling plans from the various committees but no more.[40] In the last report it issued, before what was to it the welcome abolition of the requirement, the Government Operations Committee continued to express in strong terms its reluctance to supervise other committees' oversight activities.[41] The remnants of that chore now rest with the Committee on House Administration, which reviews committee budget requests. It will probably tread lightly. Clearly the House prefers not to have its oversight activities coordinated.

Congress is reluctant to accept or to carry out large, and even small, changes that might help to coordinate oversight and provide the continuous, systematic, and especially the comprehensive overview that many reform advocates call for. Though most members like the concepts in principle, they are very uneasy about important aspects of them in practice. This is especially true of any change that means coordinating oversight behavior in a manner that helps centralized decisionmakers, including those in Congress, make decisions that might negatively affect programs or policies in the jurisdictions of substantive committees.

My data show that Congress (or, better, its committees) is willing to oversee programs and policies frequently, and even to use the products of systematic studies. But congressional committees have not shown a willingness to be bound by requirements that they oversee on a schedule fixed by others, or oversee in a manner designed to increase the possibility of central control. Committees want to make their own decisions, based when possible on the preferences of their members, the needs of their constituencies, and on what they see as the underlying needs of "their" agencies. This, I reiterate, does not preclude frequent oversight, attention to correction of errors, or even the use of systematic studies. But oversight is done in a decentralized system that gives great weight to the often overlapping needs and preferences of committee members, agencies, and the constituencies of both. The disadvantages of this system are apparent, even allowing for the positive features. There is favoritism toward established programs and groups, and there are problems that flow from lack of coordination. Programs are usually considered in isolation from one another. Administrative accountability often focuses on narrowly based congressional committees and can be blurred by conflicts between the executive and legislative branches or even within Congress. Responsiveness, accountability, and correction of errors may well exist but insulated from broader forces.

The solutions suggested for these problems usually include efforts to strengthen the party system or even to institute a parliamentary system such as Britain's, thereby coordinating control of the bureaucracy and enhancing accountability.[42] Whatever the potential benefits of such reforms in coordinated control, coherent policy, and clearer accountability to the public of elected officials, they are very likely to decrease oversight of policy and administration by the legislative branch. The more centralized and coordinated that authority in a government becomes, the less likely it is that the legislative body will be an active overseer of policy and administration. Those in control, be they the leaders of a disciplined governing party in both the legislative and executive branches or the principal ministers of a cabinet government, will have a strong interest in maintaining as much control as possible over evaluation of policy and administration.

The case of Great Britain, admittedly a polar case, is instructive. Ordinary members of Parliament, chafing under government control, have struggled to increase their influence over the executive through the establishment of a system of specialized parliamentary Select Committees. British reformers have looked to the United States for guidance.[43] However, the efforts to allow Parliament a more effective role have been only a limited success. Clive Ponting, a civil servant who achieved some notoriety in Britain when he was tried by the government for passing documents to a Labor MP about the sinking of the Belgrano during the Falklands War, says the following:

How effective have the new Select Committees been? They have certainly not caused any great tremor of fear to run through Whitehall. They bear little resemblance to the powerful Congressional Committees in the United States. They are still composed of politicians who in the last resort will give their loyalty to the party. . . . When dealing with relatively uncontroversial areas, the committees have produced some good reports but when they investigate highly political issues, the system breaks down and the members retreat into their respective party positions.[44]

Michael Rush, in his book on parliamentary government in Britain, says that the

obstacles to allowing Parliament a greater involvement in the scrutiny of the executive and the formulation of policy are three-fold. First, governments simply find it easier that way. Governments do not want to lay themselves open to wider and possibly more effective scrutiny, thus making life potentially more difficult; . . .

Second, governments do not wish to share the exercise of power any more widely than absolutely necessary. . . . Third, and arising in part out of the second point, parties in power (and those who aspire to power) do not wish to see their ability to implement their policies diminished.[45]

There is a dilemma here: the very discipline and electoral accountability of a democratic system with effectively centralized and coordinated authority over policy and administration is more than compatible with a restricted legislative role in oversight and with a situation in which an experienced civil servant can conclude that "Whitehall is not, in any real sense, accountable for the way in which it works."[46] In fact, an astute minister in this system wrote the following:

How effectively does Parliament control [a minister]? How careful must he be in his dealings with Parliament? The answer quite simply is that there is no effective parliamentary control. All this time I have never felt in any way alarmed by a parliamentary threat. . . . I can't remember a single moment in the course of legislation when I felt the faintest degree of alarm or embarrassment and I can't remember a Question Time, either, when I had any anxiety.[47]

The larger issues of accountability are beyond the scope of this book, and a brief look at one case can only whet one's appetites for more analysis, not prove a point. But it would be well worthwhile to look at legislative oversight and the broad questions of administrative accountability comparatively, choosing systems in which the roles of Parliament and the nature of party systems vary.[48] That way one can better evaluate what has just been suggested, namely, that the very system feature (disciplined, centralized decisionmaking) that seems to enhance the accountability of decisionmakers to the public may actually do more than restrict the role of legislative bodies in oversight, it may also limit bureaucratic and political accountability by increasing the ability of central decisionmakers (and civil servants) to restrict the flow of information. Whatever the nature of the tradeoffs, clearly the committees of the U.S. Congress will not easily surrender prerogatives related to policy and administration, either to the president or to central decisionmakers in Congress. Although that stance precludes serious steps toward central control of policy and administration, that may not be altogether such a bad thing.

Conclusion

To understand the motivations and behavior of political actors, one must understand institutional context and the broader political environment. This is as true for congressional oversight as for other aspects of political life. Members of Congress usually pursue self-interest as they see it, but their self-interest is defined in a changing environment.

Congress may cede much influence over administration to the executive during periods of program expansion, but it adjusts its behavior when circumstances change, and the system of separate institutions sharing powers gives it both the means and the incentives to make the adjustments. The lack of formal oversight activity and the passivity in information seeking noticed by many earlier observers made sense in light of the greater returns (both individual and institutional) then available to Congress from other activities and modes of search. The same logic can explain the more active stance now evident in these areas.

The built-in prospects in the Madisonian system for tension between the legislative and executive branches, and the loose nature of the U.S. party system, with its consequent reinforcement of the entrepreneurial tendencies of members, mean that Congress can indeed be an active overseer. And that oversight, though usually done in an advocacy context, is often vigorous and even systematic.

However, the same institutional features and motivational forces that make active oversight likely also inhibit coordinated review of policy and administration. Crisis may temporarily bridge the gaps enough to produce coordinated review, or Congress may defer to the president for a time, but the situation is inherently unstable. This inhibits democratic control of policy and administration of an idealized sort—coherent, coordinated, programmatic in the responsible parties sense—but in a real and imperfect world much can be said for it. While the U.S. political system does push bureaucrats to play a complex part in the policy process, it also subjects the bureaucracy to much scrutiny.

In essence, there are costs and benefits in any system. The one the United States has now has certain distinct advantages, and it may well fit the American pluralistic culture better than others. Given that the U.S. governmental system was not designed with a large administrative sector in mind, its ability to expose bureaucratic behavior to public scrutiny and to promote administrative responsiveness is impressive. The somewhat chaotic nature of congressional oversight of policy and administration, as of political control of policy and administration generally, is of a piece with the chaotic nature of American politics and the competition inherent in the design of U.S. institutions. A society as skeptical about authority as this one may well bear the costs of lack of coordinated direction better than the costs of coordination. We might well like the results of great change far less than what we have now, a comforting statement since we are unlikely to see big changes in the system anyway.

The knowledgeable pushing, hauling, poking, and advocacy of

Congress as it keeps a watchful eye on policy and administration can be criticized, but it is consistent with Congress's role in a system of separate institutions sharing powers. What the United States now has is far from perfect, not even pretty or neat, but we could do far worse. At least two cheers for Madison.

Appendixes

Appendix A

Research Focus, Design, and Execution

CONTROL OF ADMINISTRATION by representative institutions is a challenge for any democratic government. This study focuses on a critical aspect of congressional control in the United States—congressional oversight of administration and policy (referred to in this book as congressional oversight or oversight).

Joseph P. Harris, in an earlier Brookings study, *Congressional Control of Administration*, divides control into "legislative decisions or activities prior to the relevant administrative action" ("'control' in the narrow sense") and "oversight," or "review after the fact, . . . [including] inquiries about policies that are or have been in effect, investigations of past administrative actions, and the calling of executive officers to account for their financial transactions."[1] Both aspects of control are clearly important. I concentrate in this book on what Harris calls oversight for two basic reasons: to focus the study sufficiently to allow a manageable, reasonably precise, and systematic analysis of an important element of congressional control of administration; and to address an aspect of control (oversight) that has been of increasing concern to Congress and the focus of much recent internal reform effort in the post-World War II and, especially, the post-Watergate period.

The scientific argument in favor of the first reason is self-evident, I think, but the decision may be a bit controversial when viewed against some contemporary literature. Most studies dealing with oversight use definitions that are fundamentally in tune with Harris's (when definitions are used at all).[2] However, Morris S. Ogul, in an influential work on the subject, advocates a much broader definition and approach. "Legislative oversight is behavior by legislators and their staffs, individually or collectively, which results in an impact, intended or not, on bureaucratic behavior."[3]

Ogul's definition is designed to take the study of oversight away from a concentration found in much of the academic literature, and also in many congressional documents and studies, on particular techniques of oversight, such as staff investigations of agency activities or congressionally mandated agency reporting requirements. He wants to blur the conventional rigid distinction between legislation and oversight, thus he "seeks out oversight behavior wherever performed throughout the legislative process."[4] Politics is brought to center stage in Ogul's work, not confined to the periphery. This is a worthwhile goal, as demonstrated by Ogul's valuable treatment of what he terms "latent oversight" (found in activities not usually associated with oversight such as legislative hearings and casework), and a useful corrective to past work. However, Ogul's definition is so broad that it is hard to exclude very many congressional activities from inclusion under the oversight rubric.

In this study, therefore, I work with a traditional definition of the oversight function—congressional review of the actions of federal departments, agencies, and commissions and of the programs and policies they administer, including review during program and policy implementation as well as after the fact. I look at oversight as a part of the process by which Congress attempts to control the actions of administrators and to serve its own political interests in the complex system described in chapter 1. In this approach, much of what Congress now does when it considers proposals for new programs or even for the expansion of current programs (the nonreview aspects) is not considered oversight, even though such activities may have, in Ogul's words, "an impact . . . on bureaucratic behavior."[5] The impact of oversight—its effects on bureaucratic behavior—is conceptualized separately and, in this sense, kept distinct. The research seeks to determine the conditions that lead to oversight as defined here and to evaluate its effects and significance. Conceptualizing oversight as I do does not restrict my analysis to a specific set of techniques, nor does it force me to deemphasize the politics involved, but it does allow me to operationalize oversight in a reasonably precise manner and then analyze its role in what can broadly be called the control process.

My second reason for working with a fairly narrow definition of oversight involves Congress's own concerns. Much congressional reform effort has been devoted to oversight. As far as I know there is no standard congressional definition of oversight, but sections 136a and b of the Legislative Reorganization Act of 1946 as amended (1970) require standing committees to "review and study, on a continuing basis, the application, administration, and execution of those laws, or parts of laws, the subject of which is within the jurisdiction of that committee" and to issue a report on their activities in this regard in odd-numbered years following each Congress.[6] This central concern of Congress is compatible with the definition of oversight adopted in this study. The results, I hope, will be of value in evaluating the impact of recent reform efforts and in suggesting the strengths and limitations of possible modifications in congressional procedures and practices.

In summary, this book focuses on congressional oversight, defined as congressional review of the actions and policies of the executive branch, and viewed as an element in the process by which Congress attempts to control the behavior of the bureaucracy. Political as well as technical and institutional factors are examined for their impact on oversight. The effectiveness of oversight behavior is also considered.

Study Design and Execution

With the expansion of the federal bureaucracy and the increasingly important role played by the executive branch in program initiation, Congress has attempted to increase and improve its oversight performance. Such measures as the Legislative Reorganization Act of 1946, the 1970 amendments to that act, and the committee reforms initiated in 1974 in the House of Representatives all had important provisions that attempted to spur oversight activity. Interest in oversight was also stimulated by the intense struggle for influence between the executive and legislative branches that developed during the Nixon administration and has continued since.[7]

My goal in this study is to gain a better understanding of the complex problem of democratic control of bureaucracy in the United States. Along the way, I touch on related issues such as control of the legislative bureaucracy (that is, congressional staff) by the members of Congress. My more immediate purposes, given the potential importance of oversight efforts and the surge of interest in congressional oversight activity, are fourfold:

—To chart changes in congressional oversight behavior over time.

—To better understand why Congress does or does not do oversight. When and how is it done? Why is it done the way it is? How are the factors motivating oversight linked to the choices of techniques? What impact do senators, representatives, and staff believe that oversight has? What impact does oversight seem to have?

—To look at some elements of the issue of oversight effectiveness. How can effective oversight be achieved? What are Congress's strengths in this regard? Its weaknesses?

—To comprehend the impact of some recent reforms and the probable impact of proposed reforms aimed at increasing the incidence or effectiveness of oversight.

No single approach is adequate to achieve these deceptively simple goals, and some, of course, can only be partially achieved because of conceptual problems and prohibitive costs. For example, one can measure what effects actors in the process think oversight has on the informal behavior of administrators and, in some instances, even look at changes in statutes, regulations, and budgets, but the problem of "anticipated reactions" (behavior done in anticipation of another's action), if it can be dealt with at all, requires a detailed immersion in the day-to-day lives of the actors over a long period. Still, by focusing efforts and gathering data in a systematic manner, a good deal of progress will be made.

The study concentrates on committee oversight behavior. Why? Because David Price's comment on "the introduction, processing, and passage of a piece of legislation" is also true for oversight. "In short, most of the activities associated with [oversight], insofar as they take place within Congress, are committee-centered."[8] They either take place within committees or are eventually processed through committees (the work of relevant congressional support agencies, for example). Behavior that does not generally take place in or through committees (casework, for instance) is dealt with through evidence gathered as a by-product of the techniques used in the study, that is, from interviews with committee and executive branch respondents or from secondary sources.

Multiple Research Approaches

I employ three complementary approaches to achieving the purposes of the study. Each has limitations, but together they yield most of the information desired.

The *first approach* involves a longitudinal, comparative analysis of congressional committee oversight behavior starting in 1961.[9] I coded data from the *Daily Digest* of the *Congressional Record* for the period January 1 to July 4 of the first year of each session, that is, odd-numbered years. The *Digest* lists committee hearings and meetings for each day Congress is in session. A brief description of the subject of the hearing or meeting is included along with the listing, providing a basis for coding the event.[10] With the resulting data, I can look at trends in oversight behavior, at House-Senate similarities and differences, and at the impact on oversight frequency of such conditions as committee structure and changing levels of staff resources.

The *Digest* data are useful in the following ways:

—They provide information for a systematic, longitudinal investigation of the amount of committee hearing and meeting activity devoted primarily to oversight (that is, when oversight is the primary purpose of the hearing or meeting). Changes in the pattern of activity can be charted and analyzed with a view to providing evidence of Congress's attention to the oversight function over time.

—They provide coverage of the activities of all committees and subcommittees in Congress. The data thus allow a comprehensive analysis that is not limited to the hearing and meeting activity of a subset of congressional committees.

—They are suitable for a quantitative analysis of the impact of factors such as committee decentralization, committee structure (the existence of formal oversight subcommittees), staff size, and partisan unity or split control of the presidency and Congress on the propensity of committees to hold hearings or meetings devoted to oversight. Relationships across the entire period as well as within periods (for example, pre- and post-Watergate) can be examined.

However, the *Daily Digest* data also have shortcomings. First, the data are records of hearings and meetings, not other activities of the committees. They do not include such efforts as informal communications and staff investigations, which can be important aspects of oversight, unless those efforts are reflected in formal hearings and meetings. This deficiency can be corrected to a degree by gathering supplementary data from committee calendars, but calendars unfortunately do not consistently list such products as staff reports. Second, oversight may occur as a by-product of hearings and meetings held primarily for some purpose other than oversight (such as authorizing or appropriating funds, or amending existing legislation). However, when congressional hearings do not have oversight as a primary purpose, there is a great doubt about how great a share of committee time and effort is devoted to oversight. A third shortcoming concerns one's ability to evaluate the function and quality of the oversight activity. The descriptions in the *Daily Digest* permit crude classification of the nature of the oversight activity (ensuring that the bureaucracy implements the policy objectives of Congress, determining the effectiveness of programs and policies, and so on), but they are not very useful in analyzing the political functions (for example, satisfying discontented groups) played by the activity or in assessing the qualitative nature of the effort (is it comprehensive, systematic, and so on?). A final, and related, point is that the *Daily Digest* data are not adequate for understanding the full set of factors (structural and crudely political) that lead committees to undertake oversight, determine their approaches, and influence their effectiveness.

In light of these shortcomings, I employed a complementary *second approach*. Besides the longitudinal "events" data focused on formal hearings and meetings whose primary purpose is oversight, I used interviews to gather in-depth systematic data on the full range of oversight behavior of selected congressional committees. By necessity, the interviews were limited in focus to a short period of time—limited by resources and by the ability of the respondents to remember accurately what transpired in their committee units. Interviews were done at the end of the 95th Congress (1977–78), during the period from late 1978 to the beginning of 1980. A follow-up was done in late 1980 through 1981 to gather additional data and update relevant information.

The interviews allowed me to secure information on oversight in its many forms, both formal and informal. There are data on various types of formal hearings, investigations, and evaluations, and on informal mechanisms of oversight such as communication with agency personnel. With these data I can analyze the frequency of use of the many oversight techniques asked about. For primary-purpose oversight hearings, I can also validate the survey measures by correlating reports of activity by the respondents with objective measures drawn from the *Daily Digest* data (see appendix D). And I can use the interview data to examine how effective top staffers believe each oversight technique, formal or informal, to be.

The interview data also permit me to focus on the oversight process. How is the oversight agenda set? Why does a committee unit choose to oversee a program or agency? What is the nature of its information network? How effective does that network seem to be? Since I have unusually complete data on both formal and informal behavior, I can examine how oversight is conducted in some depth. Why do committees choose the approaches and methods employed? What roles, political and otherwise, do these activities play? The issue of oversight impact can also be approached through these data. What impact is reported? What changes ensued? Finally, issues relating to the competence of Congress to engage in oversight activity—its level of expertise and resources, and its use of expertise and resources—can be examined. And, given the design of the survey, the nature of the relationship between committee staff and members in making oversight decisions can be examined. That relationship is an issue of great importance for democratic control of bureaucracy, since oversight decisions made by staffers may not reflect the will of the elected representatives who employ them.

The interview part of the study presented a difficult design problem. Given the decision to study congressional committee behavior, what units should be chosen and who should represent them? A prior issue, of course, was whether interviews were the best way to gather data. It was clear to me after some exploration of the issue that, if I was to have sufficiently broad coverage of congressional committee behavior, interviews would be the essential data-gathering component. They would be supplemented by the examination of documents, but documentary evidence was too extensive (and vague) to serve as the primary focus. Therefore, I decided to use interviews, but I did not use a simple random sampling technique because I wanted to have enough background on the committee units studied so that I could interpret the information given me with confidence.

As a result of these considerations I chose a purposive sample of the standing committees of Congress, selected on the basis of committee prestige and subject matter of committee jurisdiction. Committees were roughly matched by chamber so that House-Senate comparisons could be made. The organizational units of analysis are subcommittee and full committee decisionmaking structures, the former included because they are important in committee decision-making in the currently decentralized Congress. In cases where committees were not sufficiently decentralized or otherwise not organized to justify a focus on subcommittees as units of analysis, alternate selection procedures were used. In each case, a top staffer was selected and interviewed. He or she served as an informant on committee unit behavior and as a representative of top committee staff.

In selecting the committees and subcommittees, my aims were to cover the spectrum of committee types as well as possible and at the same time to maximize the descriptive and analytic payoff of the study. The relevant literature on committee types, a concern with manageability, and my interest in recent oversight reforms led to selection of the following criteria: choose committees spaced along the committee prestige and (related) issue scope hierarchies; choose committees with jurisdictions spread across the spectrum of policy issues and styles of conflict resolution; and choose some committees that have separate oversight subcommittees.

I used the information available in the academic literature on committee prestige, the scope of the issues that committees handle, and the political advantages of membership to divide the committees into clusters.[11] The next task, to meet the second selection criterion, was to choose committees within the clusters to represent a variety of policy issues and styles of conflict resolution. Again taking advantage of existing analyses of committees, I selected within the clusters to maximize coverage of committees that handled different types of policy issues and used varying styles of conflict resolution.[12]

To reiterate the basic point, the goal of selecting the committee units according to the first two criteria just mentioned was to ensure coverage of a variety of committee types and political environments to maximize the descriptive and analytic payoff of the study. The sample is not, strictly speaking, statistically representative, but it does provide variation across the factors considered important in understanding congressional behavior. I often refer to the interview data as representing a sample of the standing committees, but the purist should bear in mind that the sample is purposive. (In fact, it is a universe, or as close to a universe as I could get, of the selected committee units.)

The third committee selection criterion, inclusion of some committees with separate oversight units, was related to my interest in studying oversight reform. The formation of such subcommittees was one of the principal recommendations of the 1974 House committee reforms. Analysis of their performance will help me to evaluate the impact of this device.

Based on these criteria, I selected the following eleven committees (six House and five Senate) for the study: House Ways and Means, Senate Finance; House Education and Labor, Senate Human Resources; House Interstate and Foreign Commerce, Senate Commerce, Science and Transportation; House Public Works and Transportation, Senate Environment and Public Works; House Government Operations, Senate Governmental Affairs; and relevant units of the House and Senate Appropriations Committees (roughly matched to the jurisdictions of the committees listed). The House Science and Technology Committee was also included to match up with the science jurisdiction found in the Senate Commerce Committee.

With the committees selected, a list of top staffers responsible for each unit composing the committee was drawn up. (The full committee and its subcommittee components are conceived for analytic purposes as separate organizational units.) This was a relatively easy task for all of the House committees and for the Senate Appropriations, Human Resources, and Governmental Affairs Committees. However, it was more difficult for the Senate Commerce, Environment and Public Works, and Finance Committees because of their centralized staffs.

In all cases, the staff lists in the *Congressional Yellow Book*, supplemented by other sources, were used to compile lists of the top staff appointed by the majority, either staff director, chief counsel, or other top majority staff on a unit where there was no formal staff director or chief counsel.[13] In the case of two of the three "difficult" Senate committees listed (Commerce and Environment and Public Works), top committee staffers with primary responsibility for subcommittee areas were easily identified and these judgments confirmed in the interviews conducted later. These top staff people were usually responsible primarily to subcommittee chairs. For the Finance Com-

TABLE A-1. *Top Staff Interview Data, by Chamber*

	Initial interview			Follow-up interview[a]		
Item	House	Senate	Total	House	Senate	Total
Number of cases						
Target group[b]	56	48	104	53	42	95
Completed	53	42	95	51	41[c]	92
Percent completed	95	88	91	96	98	97

a. Of the three interviews not completed in the follow-up, only one was an outright refusal. One respondent was deceased, and one was out of the country for an extended stay.

b. For three of the respondents listed on the final target group roster, there was some ambiguity resolved before placing them in the top group. In one case, a respondent divided the top staff role on his subcommittee with another. In a second case, the staff director had recently resigned and a high-level substitute was chosen. In a third case, a staffer who devoted full time to the work of a subcommittee was chosen above a nominal superior who devoted at least half of his time to another committee unit.

c. Three of the Senate interviews were done in their entirety in 1980 or 1981. These interviews combined the initial survey questions with the follow-up questions.

mittee, by far the most centralized of the committees in the sample, I identified top full committee staffers with responsibility for the main substantive areas covered by the committee.[14] In this committee personal staff play an unusually important role in serving the needs of the chairs of the subcommittees, but I confined my attention in all cases but one to the committee staff itself as the most comparable population given the centralization of decisionmaking. For the Appropriations subcommittees, which have much wider jurisdictions than the other committees, more than one subcommittee staffer was placed on the list when appropriate. Appropriations subcommittees targeted in each chamber were Labor, Health, Education, and Welfare; Public Works; State, Justice, Commerce, and Judiciary; and HUD-Independent Agencies. Appropriations staffers were selected on the basis of a rough match of their responsibilities to those handled by the other committees included in the study.

I made an attempt to interview each of the top staffers on the list, a total of 104. Table A-1 presents the results of these efforts: a success rate of 95 percent in the House and 87 percent in the Senate. The overall success rate was 91 percent. Completion on the follow-up interview attempts in 1980 and 1981 was 97 percent.

The staffers were surveyed with reference to the topics outlined earlier. All were promised anonymity. No quotations or other information will be attributed to an identified individual, even though a small number of those interviewed were willing to be identified.

The interviews were based on an open-ended yet structured survey instrument, supplemented by numerous short-answer questions of the standard survey type interspersed throughout. Discussions were often wide-ranging, with an attempt made to maintain the conversational style appropriate to an elite interview.[15] We tape recorded the interviews to facilitate ease of communication in the interview situation. Respondents tend to relax quickly in the presence of a tape recorder, especially if the interview begins with very innocuous background questions.

The survey of top staffers yields much of the information not available in the *Daily Digest* data, but it also has limitations. First, while it does concentrate on selected committees (rather than sampling purely at random among all of the full committee and subcommittee units of the Congress), it does not provide the depth one would ideally like for understanding the political and procedural subtleties of a complex phenomenon like oversight. Second, staffers, not members, are the focus of the major survey used in the analysis. Staffers are undoubtedly better informants about many aspects of committee life because their work time is devoted almost entirely to the committee's tasks, and they play a crucial role in most of the decisions made. However, one would want to supplement their reports, especially on purely political matters and on the influence structure within the committee, with reports from representatives and senators. Third, while brief case studies were developed in each interview—each respondent was asked to select the "most successful" and "least successful" oversight case the committee unit had in the 95th Congress and then was asked numerous follow-up questions— fully developed cases would be invaluable aids in developing depth and breadth of understanding. Fourth, while the top staffers provide an excellent congressional perspective on their own behavior and that of other actors such as administrators, it would be desirable to

TABLE A-2. *Supplementary Staff Interview Data, by Chamber and Status*

Interview	House	Senate	Total
Target group (number of cases)			
Majority	22	20	42
Minority	25	17	42
Total	47	37	84
Completed (number of cases)			
Majority	19	16	35
Minority	24	17	41[a]
Total	43	33	76
Percent of total			
target completed	92	89	91

a. Follow-up interviews were completed with 39 of the 41 minority respondents (22 in the House and 17 in the Senate).

gain an independent assessment of the perspectives of these other actors. And finally, there is a wealth of documentary material available for analysis that would shed light on congressional oversight behavior.

Therefore, in addition to the information on committee behavior over time coded from the *Daily Digest* and the interviews with top committee staff, I used a package of supplementary sources, which broadly constitute the *third approach* used in the research. First, to provide some of the depth needed to understand the political and procedural subtleties of oversight, a subsample of the committee units in the main sample was selected, based on the same criteria used to select the main sample, and additional (lower-level) majority staffers were interviewed. To assist further in achieving this goal, a set of top staffers appointed by the minority was also selected and interviewed. These minority staffers came from the same units as the majority subsample people. Most can be matched precisely to counterpart top majority staffers serving the same units. From time to time in the analysis "matched sample" comparisons will be done to demonstrate similarities and differences in the perspectives of the majority and minority. Table A-2 presents data on the supplementary staff interviews.

Second, to supplement staff reports, some members (representatives and senators) of the subsample units just described were

TABLE A-3. *Member Interviews*

| | Number of cases | | |
Interview	House	Senate	Total[a]
Unit chairs	20	9	29
Ranking minority members	19	7	26
Other members	20	. . .	20
Total	59	16	75

a. Completion rates were as follows: House, 87 percent (nine refusals); Senate, 67 percent (eight refusals); total, 82 percent.

interviewed. These include unit chairs and ranking minority members as well as other members. The composition of this group is displayed in table A-3. For these interviews I used an abbreviated version of the staff questionnaire, supplemented by additional questions. Member interviews were used to supplement the staff interviews in a variety of ways—to gain a better understanding of the politics of oversight, to assess staff influence and the influence structure within the committee from a nonstaff perspective, and to provide a rich stock of material for the quotations used in the text.

Third, a set of cases was developed through study of documents, attendance at congressional hearings and meetings, and interviews with participants of all types (including administrators).[16] These cases are not "representative." Their aim was to help me gain a deeper and wider understanding of oversight. The cases inform the analysis but are not developed in the text since I want to focus on the generalizations that historical and systematic interview data make possible.

Fourth, to gain an independent (nonstaff) perspective on the behavior of other actors, especially administrators, the case studies and interviews with members were further supplemented by a roundtable discussion held in June 1979 at Brookings with present and former officials of the executive branch.[17] Remarks at the conference were transcribed verbatim and analysis of the contents was useful for background and especially valuable for the discussions later in the book on the effectiveness of congressional information strategies and on the impact of oversight.

Finally, I collected *Legislative Review Activity* reports of congressional committees going back to the 92d Congress, the first Congress to require them as a consequence of the 1970 Amendments of the Legislative Reorganization Act. These reports are not consistent in content since the committees use their own discretion in deciding what to include and how much detail to provide, but they are focused on oversight behavior. Other congressional documents too numerous to catalogue here, such as committee reports and reports of support agencies, were also examined.

In short, the conclusions reached on the basis of the *Daily Digest* data and the interviews with top majority staffers are supplemented and informed by numerous additional sources. The *Digest* and interview data are the focus of the data analysis in this book, but the interpretations are backed by insights gained from other staffers, senators and representatives, case studies, federal government administrative personnel, and some of the wealth of documentary evidence available.

Summary

The data collected for the book provide the raw material for a systematic, longitudinal (historical) analysis of trends in congressional committee oversight activity and for an intensive, yet also systematic, cross-sectional analysis of committee oversight activity. The latter is based on a survey of top staffers. Numerous additional sources supplement both types of data. In the book I weave together the different strands of material in an effort to broaden and deepen our understanding of congressional oversight.

Appendix B

The *Daily Digest* Data

THIS APPENDIX supplements the brief comments in appendix A on the characteristics, particularly the limitations, of the *Daily Digest* data set that is the major data source for the analyses reported in chapters 2 and 3.

First of all, the *Digest* data set understates the amount of committee activity to some extent because the descriptions in the *Daily Digest* are inserted by the committees. If for any reason committee clerks fail to submit copy to the *Congressional Record*, there is no entry for any hearings or meetings they may have held. This, however, does not seem to be a major problem. Data of a comparable sort coded from the 1975 *Daily Digest* by the Commission on the Operation of the Senate, which was then supplemented by committee calendars and committee personnel who checked the lists of hearings and meetings, showed only minor discrepancies from my own data.[1]

Second, the descriptions submitted are not always as clear as one might hope. I guarded against error by double-coding any questionable entries in the *Digest*.

Third, the data are records of hearings and meetings, not other activities of the committees. They therefore do not necessarily include such efforts as staff investigations, which can be important aspects of oversight, unless these efforts are reflected in hearings and meetings.

Fourth, and finally, oversight may occur as a by-product of hearings and meetings held by congressional committees for other purposes such as reauthorizing programs. Accordingly, the *Daily Digest* data analyzed in this chapter underestimate the amount of oversight done by committees even in hearings and meetings because they consider only the primary purpose of each hearing or meeting as described in the *Daily Digest*.

The third and fourth shortcomings are overcome by the survey data described in appendix A. However, the survey, unlike the *Digest* data, is cross sectional and not longitudinal and therefore is not an adequate substitute for the analysis of trends and change presented in this chapter and the next.

All hearings or meetings listed in the *Daily Digest* were coded so that effort spent on oversight as measured from this source could be compared with activities devoted to other (nonoversight) purposes. Oversight was defined conceptually as indicated in appendix A (congressional review of the actions of federal departments, agencies, and commissions, and of the programs and policies they administer[2]) and operationally as hearings or meetings whose primary purpose was any of the following, either singly or in combination: (1) to review or control unacceptable forms of bureaucratic behavior; (2) to ensure that the bureaucracy implements the policy objectives of Congress; and (3) to determine the effectiveness of programs and policies. Committee hearings or meetings described in less precise terms than those above simply as efforts to review or oversee the activities of an agency were also coded as oversight. The numbered elements of the operational definition were drawn from the Congressional Research Source study for the Bolling Committee.[3] The main difference between their study and mine is that I did not code as oversight hearings or meetings designed, in their words, "to analyze national (and international) problems requiring Federal action" unless they were part of an effort to review government actions in the area.

Appendix C

Indicators and Regression Approach

THIS APPENDIX supplements the discussion in chapter 3 of the indicators and regression approach used in analyzing the *Daily Digest* data on congressional committee oversight activity for the years 1961 to 1977.[1]

Independent Variables

Indicators of the independent variables used in the analyses are as follows:

—Total days. A simple count for each congressional committee of the total days of hearings and meetings reported in the *Daily Digest* during the period January 1 to July 4 of each odd-numbered year from 1961 to 1977.

—Staff. A count of the number of staff on the payrolls of the committees in the relevant years from 1961 to 1977.1[2]

—Oversight unit. The committees in each chamber whose primary function is oversight (Government Operations in the House and Governmental Affairs in the Senate) and committees containing a subcommittee with identifying labels such as oversight or department operations were coded 1; others were coded 0—a dummy variable in the language of statistical analysis. The hypothesis, as detailed in chapter 3, is that organizational units whose jurisdiction is focused on oversight will be more likely than others to engage in oversight

My thanks to Lynn Gale and Professor Lincoln Moses of the staff of the Center for Advanced Study in the Behavioral Sciences and to Professors John Chamberlin and Mary Corcoran of the University of Michigan for their assistance and advice in doing the regression work reported in this appendix and in chapter 3.

if for no other reason than because alternative courses of action are severely limited.

—Decentralization. Finding an adequate indicator of committee decentralization (one that gets to the level of centralization or dispersal of decisionmaking power) was a bit of a challenge. Direct measures of the relative influence of the committee and subcommittee chairs were unavailable. The number of subcommittees each committee had was considered, but that measure neglected their level of activity. Therefore, I used the percentage of hearings and meeting held by subcommittees as the measure of decentralization. The underlying assumption is that the more hearings and meetings held at the subcommittee level, the more power over decisionmaking is dispersed.[3]

—Chamber. The House was coded 1 and the Senate coded 0.

—Redistributive policy issues. Committees with a heavy concentration of redistributive policy issues in their jurisdictions were coded 1, and the rest were coded 0.[4]

—Split partisan control. The years 1969, 1971, 1973, and 1975, years of Republican control of the presidency and Democratic control of the Congress, were coded 1. Others years (1961, 1963, 1965, 1967, and 1977) were coded 0.

—Number of pages in the *Federal Register*. This variable was included in preliminary work but eliminated from the final regression results presented. It was not significant when the slope dummy variables, for 1973, 1975, and 1977, which are an important part of the regression technique used, were introduced. This is almost surely because the slope dummies picked up changes in the external political environment better than a gross indicator such as the pages variable.[5]

Approach

Cross-sectional (year by year) regressions were run using all of the variables just listed except for split partisan control and pages in the *Federal Register*, which vary across time but have a constant value in any given year. These regressions were analyzed carefully to make sure that the assumptions for use of the Ordinary Least Squares regression technique were met by the data. Based on the analysis of the regressions and their diagnostics—particularly the patterns of the residuals (normal probability plots of RSTUDENT residuals), checks for influential points (deletion diagnostics for coefficient estimates, partial regression leverage plots, and the like), checks for heteroscedasticity (plots of residuals by predicted values and by each regressor), and checks for multicollinearity (condition indices and associated variance-decomposition proportions for each estimated regression coefficient)[6]—the following decisions were made:

—The dependent variable, days of oversight done by each committee, was transformed by taking its natural log. Transforming the somewhat skewed distribution found in the early years of the days of oversight series made it (the dependent variable) better meet the linear assumptions of the model.[7] Logging the dependent variable has additional virtues when one is comparing regression coefficients over time. With the means of the dependent variable rising over time, stabilizing the variance of the dependent variable by logging makes the regression coefficients comparable across years. Standard units can now be used in interpreting the coefficients. As per the examples in the chapter, one can talk about the percent increment in the dependent variable for a unit change in the independent variables.

—All predictor (independent) variables, except for pages in the *Federal Register*, could be included in the analysis. There were no problems of multicollinearity, even between committee staff and total days of committee activity where it was most feared, sufficient to eliminate other variables on the list. The tests did indicate that one committee (Senate Judiciary) should be removed in all years and one committee (Senate Governmental Affairs) in 1973.[8] This was done, although results were only slightly changed by dropping these cases.

—The years (1961–71) were clearly candidates for pooled analysis (putting the years together in one simple regression) because the unstandardized regression coefficients (slopes) for the predictor variables were similar year to year, but there was sufficient variation in the slopes in the years 1973, 1975, and 1977 to call for additional testing. The results of these tests are discussed in the next paragraph and reflected in table 3-1.

Once the variables in the analysis were identified and their form determined,[9] the data for 1961 to 1977 were pooled for a test to see which of the slopes of the independent variables should be adjusted for the years 1973, 1975, and 1977—years when there were definite signs of instability in some of the regression coefficients—and which could be estimated with a single coefficient for the entire period. The pooled test included the remaining indicator with constant values at each point in time (split partisan control of the presidency and Congress),[10] the variables in the cross-sectional regressions, and a slope-dummy variable for each of the variables and the intercepts in the cross-sectional regressions to test the joint hypothesis that $B_{61-71} = B_{73} = B_{75} = B_{77} = 0$ (B being the coefficient of the indicated year(s) dummy times the variable of interest.[11] Based on a very conservative interpretation of the F test for the hypothesis, I dropped the dummies that are best thought of as noise in the model to get the final coefficients.[12] The fit for the complete model (all variables and all slopes by years) is $R^2 = 0.59$. For the final (reduced) model presented in table 3-1 it is just slightly lower, $R^2 = 0.58$. Little is lost by the procedure and much is gained in clarity.

Appendix D

Validity of the Measures

IT IS USUALLY difficult to validate the answers to questions in a survey study. Though I cannot validate all of the measures used in the study, it is possible to check top staffers' reports on the frequency of use by their units of primary-purpose oversight hearings in the 95th Congress against objective, independently gathered data on oversight hearings in the 95th Congress coded for the analyses reported earlier in chapters 2 and 3. The match is not perfect since the available objective data coded from the *Daily Digest* to the *Congressional Record* covers only the first year of the two-year Congress, but if the results match up reasonably well, then we can have great confidence in the survey indicator on primary-purpose oversight hearings and, by implication, in the other behavioral and even nonbehavioral (motivational) indicators from the survey as well.[1]

The validating analysis is straightforward: average the scores on the oversight behavior survey indicator as reported by the top staffers (subcommittee and full committee) of each committee and compare them with the number of days of oversight hearings and meetings recorded for each of the relevant committees in the *Daily Digest* data.[2] When this is done, the rank order correlation (R_s) between the two measures is a very robust 0.809. Clearly the measure is quite valid. (And, coincidentally, we gain confidence that the top staff respondents whose answers are the basis for much of this analysis are reliable informants.)

The high correlation between answers to the survey item on primary-purpose oversight hearings and objectively measured counts of oversight hearings days is the best way to check the validity of the survey measure, but obviously it covers the survey measure of oversight hearings alone. The result gives me great confidence in the oversight measure on the survey, and, by inference, in the other survey measures, but there is a supplementary test that adds to my confidence.

As I noted in appendix A, a subsample of top minority staffers was interviewed for the study. They were matched to top majority staffers on the same units so that it is possible to check their answers to the questions on oversight behavior against those of their top majority counterparts. If both gave the same answers, one's confidence in the measures of oversight behavior increases. Since this test is not confined to the primary-purpose oversight hearings measure, it has the further advantage of checking each of the measures of oversight behavior used. (See tables 6-1 and 6-2 for a list of the measures.)

The appropriate statistic is a test of the mean of pair-by-pair differences in which a comparison is done by obtaining a difference score for each matched pair.[3] Results of the test show significant differences ($p \leq 0.10$) between the reports on oversight behavior frequency or effectiveness for only four of the twenty-eight measures used, and three of these are easily explained because they gauge the frequency or effectiveness of behavior when the majority and minority would have different experiences and, therefore, different perspectives. Each of the three easily explained differences involves reports of staff or member communication with agency personnel for oversight purposes. Not surprisingly, the majority staffers were significantly more likely to report greater frequency of such communications, with greater effectiveness reported by majority staffers when assessing the communications of senators and representatives with agency personnel. It is highly likely that the majority does use these techniques more often than the minority (and that the minority is not aware of all of the contacts taking place), and that administrators are somewhat less responsive to the communications of minority senators and representatives than to those of the majority.[4] All in all, then, the measures seem to be valid.[5]

Notes

Notes to Chapter One (pages 1–4)

1. Max Weber, "Bureaucracy" in H. H. Gerth and C. Wright Mills, trans. and eds., *From Max Weber: Essays in Sociology* (New York: Oxford University Press, 1958), p. 232.

2. Robert D. Putnam, "The Political Attitudes of Senior Civil Servants in Western Europe: A Preliminary Report," *British Journal of Political Science*, vol. 3 (July 1973), p. 257.

3. Putnam, "Political Attitudes," pp. 260, 290.

4. Richard E. Neustadt, *Presidential Power: The Politics of Leadership with Reflections on Johnson and Nixon*, 3d ed. (John Wiley and Sons, 1976), p. 101.

5. Robert A. Dahl, *Democracy in the United States: Promise and Performance* (Rand McNally, 1976), p. 73.

6. Alexander Hamilton, John Jay, and James Madison, *The Federalist* (Random House, The Modern Library, 1937), p. 337.

7. James MacGregor Burns, *The Deadlock of Democracy: Four-Party Politics in America* (Prentice Hall, 1963), p. 22.

8. James Q. Wilson, "The Rise of the Bureaucratic State," *Public Interest*, no. 41 (Fall 1975), p. 77.

9. Herbert A. Simon, Donald W. Smithburg, and Victor A. Thompson, *Public Administration* (Alfred A. Knopf, 1950), p. 533.

10. Richard E. Neustadt, "Politicians and Bureaucrats," in David B. Truman, ed., *Congress and America's Future*, (Prentice Hall, 1965), p. 103.

11. Neustadt, "Politicians and Bureaucrats," pp. 114–15.

12. Joel D. Aberbach and Bert A. Rockman, *The Administrative State in Industrialized Democracies* (Washington: American Political Science Association, 1985), p. 19. See also Joel D. Aberbach, Robert D. Putnam, and Bert A. Rockman, *Bureaucrats and Politicians in Western Democracies* (Harvard University Press, 1981), pp. 95–96, particularly the following: "Fragmented accountability forces American bureaucrats to be risk takers and forceful advocates for positions they hold privately. . . . In a political system that rewards entrepreneurs, neither protected by anonymity nor clearly serving a single master, American bureaucrats must find allies where they can."

13. I often discuss congressional oversight of policy and administration

in broad terms and do not divide administrators into political appointees and career civil servants. When appropriate, however, I will make the distinction and refer to the two types separately.

14. Hugh Heclo, *A Government of Strangers: Executive Politics in Washington* (Brookings, 1977).

15. See, for example, Joel D. Aberbach and Bert A. Rockman, "Clashing Beliefs within the Executive Branch: The Nixon Administration Bureaucracy," *American Political Science Review*, vol. 70 (June 1976), pp. 456–68; Joel D. Aberbach and Bert A. Rockman, "From Nixon's Problem to Reagan's 'Achievement'—The Federal Executive Reexamined," paper prepared for the Conference on the Legacy of the Reagan Presidency, sponsored by the Institute of Governmental Affairs, University of California, Davis, 1988; Richard F. Fenno, Jr., *The President's Cabinet: An Analysis of the Period from Wilson to Eisenhower* (Harvard University Press, 1959); Heclo, *Government of Strangers*; Richard P. Nathan, *The Plot That Failed: Nixon and the Administrative Presidency* (Wiley, 1975); and Richard P. Nathan, *The Administrative Presidency* (Wiley, 1983).

16. Nathan, *The Plot That Failed* and *The Administrative Presidency*.

17. The Civil Service Reform Act of 1978, for example, increased the president's leverage with top civil servants. For descriptions and evaluations of the reform, see *Senior Executive Service*, Hearings before the Subcommittee on Civil Service of the House Post Office and Civil Service Committee 98 Cong. 1 and 2 sess (Government Printing Office, 1984). For evidence of the president's ability to use the reform, see Aberbach and Rockman, "From Nixon's Problem." The quotation from Norton E. Long comes from "Power and Administration," *Public Administration Review*, vol. 9 (Autumn 1949), pp. 257–64, as quoted on p. 16 of Francis E. Rourke, *Bureaucratic Power in National Politics*, 3d ed. (Little, Brown, 1978).

18. Heclo, *Government of Strangers*, pp. 84, 103. Twenty-two months is the average stay for an assistant secretary. Heclo identifies a third category of administrators he calls "public careerists," a "de facto, higher civil service" of individuals who do not make a career of government yet know the issues and processes of government. How large a cadre of people the public careerists represent is unclear (many of those identified in the Heclo article as possible public careerists are long-time civil servants who served in appointee positions during the early Nixon administration, but the group should be investigated more closely). See Hugh Heclo, "The State and America's High Civil Service," a paper presented to the Wilson Center Conference on the Role of the State in Recent American History, October 23–24, 1982, especially pp. 14–18, and table 3, p. 16.

19. A good discussion of "purposeful collective direction: the cabinet ideal" and the reasons it cannot be implemented in Washington can be found in Richard Rose, *The Capacity of the President: A Comparative Analysis*, Studies in Public Policy, no. 130 (Glasgow: University of Strathclyde, Center for the Study of Public Policy, 1984), pp. 42–47.

20. Aberbach and others, *Bureaucrats and Politicians*, p. 94.

21. Aberbach and others, *Bureaucrats and Politicians*, p. 233.

22. In the direct linkage countries—where "simultaneous linkage" prevails—"MPs and civil servants report a high level of contact with each other and with the minister." Aberbach and others, *Bureaucrats and Politicians*, p. 235.

23. Aberbach and others, *Bureaucrats and Politicians*, p. 235.

24. For example, "American bureaucrats focus on facilitating [specific] interests to a far greater extent than bureaucrats in other systems." Aberbach and others, *Bureaucrats and Politicians*, p. 99.

25. Aberbach and others, *Bureaucrats and Politicians*, p. 99.

26. This section and the next two subsections are adapted from Aberbach and Rockman, *The Administrative State*, pp. 10–19.

27. Aberbach and Rockman, *The Administrative State*, p. 11.

28. Richard Rose, "Government against Sub-Governments: A European Perspective on Washington," in Richard Rose and Ezra N. Suleiman, eds., *Presidents and Prime Ministers* (Washington: American Enterprise Institute for Public Policy Research, 1980), p. 288.

29. Reality is more complex. France is the main but still partial exception, with a mixed presidential and cabinet parliamentary system.

30. Cabinet governments are not uniformly strong, by any means. The strong cabinet system found in Britain is the "ideal type" described in most texts and used as a model here. However, formal cabinet authority and whatever informal advantages go with that authority is the rule in most Western democratic systems.

31. The word *if* should be emphasized. Authority is often delegated to corporatist subgovernments. Also, while this point is important in comparative terms, one should bear in mind that cabinet officials are limited in their execution of these control activities by the prestige of the civil service elite, the traditions of bureaucratic professional responsibility and representation of state interests that go with that prestige, and the natural disinclination of the cabinet to evaluate negatively its own programs or to admit to management failures. The expertise of the bureaucracy, Weber's point made at the beginning of the chapter, is also an important limit on the relative power of cabinet officials.

32. Rose, "Government against Sub-Governments," p. 284.

33. Kenneth H. F. Dyson, *The State Tradition in Western Europe: A Study of an Idea and Institution* (New York: Oxford University Press, 1980), p. 271.

34. Richard F. Fenno, Jr., "If, as Ralph Nader Says, Congress Is 'The Broken Branch,' How Come We Love Our Congressmen So Much?" in Norman J. Ornstein, ed., *Congress in Change: Evolution and Reform* (Praeger, 1975), pp. 277–87. See also Glenn R. Parker and Robert H. Davidson, "Why Do Americans Love Their Congressmen So Much More Than Their Congress," *Legislative Studies Quarterly*, vol. 4 (February 1979), pp. 53–61.

35. Aberbach and Rockman, *The Administrative State*, p. 14.

36. Morris P. Fiorina, *Congress: Keystone of the Washington Establishment* (Yale University Press, 1977), pp. 48–49.

37. For a critique of the "congressional dominance" view, see Terry M. Moe, "An Assessment of the Positive Theory of 'Congressional Dominance'" *Legislative Studies Quarterly*, vol. 12 (November 1987), pp. 475–520.

38. Woodrow Wilson, *Congressional Government: A Study in American Government* (Mentor Books, 1954), p. 79.

39. Roger H. Davidson, "Subcommittee Government: New Channels for Policy Making," in Thomas E. Mann and Norman J. Ornstein, eds., *The New Congress* (Washington: American Enterprise Institute for Public Policy Research, 1981), p. 108.

40. Norman J. Ornstein, Thomas E. Mann, and Michael J. Malbin, *Vital Statistics on Congress, 1987–1988* (Washington: Congressional Quarterly, 1987), pp. 128–29.

41. Aberbach and Rockman, *The Administrative State*, p. 18.

42. See, for example, Nelson W. Polsby, "The Institutionalization of the U.S. House of Representatives," *American Political Science Review*, vol. 62 (March 1968), pp. 144–68.

43. For an extended treatment of congressional staffs, see Harrison W. Fox, Jr., and Susan Webb Hammond, *Congressional Staffs: The Invisible Force in American Lawmaking* (Free Press, 1977). For recent data on staff, see Ornstein and others, *Vital Statistics*, chap. 5. An extended treatment of the role of the General Accounting Office is available in Frederick C. Mosher, *The GAO: The Quest for Accountability in American Government* (Westview, 1979).

44. Rose, "Government against Sub-Governments," p. 299.

45. Calvert, Moran, and Weingast, for example, in summarizing the oversight literature say, "There seems little doubt that formal congressional oversight and monitoring are infrequent and ad hoc." Randall L. Calvert, Mark J. Moran, and Barry R. Weingast, "Congressional Influence Over Policy Making: The Case of the FTC," in Mathew D. McCubbins and Terry Sullivan, eds., *Congress: Structure and Policy* (Cambridge University Press, 1987), p. 496.

46. Calvert and others, "Congressional Influence," p. 500. See the extensive discussion of this point in chap 4. Probably the most influential work in this area is Mathew D. McCubbins and Thomas Schwartz, "Congressional Oversight Overlooked: Police Patrols versus Fire Alarms," *American Journal of Political Science*, vol. 28 (February 1984), pp. 165–79.

47. Joseph Cooper and Cheryl D. Young, "Bill Introduction in the Nineteenth Century: A Study of Institutional Change," *Legislative Studies Quarterly*, vol. 14 (February 1989), p. 99.

Notes to Chapter Two

1. James Q. Wilson, "The Rise of the Bureaucratic State," *Public Interest*, vol. 41 (Fall 1975), pp. 81–82.

2. Allen Schick draws this point from Leonard D. White. See Schick's excellent essay, "Politics through Law: Congressional Limitations on Executive Discretion," in Anthony King, ed., *Both Ends of the Avenue: The Presidency, the Executive Branch, and Congress in the 1980s* (Washington: American Enterprise Institute for Public Policy Research, 1983), pp. 154–84, especially p. 157.

3. Schick, "Politics through Law," pp. 157–58.

4. Wilson, "Rise of the Bureaucratic State," p. 88.

5. Schick, "Politics through Law," p. 158.

6. See Nelson W. Polsby, "The Institutionalization of the U.S. House of Representatives," *American Political Science Review*, vol. 62 (March 1968), pp. 144–68.

7. Schick, "Politics through Law," p. 158.

8. Schick, "Politics through Law," p. 159.

9. Schick, "Politics through Law," pp. 159–60.

10. Schick, "Politics through Law," p. 160.

11. See, for example, Richard E. Neustadt, "Presidency and Legislation: The Growth of Central Clearance," *American Political Science Review*, vol. 48 (September 1954), pp. 641–71.

12. Schick, "Politics through Law," p. 161.

13. *A Compilation of the Legislative Reorganization Act of 1946 with Amendments through the First Session of the Eighty-Third Congress*, S. Doc 71, 83 Cong. 1 sess. (Government Printing Office, 1953), p. 26.

14. Roger H. Davidson and Walter J. Oleszek, *Congress against Itself* (Indiana University Press, 1977), p. 7.

15. Davidson and Oleszek, *Congress against Itself*, p. xiii.

16. Lawrence C. Dodd, "Congress and the Quest for Power," in Lawrence C. Dodd and Bruce I. Oppenheimer, eds., *Congress Reconsidered* (Praeger, 1977), p. 282.

17. This famous expression is, I believe, generally attributed to Representative Sam Rayburn, Speaker of the House from 1940 to 1947, 1949 to 1953, and 1955 to 1961.

18. Joseph P. Harris, *Congressional Control of Administration* (Brookings, 1964), pp. 264–66.

19. Harris, *Congressional Control*, p. 282.

20. Harris, *Congressional Control*, p. 270.

21. Harris, *Congressional Control*, p. 270.

22. Harris, *Congressional Control*, pp. 270–71.

23. Harris, *Congressional Control*, p. 2.

24. A very strong version of this argument can be found in Norton E. Long, *The Polity* (Rand McNally, 1962), chap. 5.

25. Harris, *Congressional Control*, pp. 269–78.

26. Harris, *Congressional Control*, p. 295.

27. John F. Bibby, "Congress' Neglected Function," in Melvin R. Laird, ed., *The Republican Papers* (Anchor, 1968), pp. 477–88.

28. Bibby, "Congress' Neglected Function," pp. 487–88. I will discuss later the reasons for notions held by some of widespread oversight at this time. See chap. 4 especially.

29. Harris, *Congressional Control*, p. 297.

30. Bibby, "Congress' Neglected Function," p. 488.

31. Bibby, "Congress' Neglected Function, p. 484.

32. Richard P. Nathan, *The Plot That Failed: Nixon and the Administrative Presidency* (Wiley, 1975), especially pp. 73–76. An update of the book is entitled *The Administrative Presidency* (Wiley, 1983).

33. *Committee Reform Amendments of 1974*, H. Rept. 93-916, 93 Cong. 2 sess. (GPO, 1974), p. 63.

34. Walter J. Oleszek, "Overview of Legislative History and Methods," in *Workshop on Congressional Oversight and Investigations*, H. Doc. 96-217, 96 Cong. 1 sess. (GPO, 1979), p. 10.

35. See *Committee Reform Amendments of 1974: Explanation of H. Res. 988 as Adopted by the House of Representatives, October 8, 1974*, Committee Print, House Select Committee on Committees, 93 Cong. 2 sess. (GPO, 1974), pp. 54–61.

36. *Toward A Modern Senate: Final Report of the Commission on the Operation of the Senate*, S. Doc. 94-278, 94 Cong. 2 sess. (GPO, 1976), pp. 47–50.

37. Leroy N. Rieselbach, "The Forest for the Trees: Blazing Trails for Congressional Research," in Ada W. Finifter, ed., *Political Science: The State of the Discipline* (Washington: American Political Science Association, 1983), p. 175.

38. *Committee Reform Amendments of 1974*, H. Rept. 93-916, pp. 68–69; Davidson and Oleszek, *Congress against Itself*, p. 213; and Dodd, "Congress and the Quest for Power," p. 295.

39. *Committee Reform Amendments of 1974*, H. Rept. 93-916, pp. 66–67.

40. Davidson and Oleszek, *Congress against Itself*, pp. 262–64.

41. Norman J. Ornstein, "Causes and Consequences of Congressional Change: Subcommittee Reforms in the House of Representatives, 1970–73," in Norman J. Ornstein, ed., *Congress in Change: Evolution and Reform* (Praeger, 1975), pp. 105–09.

42. Davidson and Oleszek , *Congress against Itself*, esp. p. 264.

43. See Roger H. Davidson, "Subcommittee Government: New Channels for Policy Making," in Thomas E. Mann and Norman J. Ornstein, *The New Congress* (Washington: American Enterprise Institute for Public Policy Research, 1981), pp. 99–133.

44. For a brief catalogue of reforms, see table 15-4, "The Decade of Congressional Reform, 1970–1979," in Charles O. Jones, *The United States Congress: People, Place, and Policy* (Dorsey Press, 1982), p. 429.

45. Davidson and Oleszek, *Congress against Itself*, p. 218.

46. Dodd, "Congress and the Quest for Power," p. 290. See also Ornstein, "Subcommittee Reform," on the "Subcommittee Bill of Rights."

47. *Compilation of the Legislative Reorganization Act of 1946*, S. Doc. 71, p. 26.

48. For example, in the first study I know of that tried to gauge both the absolute and relative level of committee activity with oversight as the primary purpose, oversight activities took up barely 11 percent of the hearing and meeting time of House committees. See *Committee Reform Amendments of 1974*, H. Rept. 93-916, p. 268.

This figure, by the way, surely overstates the amount of oversight since it includes hearings and meetings "to analyze national (and international) problems requiring Federal action" as well as the more traditional purposes usually included within the oversight rubric: "1) To review and control unacceptable forms of bureaucratic behavior; 2) To ensure that the bureaucracy implements the policy objectives of the Congress; 3) To determine the effectiveness of legislative programs and policies." (p. 267).

49. See, for example: Scher, "Conditions for Legislative Control"; Bibby, "Congress' Neglected Function"; and Morris S. Ogul, *Congress Oversees the Bureaucracy: Studies in Legislative Supervision* (University of Pittsburgh Press, 1976).

50. *Committee Organization in the House*, Panel Discussions before the House Select Committee on Committees, vol. 2, 93 Cong. 1 sess. (GPO, 1973), pt. 1, pp. 15–16. See also the comments by Nelson Polsby, Morris Ogul, and John Bibby in the same volume.

51. *Committee Organization in the House*, Hearings before the House Select Committee on Committees, 93 Cong. 1 sess. vol. 1 (GPO, 1973), pt. 1, p. 66.

52. *Committee Reform Amendments of 1974*, H. Rept. 93-916, pp. 62–63.

53. *Committee Reform Amendments of 1974*, H. Rept. 93-916, p. 63.

54. Bibby, "Congress' Neglected Function," p. 484.

55. Ogul, *Congress Oversees*, p. 181.

56. *Committee Reform Amendments of 1974*, H. Rept. 93-916, p. 68.

57. The review schedule of the Muskie version of Sunset reform was linked to the budget function categories of the budget process. It was highly suspect as a result since many saw it as a power play by the Budget Committee, which Senator Muskie chaired.

58. Rieselbach, "Forest," p. 175.

59. See appendixes A and B for a full description of the *Daily Digest* data set used here. Appendix B, particularly, focuses on the limitations of the *Daily Digest* data.

60. See, for example, Harris, *Congressional Control*; *Committee Reform Amendments of 1974*, H. Rept. 93-916, pt. 2, pp. 267–75; and *Legislative Activity Sourcebook: United States Senate*, prepared for the Commission on the Operation of the Senate, 94 Cong. 2 sess. (GPO, 1976), pp. 6–16.

61. Data for 1979 were not coded because of budget limitations. My quick perusal of the sources indicates that the 1979 data, when available, will not modify significantly any general findings reported in this book.

62. The hearings or meetings of formal joint committees (for example, the Joint Economic Committee) and those held jointly by House and Senate committees were also excluded from the analysis.

63. A series is defined as a set of hearings and meetings dealing with one

subject, topic, or theme. The unusually long series in 1969 lasted thirty-three days. The next longest series in the data set lasted only sixteen days.

64. The exception is the Reagan administration, but even here the huge Omnibus Reconciliation Act of 1981 (PL 97-35, over 900 pages) is probably partially responsible. Note the sharp blip in the pages per statute entry for 1981, up to 9.2 pages per statute.

65. See note 64. The dropoff in 1981–1982 is probably exaggerated.

66. Schick, "Politics through Law," p. 167.

67. Schick, "Politics through Law," pp. 168–69. For a related interpretation focusing on "rationalizing politics," see Lawrence D. Brown, *New Policies, New Politics: Government's Response to Government's Growth* (Brookings, 1983).

68. Schick, "Politics through Law," pp. 166–79 on "The New Congressional Assertiveness." For details, see also Allen Schick, "Budgeting," in Norman J. Ornstein, Thomas E. Mann, Michael J. Malbin, and John F. Bibby, *Vital Statistics on Congress, 1982* (Washington: American Enterprise Institute for Public Policy Research, 1982).

69. The exact wording of the item was, "Observers of Congress have noted a great increase in congressional oversight activity since the early 1970s. Is this perception accurate?" Eighty-eight percent of the top House staffers responding to the item said this perception was accurate. Ninety percent of top Senate staffers agreed.

70. The influence of staff on the increase in oversight and on oversight decisions will be examined in greater detail in chaps. 3 and 5.

71. There is a legislative appropriations bill, but it is not tampered with by the executive.

72. Relevant information for the Appropriations, Rules, and Administration Committees in each chamber has been excluded from the counts for the reasons mentioned above.

73. The falloff in the rate of increase for committee staff in 1977 is a function of the Senate committee reform in that year, which reduced the number of standing committees.

74. See Ornstein and others, *Vital Statistics*, p. 129. See the text and figure 2-2 for data on pages in the *Federal Register*. Data for 1983 come from Norman J. Ornstein, Thomas E. Mann, and Michael J. Malbin, *Vital Statistics on Congress, 1987–88* (Washington: Congressional Quarterly, 1987), p. 170.

75. In light of the discussion of the large number of staff who identified negative public reactions to government size or efficiency as a contributor to increased congressional oversight activity (table 2-3), note that the correlation between the trend in pages in the *Federal Register* (increasing) and the Center for Political Studies political trust scale (decreasing) is almost perfectly negative (-0.92) over the period covered by each measure. This is exactly what the staffer explanations would predict. Trust measures were taken in the fall of each even-numbered year up to 1980, the last year in which the full series of questions was asked. Measures for 1960 and 1962 are extrapolated from the 1958 and 1964 data because the relevant questions were not asked in 1960 or 1962. See Warren E. Miller, Arthur H. Miller, and Edward J. Schneider,

American National Election Studies Data Sourcebook: 1952–1978 (Harvard University Press, 1980), p. 268; and *American National Election Study, 1980*, vol. 1 (Ann Arbor: Inter-University Consortium for Political and Social Research, 1982), pp. 220–21.

76. In chap. 3 I will analyze the post-1971 data separately from the rest.

77. In the period covered by this study, the environmental stimuli almost always worked in tandem. In other conceivable situations, they might work against one another. Also, one would not be surprised if there were significant lags in the relationship between indicators such as pages in the *Federal Register* and oversight hearings in a period of change. Under most circumstances, for example, once Congress has established a routine for actively doing oversight, it would probably continue its pattern of active oversight for a period of time beyond the actual "demand" for it.

78. See, for example, Ogul, *Congress Oversees*, p. 199. He saw the oversight increases of the early 1970s as "a transitory phenomenon."

79. Interview, May 22, 1979.

Notes to Chapter Three

1. Making inferences about linkages between the level of oversight and external environmental factors such as increases in the size and complexity of government obviously presents some difficulties. These difficulties are less relevant to establishing links between changes in internal congressional organization and procedures and oversight behavior, but even here they should be kept in mind. For example, the strength of the relationship between decentralization of committee decisionmaking and the level of oversight changed over time. The argument will emphasize that the meaning of the decentralization indicator has changed because of changes in congressional rules and procedures. Whereas in the past, full committee chairs had much influence over what went on in subcommittees, the "subcommittee bill of rights" in the House and related changes in the Senate altered that significantly. At one time the decentralization of hearings and meetings to subcommittees was based on the consent of committee chairs; now it is more a matter of right. Therefore, the relationship between the indicator of decentralization used in the study and oversight activity changed. A change in the nature of the internal environment had a marked impact on the cross-sectional relationships between decentralization and oversight activity.

2. Based on an analysis of the stability of regression coefficients, some relationships will be summarized with one coefficient and others will be allowed to vary with time. See appendix C.

3. The analysis was supplemented by use of an approach developed by demographers called "components-of-a-difference technique," which was used to estimate how much of the change in the average level of committee oversight activity from one point in time to another could be attributed to changes in the levels (means) of the independent variables and how much

to changes in the effects (slopes) of the independent variables. The components analysis reinforced the conclusions drawn here. I am grateful to Professor Robert Mare of the Department of Sociology at the University of Wisconsin, my colleague at the Center for Advanced Study in the Behavioral Sciences, 1983–84, for bringing this technique to my attention and helping me to apply it to the data at hand.

4. See the text of appendix C on exclusion of the Senate Judiciary Committee in the regression analyses.

5. Charles O. Jones, *The United States Congress: People, Places, and Policy* (Dorsey Press, 1982), p. 266.

6. Data on committee assignments show how many more affiliations (committee and subcommittee) each senator has when compared with the typical representative. In 1971 the typical senator served on 2.5 standing committees and 9.5 subcommittees of standing committees, and 3.3 "other" assignments on special and select committees for a total of 15.3 assignments per senator. In 1979, after the 1977 committee reforms that cut back the number of committees and assignments, the comparable figures still stood at 2.3, 6.6, and 1.5 for a total of 10.4. In the House, the comparable totals were 5.1 in 1971 (1.5, 3.2, and 0.4) and 5.8 in 1979 (1.7, 3.6, and 0.5). Norman J. Ornstein, Thomas E. Mann, Michael J. Malbin, and John F. Bibby, *Vital Statistics on Congress, 1982* (Washington: American Enterprise Institute for Public Policy Research, 1982), p. 100.

7. See the seminal piece by Theodore J. Lowi, "American Business, Public Policy, Case-Studies, and Political Theory," *World Politics*, vol. 16 (July 1964), pp. 677–715.

8. For a good critique of Lowi, see George D. Greenberg, Jeffrey A. Miller, Lawrence B. Mohr, and Bruce C. Vladek, "Developing Public Policy Theory: Perspectives from Empirical Research," *American Political Science Review*, vol. 71 (December 1977), pp. 1532–43. See app. A, note 12 for discussion of why George Goodwin's breakdown of committees was used.

9. Randall B. Ripley and Grace A. Franklin, *Congress, the Bureaucracy, and Public Policy*, 4th ed. (Dorsey, 1987), pp. 246–48.

10. According to Randall B. Ripley and Grace A. Franklin, "oversight does not come naturally or easily to Congress, and there is no reason to expect that it ever will." See Ripley and Franklin, *Congress, the Bureaucracy, and Public Policy*, p. 225.

11. Strategic foreign and defense issues are also unlikely targets for oversight, but, as Ripley and Franklin point out, ordinary subgovernmental relations, which involve congressional subcommittees, tend often to occur in the strategic and defense areas because of Congress's tendency to redefine defense and foreign policy issues into "structured" ones involving procuring and deploying military personnel and matériel. See *Congress, the Bureaucracy, and Public Policy*, pp. 238–45, especially pp. 244–45 on the comparison between the tendencies for subgovernments to play a role in the redistributive and foreign and defense policy arenas. Note also that redistributive programs

are more often run by formulas than other programs, and therefore there is less discretionary bureaucratic behavior to examine.

12. See George Goodwin, Jr., *The Little Legislatures: Committees of Congress* (University of Massachusetts, 1970), pp. 102–03 for a guide to the assignment of committees by policy arena. Committees covering more than one arena were assigned to each.

13. The average correlation coefficients for the nine cross-sections (years) were 0.01 and 0.06 for distributive and regulatory units, respectively, and −0.09 for redistributive committees.

14. See the Bolling Committee proposal to create oversight subcommittees on House committees for a good example of reformers' views. *Committee Reform Amendments of 1974*, H. Rept. 93-916, 93 Cong. 2 sess. (GPO, 1974), pt. 2, pp. 63–65.

15. For an exposition of these points, see Seymour Scher, "Conditions for Legislative Control," *Journal of Politics*, vol. 25 (August 1963), pp. 526–51; and Morris S. Ogul, *Congress Oversees the Bureaucracy: Studies in Legislative Supervision* (University of Pittsburgh Press, 1976).

16. Fred Kaiser makes the related argument that a "restricted legislative jurisdiction" encourages oversight since there is little else to do. Fred Kaiser, "Oversight of Foreign Policy: The U.S. House Committee on International Relations," *Legislative Studies Quarterly*, vol. 2 (August 1977), p. 261.

17. See Kaiser, "Oversight of Foreign Policy," p. 259; John F. Bibby, "Committee Characteristics and Legislative Oversight of Administration," *Midwest Journal of Political Science*, vol. 10 (February 1966), pp. 84–87; and Ogul, *Congress Oversees*, p. 15.

18. Bibby, "Committee Characteristics," p. 97.

19. Ogul, *Congress Oversees*, p. 15.

20. Ogul, *Congress Oversees*, p. 15.

21. Ogul, *Congress Oversees*, pp. 14–15.

22. For a review of the relevant literature, see Susan Webb Hammond, "Legislative Staffs," *Legislative Studies Quarterly*, vol. 9 (May 1984), pp. 271–317.

23. See Norman J. Ornstein, Thomas E. Mann, and Michael J. Malbin, *Vital Statistics on Congress, 1987–1988* (Washington: Congressional Quarterly, 1987), chap. 5, especially pp. 146–49.

24. Ogul, *Congress Oversees*, p. 13.

25. In the first fifty Congresses (1789 to 1889), different parties controlled the presidency and either house of Congress only eleven times (22 percent). The comparable figures for the next fifty Congresses (1889–1989) is 17 (34 percent). Since 1961 this situation has occurred eight times out of fourteen, that is, 57 percent of the time.

26. Joel D. Aberbach, "Changes in Congressional Oversight," in Carol H. Weiss and Alan H. Barton, eds., *Making Bureaucracies Work* (Beverly Hills, Calif.: Sage, 1980), pp. 67–68.

27. Ogul, *Congress Oversees*, p. 18.

28. See, for example, Ogul, *Congress Oversees*, pp. 19–22; and Scher, "Conditions," pp. 526–51.

29. Correlations using Americans for Democratic Action (ADA) scores are weak in magnitude and inconsistent. See *Congressional Quarterly Almanac* (Washington: Congressional Quarterly, various years).

30. The percentage figure, incidentally, is derived by taking the antilog of the coefficient, subtracting one from it, and multiplying the results time 100. The antilog of 0.233 is 1.262. That figure minus 1 equals 0.262, which yields 26.2 when multiplied by 100.

31. Both of these figures delete the Senate Judiciary Committee totals to conform to the data in the regressions, although the effects of the deletions are trivial. With all committees included, the means are 55.4 in 1961–71 and 82.4 in 1977.

32. The zero-order coefficients are 0.008 in 1961–71, 0.014 in 1973, 0.015 in 1975, and 0.016 in 1977.

33. See the discussion in appendix A.

34. A nonoversight unit is one whose named function is not oversight, department operations, government operations, or the like.

35. The mean percentage for 1961–71 is 17.4. The percentages for 1973, 1975, and 1977 are 31.5, 44.3, and 57.7, respectively. The percentages are based on the activities of all committees except Appropriations, Rules, and Administration.

36. Data for the full year available for 1977 show that this finding is not an artifact of the fact that data for only the first six months of the year are used in these calculations. For the full-year data, the 1977 difference is a tiny 9.8 percent.

37. See Everett M. Rogers, *Diffusion of Innovations*, 3d ed. (Free Press, 1983); and Jack L. Walker, "The Diffusion of Innovations among the American States," *American Political Science Review*, vol. 68 (September 1969), pp. 880–99.

38. The survey of top staffers was not designed with the diffusion model in mind, but data from it do suggest that some variant of the model might be fruitful. Most top staffers (95 percent) reported "keeping up" to some extent with the oversight activities of their counterpart units in the other chamber, and 57 percent reported keeping up at least sometimes with oversight activities of the Government Operations/Governmental Affairs Committees.

39. Tests indicate no multicollinearity problems with the predictor variables used in the regression reported in table 3-1. See appendix C.

40. John W. Kingdon, *Agendas, Alternatives, and Public Policies* (Little, Brown, 1984), p. 93. See also Michael D. Cohen, James G. March, and Johan P. Olsen, "A Garbage Can Model of Organizational Choice," *Administrative Science Quarterly*, vol. 17 (March 1972), pp. 1–25; and Rogers, *Diffusion*, pp. 362–63.

41. The 1981 figure was up a bit but was still less than 2.0 percent (1.8 percent). This figure stayed the same (1.8 percent) in 1983.

42. See chap. 2, table 2-1, for the data.

43. See David W. Rohde, "Committee Reform in the House of Representatives and the Subcommittee Bill of Rights," *Annals of the American Academy of Political and Social Sciences*, vol. 411 (January 1974), pp. 39–47.

44. Norman J. Ornstein, "The House and the Senate in a New Congress," in Thomas E. Mann and Norman J. Ornstein, eds., *The New Congress* (Washington: American Enterprise Institute for Public Policy Research, 1981), p. 378.

45. See Roger H. Davidson, "Subcommittee Government: New Channels for Policy Making," in Mann and Ornstein, eds., *The New Congress*, pp. 103–04.

46. Davidson, "Subcommittee Government," p. 107.

47. The coefficient for the decentralization variable was actually .00 in the 1971 cross-sectional multiple regression. It went up to .018 in the 1973 cross-sectional multiple regression.

48. Davidson, "Subcommittee Government," p. 117.

49. The zero-order coefficients for the log of oversight days regressed on committee decentralization also increased. They are as follows: 1961–71 = 0.010; 1972 = 0.018; 1975 = 0.025; and 1977 = 0.021.

50. See, for example, James L. Sundquist, *The Decline and Resurgence of Congress* (Brookings, 1981), p. 394.

51. They are 0.25 and 0.33 for the House and Senate, respectively, for 1961–71. The average correlation coefficients for 1973, 1975, and 1977 are 0.63 for both the House and the Senate.

52. The coding was done after the analyses, reported in chaps. 2 and 3, were completed.

53. Data for subsequent years of the Reagan administration—1985 and 1987—are now being coded and will be reported when ready. I do not expect these data to change significantly the conclusions reached here.

54. Hearings and meetings held by Appropriations, Rules, Administration, and joint committees were excluded.

55. See chap. 2 of this book; and Ornstein and others, *Vital Statistics*, pp. 165–67.

56. The variables were the same as those listed in table 3-1 except, of course, for split partisan control, which was deleted. The Senate Armed Services Committee was deleted for 1981.

57. This approach was suggested to me by John Chamberlin of the Institute of Public Policy Studies at the University of Michigan.

58. See appendix C for a brief discussion of year adjustments. The year 1977 was the base year for the tests when data were pooled for 1977, 1981, and 1983. The Senate Armed Services Committee was deleted for 1981. The years 1981 and 1983 were coded as years of split partisan control (regression coefficient 0.054; $p < 0.14$).

59. P was 0.77 or greater for all other coefficients.

60. In the pooled model of data from 1961 to 1977 reported earlier in the chapter, committees with heavy concentration of redistributive policy issues

in their jurisdictions averaged 32.7 percent fewer days of oversight than other committees. That figure dropped to 8.8 percent fewer in 1981. In 1983 it went to 73.9 percent *more* days of oversight, certainly causing one to question the notion that redistributive committees in Congress will always be relatively quiescent about oversight.

61. R^2 for the revised model (including the redistributive policy year adjustment), incidentally, equals 0.69.

62. Coefficients of variability of the committee oversight activity were 0.374 in 1977, 0.450 in 1981, and 0.407 in 1983. See table 3-5 for other years and a fuller explanation.

63. The pooled coefficient for 1977–83 was 0.015. The year estimate for 1977 was 0.018. See table 3-1.

64. Holding total days and decentralization constant, the average Senate committee was 24.9 percent more active than the average House committee in 1977. (See table 3-3.) The comparable figures for 1981 and 1983 were 12.6 and 48.1 percent, respectively.

Notes to Chapter Four

1. See chap. 1, especially the reference to Max Weber, "Bureaucracy," in H. H. Gerth and C. Wright Mills, eds. and trans., *From Max Weber: Essays in Sociology* (New York: Oxford University Press, 1958), pp. 196–244.

2. Fifty-three percent of a 1971 sample of the House of Representatives were lawyers. See Joel D. Aberbach and Bert A. Rockman, "The Overlapping Worlds of American Federal Executives and Congressmen," *British Journal of Political Science*, vol. 7 (January 1977), p. 30.

3. For an extended discussion of expertise on the Appropriations Committee in the pre-reform Congress, see Richard F. Fenno, Jr., *The Power of the Purse: Appropriations Politics in Congress* (Little, Brown, 1966). For data on the declining length of service prior to achieving a subcommittee chairmanship, see Steven S. Smith and Christopher J. Deering, *Committees in Congress* (Washington: Congressional Quarterly, 1984), pp. 191–93. The same set of reforms that increased the prospects that less experienced members would receive a subcommittee chairmanship also seem to give members an incentive to remain with their initial committee (although not necessarily subcommittee) assignment. If so, notions of a great diminution of committee member expertise are exaggerated. See Gary W. Copeland, "Committee Mobility and the Revised Seniority Rule," paper prepared for the 1984 annual meeting of the American Political Science Association.

4. See appendix A for details on the interviews with top committee staffers. For descriptions of the earlier study, see Aberbach and Rockman, "Overlapping Worlds," pp. 23–47; Joel D. Aberbach, James D. Chesney, and Bert A. Rockman, "Exploring Elite Political Attitudes: Some Methodological Lessons," *Political Methodology*, vol. 2, no. 1 (1975), pp. 1–28; and Joel D. Aberbach, Robert D. Putnam, and Bert A. Rockman, *Bureaucrats and Politicians*

in Western Democracies (Harvard University Press, 1981). All of the top career and noncareer executives interviewed from the following agencies were included in the subsample analyzed in this chapter. The numbers are as follows: Department of Commerce (N = 11); Department of Health, Education, and Welfare (N = 21); Department of Labor (N = 10); Department of Treasury (N = 5); General Services Administration (N = 8); Office of Economic Opportunity (N = 4); Federal Communications Commission (N = 2); Federal Trade Commission (N = 3); Interstate Commerce Commission (N = 4); and the Securities Exchange Commission (N = 1). Total N = 69; Top Career = 44; Top Noncareer = 25. My thanks to Professor Bert A. Rockman of the University of Pittsburgh for help in constructing the subsample.

5. The administrative personnel came from the ranks of top career civil service executives (GS-16–18s at the top of their administrative hierarchies) and top political (executive level) appointees. From this framework one gets an indication of how top congressional staff compare with the two major sets of actors in their administrative environment.

6. The top Senate staffers, who were younger than House staffers, also had a slightly larger proportion of females. Seventeen percent of the Senate staffers were female contrasted to 12 percent in the House. Eighty-four percent of the top congressional staffers interviewed had been to graduate school, and 75 percent earned at least one graduate degree.

7. Eighty percent of the subsample of top career civil servants attended graduate school, and 73 percent had at least one graduate degree. Seventy-six percent of the politically appointed executives in the subsample attended graduate school, and 56 percent had at least one graduate degree.

8. Twenty-one percent of the top congressional staffers did their undergraduate work at Ivy League or other prestigious private institutions. The comparable percentages for the top noncareer and career executives in the subsample are 33 percent and 21 percent, respectively. See Aberbach and Rockman, "Overlapping Worlds," p. 29, table 2B, for the sources and method used to classify institutions.

9. These percentages are based on the total Ns, that is, those who have no postgraduate training were included.

10. Aberbach, Putnam, and Rockman, *Bureaucrats and Politicians*, p. 67.

11. Within a year of the original interview, 22 percent of the top staffers had already left Congress. And this was before the change in party control in the Senate, which occurred in 1981. Close examination of the data also shows that the average top staffer has worked for his or her employing committee (in any capacity, either for a subcommittee or the full committee) for 7.1 years and in his or her current position as top staffer for just over 4.7 of these years. In fact, 65 percent of the top staffers started work for the committee employing them at the time of the study in their current position as top staffer in the unit.

12. Noncareer people in office in 1971—a bit more than two years into a new administration—were, of course, predominantly inexperienced in the agency.

13. The lower tenure of Senate staffers in my data is not a function of the 1978 Senate reorganization since it was a fact well before reorganization took place. See Harrison W. Fox, Jr., and Susan Webb Hammond, *Congressional Staffs: The Invisible Force in American Lawmaking* (Free Press, 1977), p. 61.

14. For details on these data, see Joel D. Aberbach, "The Congressional Committee Intelligence System: Information, Oversight, and Change," *Congress and the Presidency*, vol. 14 (Spring 1987), p. 56, table 3.

15. Just about 32 percent of top Senate staffers had formal education in a specialized area covered by their committee unit's jurisdiction. The same is true of 23 percent of top House staffers. Many staffers, of course, had both formal training and work experience in a relevant field. Therefore, the results described in the text are less than the sum of the two figures. House Government Operations and Senate Governmental Affairs staffers were not counted as having experience in the areas covered by their units' jurisdiction if they studied general public administration or government. See Aberbach, "Congressional Committee," p. 56, table 3.

16. Even the most specialized congressional committee units usually cover more than one agency and almost always more than one bureau.

17. Committee level staffers were asked about areas in the committee's jurisdiction; subcommittee staffers about officials in the subcommittee's jurisdiction.

18. Oversight unit staffers report fewer contacts, which accounts for the difference.

19. Aberbach, Putnam, and Rockman, *Bureaucrats and Politicians*, pp. 233–36.

20. Bravado, more than fact, may also account for the reported differences, with Senate staffers claiming to be in charge, but other data reported in the next section of this chapter buttress the inference in the text.

21. Forty-one percent report their contacts are mainly with the same individuals; 43 percent say that ad hoc contacts are their main sources, and the rest said the pattern is too mixed to characterize in this manner. These data are based on answers to the following question asked only of those who reported relevant lower-level contacts in the bureaucracy: "Are these mainly contacts with the same individuals or ad hoc contacts?"

22. Only about 7 percent say that noncooperation for this reason happens often, while 39 percent say that it never happens, and 21 percent say it is rare. This conclusion is based on answers to the following question: "Have you often, sometimes, rarely, or never found agency staff unwilling to cooperate with you due to fear of reprisal by others in the agency?"

23. Aberbach, Putnam, and Rockman, *Bureaucrats and Politicians*, pp. 234–35.

24. Aberbach, Putnam, and Rockman, *Bureaucrats and Politicians*, p. 235.

25. No ways of keeping track were suggested to respondents by the interviewer. All ways of tracking in the coded answers, therefore, were volunteered by the respondents.

26. Multiple responses in a category were counted only once in the table.

27. Note that these are agency sources giving information outside of the hearing room. Information from agency and other sources attributed to hearings is coded under the hearings heading in the table.

28. Agency sources together were cited as sources of information by 73 percent of the respondents, a figure smaller than the sum of 56 and 35 because there is some overlap between the categories where respondents mentioned both complaints and information.

29. Interviews, April 23, 1979; February 14, 1979; and December 12, 1978.

30. The figure is smaller than the sum of the entries because of overlap between the two.

31. "Other government sources" in any form were mentioned by 25 percent of the top staffers. Obviously, there was very little overlap between the complaints and information categories.

32. In answer to a question, "How often, if at all, do you attend public meetings or conventions of professional or interest groups specializing in the area of the [sub]committee's interest?" 37 percent of the top committee staffers said often (defined as five or more times a year for those giving numerical answers) and only 3 percent said never.

33. These are the percentages of the total sample who reported using complaints or criticisms of any type to track what goes on in agencies or programs.

34. House oversight units are the big mass media users—73 percent of House oversight units use the mass media for keeping track compared with 21 percent of nonoversight House units, which use the mass media.

35. Coders were asked to do the following: "Code how well developed an information network R's [sub]committee seems to have for keeping track of what's going on in the programs or agencies under its jurisdiction." The "[sub]committee" construction was used to signal the coder to code R's unit as appropriate.

36. There was also a code for "can't tell"—which was appropriate for five Senate staffers—where the quality of the recorded responses was insufficient to allow a reliable assignment of a score.

37. Committees other than Appropriations and specialized oversight units do not stand out.

38. The finding conforms to the expectation one would draw from the literature. See Fenno, *Power of the Purse,* especially pp. 321–24.

39. Fifty-three percent of the oversight unit respondents report using the mass media to keep track of agency and programs, compared with 26 percent of nonoversight respondents.

40. The correlation is negative because the high end of the information development measure is scored 1 (well-developed network) and the low end (poorly developed network) is scored 5.

41. The correlation (r) between number of sources (running from two to seven) and a dummy variable for oversight unit (O = oversight unit,

1 = nonoversight unit) is +0.12. The sign is the reverse of what one would expect if oversight units had fewer contacts.

42. Slightly over 2 percent of the top staffers mentioned "squeaky wheel" as their unit's major approach.

43. See the "Implications" section for a full discussion of the "fire-alarm" style, which is reactive in nature. The analysis referred to in the text is presented in Mathew D. McCubbins and Thomas Schwartz, "Congressional Oversight Overlooked: Police Patrols and Fire Alarms," *American Journal of Political Science*, vol. 28 (February 1984), pp. 165–79.

44. For a detailed analysis of the relationships between the various measures of contacts with officials and the information network development and tracking approach measures, see Joel D. Aberbach, "The Congressional Committee Intelligence System," paper prepared for the 1985 annual meeting of the American Political Science Association.

45. See table 11 in my 1985 APSA paper, "Congressional Committee," from which these figures can be derived. They are based on "total" percentages.

46. John F. Bibby, "Congress' Neglected Function," in Melvin R. Laird, ed., *The Republican Papers* (Anchor, 1968), pp. 477–88.

47. McCubbins and Schwartz, "Congressional Oversight," p. 165.

48. McCubbins and Schwartz, "Congressional Oversight," p. 166.

49. McCubbins and Schwartz, "Congressional Oversight," p 166. Police-patrol oversight is described in full as follows: "Analogous to the use of real police patrols, police-patrol oversight is comparatively centralized, active, and direct: at its own initiative, Congress examines a sample of executive-agency activities, with the aim of detecting and remedying any violations of legislative goals and, by its surveillance, discouraging such violations."

50. McCubbins and Schwartz, "Congressional Oversight," p. 166.

51. McCubbins and Schwartz, "Congressional Oversight," pp. 167–68. As should be evident, the McCubbins and Schwartz model owes much to the work of contemporary organization theorists, in particular James March and his colleagues. The fire-department concept (analogous to the fire-alarm notion by McCubbins and Schwartz) was, to the best of my knowledge, first developed in Richard M. Cyert and James G. March, eds., *A Behavioral Theory of the Firm* (Prentice Hall, 1963), p. 119. The notion of "problemistic search" that Cyert and March develop is similar to the ideas developed by McCubbins and Schwartz to describe the police-patrol strategy, although problemistic search has elements of the fire-alarm strategy since it may be motivated by a problem that is brought to the organization's attention.

52. McCubbins and Schwartz, "Congressional Oversight," p. 171.

53. McCubbins and Schwartz, "Congressional Oversight," p. 172.

54. McCubbins and Schwartz, "Congressional Oversight," p. 172, try to answer such criticisms.

55. McCubbins and Schwartz, "Congressional Oversight," p. 171.

56. McCubbins and Schwartz, "Congressional Oversight," p. 166. See also p. 176 where the same distinction is stressed.

57. An additional, and related, reason for active search can be understood in terms of the "garbage can model of organizational choice" developed by James March and colleagues (Michael Cohen and Johan Olsen in the garbage can case). The garbage can model is an amendment to their original formulation, which conceived of organizations' search as stimulated by problems and terminated by satisfactory (but nonoptimal) solutions. In the garbage can conception, however, solutions look for problems to which the solutions can be answers. "Search is a form of mating, and the level of discovery through search depends not only on the activity of problems looking for solutions but also on solutions looking for problems." James G. March, "Decisions in Organizations and Theories of Choice," in Andrew M. Van de Ven and William F. Joyce, eds., *Perspectives on Organization, Design and Behavior* (Wiley, 1981), p. 213. One example of a "garbage can"-like stimulus to active search may well be the decentralization of Congress in the 1970s. Designed to democratize the Congress (solve the problems of participation and nonrepresentativeness), decentralization fostered the creation of more autonomous decision units (the solution) with an incentive to find problems to address (hence more active search). Many other factors encouraging active search, such as the elaboration of staff resources, can be thought of in the same way.

58. The fourth point, that the concept of police-patrol oversight may confuse two elements best left separate, was discussed at length in the text when it was raised and will not be recapitulated here.

59. Recall that the two variables are coded in opposite directions so that a negative coefficient indicates a positive relationship.

60. See Morris P. Fiorina, *Congress: Keystone of the Washington Establishment* (Yale University Press, 1977), particularly pp. 48–49, for a concise argument making this point.

61. McCubbins and Schwartz, "Congressional Oversight," p. 166.

62. See Max Weber, "Bureaucracy," pp 196–244, especially section 12, pp. 232–35, on "The Power Position of Bureaucracy." I wish to thank Charles Nixon of the Department of Political Science at UCLA for emphasizing to me the import of secrecy in Weber's treatment of this problem.

63. Weber, "Bureaucracy," p. 232.

64. See, for example, Seymour Scher, "Conditions," pp. 526–51; Bibby, "Congress' Neglected Function," pp. 477–88; Morris S. Ogul, *Congress Oversees the Bureaucracy: Studies in Legislative Supervision* (University of Pittsburgh Press, 1976); and McCubbins and Schwartz, "Congressional Oversight," pp. 165–79.

Notes to Chapter Five

1. See John W. Kingdon, *Agendas, Alternatives, and Public Policies* (Little, Brown, 1984), p. 4, for a discussion of what he calls the " *decision* agenda, or the list of subjects within the governmental agenda [those subjects getting attention] that are up for active decision."

2. For academic literature cataloging these factors, see Seymour Scher, "Conditions for Legislative Control," *Journal of Politics*, vol. 25 (August 1963), pp. 526–55; Morris S. Ogul, *Congress Oversees the Bureaucracy: Studies in Legislative Supervision* (University of Pittsburgh Press, 1976); and Joel D. Aberbach, "Changes in Congressional Oversight," in Carol H. Weiss and Allen H. Barton, eds., *Making Bureaucracies Work* (Sage, 1980), pp. 65–87.

3. The wording of the question staffers were asked is in the text under "Choosing Agencies or Programs for Oversight." The full wording of the individual items is listed in table 5-1.

4. The exact wording of the question members were asked was, "What were the major factors leading the [sub]committee to select the agencies and programs you concentrated on in your oversight work in the 95th Congress?"

5. Interview, June 18, 1979.

6. Interview, December 7, 1979.

7. Interview, June 5, 1979.

8. Interview, July 17, 1979.

9. Interview, May 10, 1979.

10. Interview, 1979.

11. Interview, December 4, 1979.

12. Interview, August 28, 1979.

13. Data are reported only for cases in which respondents completed cards for both members and staff.

14. See table 5-2 and the related discussion.

15. Committee staffers, while well attuned to committee members' needs, were least likely to know about casework problems, which are usually handled through district or personal offices. Staffers were also less likely to be influenced by publicity potential, especially of the general type implied by the question.

16. See the appropriate footnote to table 5-2 for a list of the verbal descriptions attached to each point on the scale.

17. See the definition in *Webster's New World Dictionary*, 2d college ed. (Simon and Schuster, 1980), p. 705.

18. See Ogul, *Congress Oversees*, p. 22. These are the core "conversion factors" Ogul identifies, those that "define the most common situations in which propensities [to oversee] are converted to behavior. They seem to account most directly and immediately for specific oversight efforts."

19. Ogul develops a model in which a series of "opportunity factors"— "conditioning factors making oversight more likely"—"enhance or lessen the potential for oversight" and are converted into behavior in the presence of the "conversion factors" mentioned in the text and defined in note 18. Ogul, *Congress Oversees*, p. 11–23. The model is difficult to apply operationally because the conversion and opportunity factors are not always easy to separate—for example, "member priorities," one of the opportunity factors that Ogul identifies, are intricately linked to, if not inseparable from, the conversion factors, especially if one adopts Ogul's view that members give priorities to oversight based on its expected political payoff. Using my data,

I tested a version of the Ogul model. My results indicate that the model does not hold up, and therefore I do not treat the conversion factors as unique intervening variables in the manner required by Ogul's model.

20. See David R. Mayhew, *Congress: The Electoral Connection* (Yale University Press, 1974), for a stark presentation of this perspective on the motivations of congressional behavior.

21. The basic assumption of the work done by Ogul and by Seymour Scher, on whom he relied, is that the potential for oversight is enhanced when some circumstance exists such that it yields greater payoffs for a senator's or representative's electoral and legislative position than alternative uses of his time. See Scher, "Conditions," pp. 528–29; and Ogul, *Congress Oversees*, pp. 19–21.

22. See, for example, Richard F. Fenno, Jr., *The Power of the Purse* (Little, Brown, 1966); and Aaron Wildavsky, *The Politics of the Budgetary Process* (Little, Brown, 1964).

23. The average correlation (r) between scores for the individual factors is 0.65. Even those with significant differences in means have an average correlation (r) of 0.61.

Note that the appropriate difference of means test for paired data is a paired t-test. Top staffers' ratings of their own and member importance scores were treated as paired data, and the means and significance levels reported are based on paired t-tests. (Incidentally, when I used "ordinary" difference of means tests with larger but uneven numbers of cases, the results did not change.)

24. The reader will note that the numbers of cases are higher in table 5-3 than in table 5-2. This occurs because only staff data are included in table 5-3, while the analysis in table 5-2 (and 5-1) required that the top staffer have completed assessments for both members and staff.

25. The main importance scores sensitive to committee unit type are scandal, especially important to the oversight units, and reauthorization, especially unimportant to the oversight units. Since the House has more oversight units, removing oversight units from the sample increases the rank correlation between the mean scores slightly to (R_s) 0.953.

26. The committees in the two chambers were not treated as matched pairs because they operate as quasi-independent entities, each with its own members and chair, and most with imperfectly matched jurisdictions.

27. The findings on chamber differences using the importance scores that staffers ascribe to members are essentially the same as those just described in the text, although there are a few differences. The rank correlation (R_s) for members between the scores by chamber is a very robust 0.819, and a pooled difference of means test shows no significant difference. Significant differences in individual means are, however, present between scores for malfeasance (scandal) and publicity. In both cases, the factor is more important to senators than to representatives. This is especially true for publicity (difference $= 0.74$, $p = 0.01$).

28. Hayward R. Alker, Jr., and Bruce M. Russett, *World Politics in the*

General Assembly (Yale University Press, 1965), p. xxii. For recent treatments on the use of factor analysis, see Jae-On Kim and Charles W. Mueller, *Introduction to Factor Analysis: What It Is and How To Do It* (Sage Publications, 1978) and Jae-On Kim and Charles W. Mueller, *Factor Analysis: Statistical Methods and Practical Issues* (Sage Publications, 1978). To prevent confusion, from now on I will refer to the individual variables as measures, indicators, and the like, rather than as factors. The term "factor" will be reserved for the products of the factor analysis itself.

29. Factor analyses done adding scandal (malfeasance) alone to the matrix or scandal and reauthorization do not yield appreciably different results, although the numbers of cases are lower. Dropping the policy crisis variable, which is the second most skewed (skewness 1.562), yields results similar to those reported in table 5-4, with, of course, the policy crisis factor eliminated.

30. The Midas program package developed at the University of Michigan was used for the analysis. Principal component factors with eigen-values (amount of variance explained) greater than one (that is, when a factor explained more than the variance contained in one importance item) were rotated. For full documentation, see Daniel J. Fox and Kenneth E. Guire, *Documentation for Midas* (University of Michigan: Statistical Research Laboratory, 1976), pp. 105–06, 141–42.

31. Interview, June 26, 1979.

32. See, for example, Barry R. Weingast and Mark J. Moran, "Bureaucratic Discretion or Congressional Control? Regulatory Policymaking by the Federal Trade Commission," *Journal of Political Economy*, vol. 91 (October 1983), pp. 765–800.

33. Aberbach, "Changes," pp. 68–69.

34. The desire to assist an agency or program favored by the committee does not necessarily take place in an atmosphere of unalloyed mutual admiration between Congress and agency administrators. Note that the "low regard" item loads at the 0.3 level on the factor. To cite a more specific example, in a case study on oversight of the Rehabilitation Services Administration (RSA) that I did as background for this book, the subcommittees involved had close ties to the career administrators in the program, but they had low regard for the political appointees above RSA and ambivalent relations with the civil servant serving in an acting capacity as program chief.

35. See Ogul, *Congress Oversees*; and Scher, "Conditions."

36. To quote the pithy conclusion of one of the more experienced House staffers on members' often frustrated aspirations for publicity through oversight, "They live in hope."

37. Stephen Hess, *The Washington Reporters* (Brookings, 1981), pp. 101–02; see also Stephen Hess, *The Ultimate Insiders: U.S. Senators in the National Media* (Brookings, 1982), p. 90.

38. See chap. 8, which makes the argument on political context in detail.

39. See Herbert Kaufman, *The Administrative Behavior of Federal Bureau Chiefs* (Brookings, 1981), for examples of the tremendous attention federal

bureau chiefs give to the nurturing of Congress and to the demands of its personnel.

40. In addition, programs reach the oversight agenda when they are up for reauthorization (see table 5-3). The legislative schedule thus is important in determining whether or not an agency or program is selected for oversight. For more detailed information, see chap. 7 and the data on annual authorizations in Norman J. Ornstein and others, *Vital Statistics on Congress, 1982* (Washington: American Enterprise Institute for Public Policy Research, 1982), p. 151.

41. See, for example, the discussion of staff influence in Steven S. Smith and Christopher J. Deering, *Committees in Congress* (Washington: Congressional Quarterly, 1984), especially p. 219, where they note, "Staff are . . . an important causal agent in congressional and committee politics. [And quoting a senior Representative:] 'We see the committee staffs determining priorities,' says House Republican James M. Collins of Texas. 'We must put an end to this growth [of staff] and return policymaking to the elected membership.'"

See also the concerns of Malbin on this issue, particularly in Michael J. Malbin, "Congressional Committee Staffs: Who's in Charge Here?" *The Public Interest*, vol. 47 (Spring 1977), pp. 16–40; and Michael J. Malbin, *Unelected Representatives: Congressional Staff and the Future of Representative Government* (Basic Books, 1980).

42. Committee and subcommittee chairs are, of course, the people who in most cases hire top staffers and always have the option of removing them. See Robert H. Salisbury and Kenneth A. Shepsle, "Congressional Staff Turnover and the Ties-That-Bind," *American Political Science Review*, vol. 75 (June 1981), pp. 381–96, especially pp. 383–84, 389–90.

Naturally enough, full committee top staffers were more likely to see committee chairs as most influential than were subcommittee top staff, and subcommittee top staffers were more likely to mention subcommittee chairs.

43. For the committee or subcommittee chairs (twenty-nine of the seventy-five members interviewed), the question "Who has the major influence in deciding which agencies or program areas to oversee?" was introduced by the phrase "aside from yourself." This was done in part to make the question more comfortable for the chairs (who might find nominating themselves slightly embarrassing, although I should have guessed that their monumental egos made embarrassment unlikely), but mainly to prevent the interviewer from appearing grossly unfamiliar with the committee unit's mode of operation.

44. While the phrasing of the question discouraged unit chairs from nominating themselves, seven of the twenty-four who were asked the question said that they were by far the most important.

45. Even more suggestive is the fact that when only unit chairs are considered, the percentages are 43 percent in the Senate and only 16 percent in the House.

46. Interview, July 17, 1979.

47. After the question about major influence in oversight agenda setting, respondents were asked (if staff were not named as the figures with major influence), "What role do the [unit] staff play in choosing oversight topics?"

48. There are no chamber differences.

49. Interview, June 2, 1980.

50. Among the majority and minority staffers, for example, only 3 percent of the majority staffers and 8 percent of the minority staffers ascribed major influence in oversight agenda setting to the ranking members of their units. The minority staffers, then, are a bit more likely to ascribe major influence to their principals but only a bit. See note 52 for data on members.

51. The figures for members are remarkably consistent with those for the staff. Eighty-four percent of the Democratic representatives and senators gave answers in the yes range to the agreement question, that is, they reported general agreement in their committee units about what the units should oversee, and 63 percent of the Republicans gave similar responses. Incidentally, chamber differences are as expected but not very substantial. Among the top staffers (where the number of cases is large enough for reliable statistics), Senate staffers are more likely to report agreement (76 percent say yes without qualification) than House staffers (57 percent say yes).

52. When asked about the role played by the ranking minority member of their subcommittee in choosing oversight topics, only 20 percent of the minority subcommittee staffers in the matched sample felt that the ranking minority member of their unit played no role or an unimportant role.

53. These data are from the matched minority sample of top staffers. The comparable data for the matched majority are 71 percent who say the minority members are consulted, and 10 percent who say that the minority members are not consulted, but can get items on the oversight agenda if they want to.

54. Malbin, *Unelected*, p. 4. For other noteworthy treatments of the role of staff, see Susan Webb Hammond, "Legislative Staffs," *Legislative Studies Quarterly*, vol. 9 (May 1984), pp. 271–317; Salisbury and Shepsle, "Congressional Staff Turnover," pp. 381–96; and, especially, David E. Price, "Professionals and 'Entrepreneurs': Staff Orientations and Policy Making on Three Senate Committees," *Journal of Politics*, vol. 36 (May 1971), pp. 316–36. For a study of staff concluding that "chairs are in far better control of the policy outcomes of their subcommittees than the critics would have us believe," see Christine De Gregorio, "Professionals in the U.S. Congress: An Analysis of Working Styles," *Legislative Studies Quarterly*, vol. 13 (November 1988), p. 473.

55. Malbin, *Unelected*, p. 243.

56. These data are derived from answers to the question "How do you convince the members that some oversight effort you think is important ought to be pursued?"

57. Interview, January 24, 1979.

58. Interview, April 6, 1981.

59. For a review of the principal-agent literature and of its strengths and

weaknesses in application to problems in the American political arena, see Terry M. Moe, "The New Economics of Organization," *American Journal of Political Science*, vol. 28 (November 1984), pp. 739–77. Moe pays special attention to the problems in applying formal principal-agent theory to the question "How Can Politicians Control Bureaucrats?" pp. 765–72.

Notes to Chapter Six

1. See Morris Ogul, *Congress Oversees the Bureaucracy: Studies in Legislative Supervision* (University of Pittsburgh Press, 1976), chap. 6, especially p. 153.

2. Before respondents were given the list of oversight techniques, they were read this statement: "A wide variety of techniques is used for oversight. We'd like to get some idea about the advantages and disadvantages of various techniques you may use in conducting oversight." Respondents were then given a card for rating the 14 techniques listed verbatim in table 6-1, prefaced as follows: "The following is a list of oversight techniques used by congressional committees in overseeing the programs and agencies of the government. Please indicate, by checking the appropriate blanks, how frequently the ____ [sub]committee used each technique in the 95th congress and how effective you judged each to have been."

3. Empirically, however, of those committees having any (that is, one or more) of their programs on periodic reauthorization schedules, the overwhelming majority (90.7 percent) reported that they spent much time on oversight when considering the case for reauthorization. Only 3 percent reported spending most of the time in hearings considering the case for adding new programs. The fact that our survey measure gauges frequency of use of a technique for oversight (and not for other purposes) does not affect the measurement validity check discussed in appendix D because there the actual primary-purpose oversight hearings coded from the *Daily Digest* are checked against the item on the card focused also on primary-purpose oversight hearings. These hearings may not involve systematic oversight of the type evaluation experts generally prefer, and they may have subtle purposes beyond oversight, but they do focus on oversight by definition and in fact.

4. No respondent checked a box lower than 3 (occasionally) for staff communication, the only variable with this characteristic. The standard deviation is 0.472. The next lowest standard deviation is 0.729 on program evaluations done by the agencies.

5. Members' time, a scarcer resource, is the ninth most frequently used technique with a mean of 2.802.

6. GAO (General Accounting Office) evaluations are most frequently used, followed by CRS (Congressional Research Service) evaluations. CBO (Congressional Budget Office) and OTA (Office of Technology Assessment) studies are rarely used, the top staffers report.

7. William J. Keefe and Morris S. Ogul, *The American Legislative Process: Congress and the States* (Prentice Hall, 1985), pp. 182–83.

8. Ogul, *Congress Oversees*, p. 159.

9. See Herbert Kaufman, *The Administrative Behavior of Federal Bureau Chiefs* (Brookings, 1981).

10. See appendix A for an account of the Brookings roundtable.

11. See chap. 9 for additional evidence on this point.

12. See note 3.

13. Based on internal Congressional Budget Office memos. See also Allen Schick, "Budgeting," in Norman J. Ornstein and others, *Vital Statistics on Congress, 1982* (Washington: American Enterprise Institute for Public Policy Research, 1982), p. 144. Schick mentions "a trend toward temporary authorizations; moreover, annual authorizations . . . now constitute almost 20 percent of the total budget authority . . . acted on by Congress each year."

14. See chap. 2 for evidence.

15. Clark Norton, the CRS expert on the subject, defines the "legislative or congressional veto" as "laws authorizing either or both Houses of Congress, and sometimes merely congressional committees, to approve or disapprove executive proposals in advance of their implementation." See Clark F. Norton, "Congressional Veto Legislation in the 96th Congress: Proposals and Enactments," Report 82-26-G (Washington, Congressional Research Service, February 1982), p. 1.

16. The pioneer act in this area was P. L. 72-212, which became law in 1932. See Clark F. Norton, "Congressional Review, Deferral and Disapproval of Executive Actions: A Summary and an Inventory of Statutory Authority," Report 76-88-G (Washington, Congressional Research Service, April 1976), p. 3. See also Barbara H. Craig, *The Legislative Veto: Congressional Control of Legislation* (Westview, 1983).

17. Only 2.4 percent of the staff in my survey reported that their committee units used the legislative veto frequently or very frequently.

18. For a detailed account of the *Chadha* case, see Barbara H. Craig, *Chadha: The Story of an Epic Constitutional Struggle* (New York: Oxford University Press, 1988).

19. A revealing discussion of "noncompliance with Chadha" by Congress is found in Louis Fisher, "The Separation Doctrine in the Twentieth Century," paper prepared for the Bicentennial Research Conference on "Understanding Congress," sponsored by the Congressional Research Service, February 1989. I thank Steven S. Smith for bringing this paper to my attention.

20. See table 6-2 for the scale.

21. Indeed, the rank correlation (Spearman's rho) between the two is 0.697. And the rank correlation is slightly higher (0.702) if the means and ranks on the frequency of use measures are recalculated to eliminate the 5 (never) scores so that the two sets of means are calculated on the basis of similar Ns (numbers)—recall that those answering "never" did not then rate a technique's effectiveness.

22. See, for example, Harold H. Bruff and Ernest Gellhorn, "Congressional Control of Administrative Regulation: A Study of Legislative Vetoes," *Harvard*

Law Review, vol. 90 (May 1977), p. 1420. Bruff and Gellhorn, like many observers, do not evaluate the veto positively. For a detailed analysis, see Craig, *Legislative Veto.* For a positive perspective on the legislative veto, see Joseph Cooper, "The Legislative Veto in the 1980s," in Lawrence C. Dodd and Bruce I. Oppenheimer, eds., *Congress Reconsidered,* 3d ed. (Washington: Congressional Quarterly, 1985), pp. 364–89.

23. A possible reason for the veto not receiving a higher effectiveness score, even from those using it, is that "nonstatutory substitutes" for the veto seem to work equally well. Perhaps this fact lowers the rating given to the formal veto device. See Fisher, "Separation," p. 14.

24. These correlations are based on a truncated version of the frequency variable, that is, cases in which the respondent answered "never" were dropped since those who reported that their units never used a technique did not rate its effectiveness.

25. The member communication variable is obviously a candidate for further analysis. Overall, however, and not surprisingly, my tests indicate great similarities in the behavior of the two sets of measures.

26. Oversight units include all units of the Senate Governmental Affairs and House Government Operations Committees, as well as the oversight subcommittees of the House Commerce, Public Works, and Ways and Means Committees.

27. Other major (that is, statistically significant) differences between the oversight units taken as a group and other committee units are in the use of staff investigations, support agency evaluations, and oversight hearings, all of which are used more often by oversight units. The first reflects the vigor of oversight unit staffs, which are generally quite large. The second is a function of particularly close ties between the Government Operations Committees and the General Accounting Office. The third (oversight hearings) is discussed in the text.

28. For the record, the rank order correlation (R_s), by chamber, between the techniques rises from 0.543 to 0.785 when respondents from oversight units are excluded.

29. The correlation (r) between chamber and staff investigations is 0.27 ($p \leq 0.01$). With committee decentralization (percentage of hearings held at the subcommittee level) controlled, the correlation drops to 0.16 (no longer statistically significant at the 0.05 level). Controlling further for staff size drops the correlation to 0.13. With decentralization, staff size, and committee role (oversight versus nonoversight) controlled, the correlation between chamber and staff investigations fades to 0.10.

30. Table 6-3 shows that House committee units use all the activities listed more frequently for oversight except the reauthorization and amendment hearings just discussed. Most of the differences are very small, but they are consistent. In addition to those discussed in the text, only the differences in the means on use of program evaluations done by the agencies and congressional support agency program evaluations are statistically significant.

31. See the relevant sections of chap. 5, including footnotes. The factor

analysis reported in this chapter was done using the SAS program package. See *SAS User's Guide: Statistics, Version 5 Edition* (Cary, N.C.: SAS Institute, 1985), pp. 335–75.

32. See the discussion of these terms earlier in this chapter under "Oversight Techniques." See also chap. 9.

33. The correlation coefficient between use of primary-purpose oversight hearings and program reauthorization hearings is 0.19. All coefficients are based on data reported on non-Appropriations units alone, since the reauthorizations and amendment items were asked only of the top staffers of these units.

34. See table 6-2 and the discussion accompanying it of program evaluation effectiveness.

35. See chap. 7 for discussion of separate analyses of the staff evaluation and staff investigations measures.

36. The mean rank for the piecemeal review variables is 10 ($\bar{x} = 3.05$). It is 11 ($\bar{x} = 2.99$) for the comprehensive techniques with the support agency program analysis variable excluded from the calculation, and 9 ($\bar{x} = 2.84$) with it included.

37. As Keefe and Ogul note, "No student of legislatures describes committee hearings as models of efficiency or of objectivity. The assessment usually is just the reverse. The most serious charges deal with problems of misinformation, unrepresentative opinions, bias and staging." Keefe and Ogul, *American Legislative Process*, p. 182.

Notes to Chapter Seven

1. The original indices were coded 1 for frequently and 5 for never. The scores along the entire scale were reversed so that, for the regression analyses presented in this chapter, 5 equals frequently and 1 equals never.

2. See chap. 4 on Appropriations Committee information search behavior, for example. The Appropriations dummy allows me to control for the effects of the Appropriations Committees when relevant. This facilitates comparisons between coefficients in the equations for reauthorization and program amendment hearings that Appropriations units do not conduct and coefficients in the equations for the other oversight techniques that all committees use. See table 7-1 and text.

3. Indicators of decentralization, staff size, and total of hearings were not included in the main analysis of this chapter for two reasons. First, the only available measures of the three indicators listed were at the committee level and, therefore, not as satisfactory as one might wish for data using units of committees as the focus of analysis. The analysis in chap. 3, you will recall, used committees as a whole as the units of analysis. Second, the addition of the three variables would increase the number of variables in the regression analyses from ten to thirteen. As it is, the number is unwieldy enough and, given the limitations of the available indicators of the additional variables

just discussed in point one, I decided not to add them to the analyses reported in the text.

4. The oversight units consist of all House Government Operations and Senate Governmental Affairs units and the specialized oversight subcommittees of House Commerce, House Public Works, and House Ways and Means. Note that for this variable and for the redistributive policy issues variable, each unit of the committee is given a score, but for the comparable variables in chap. 3, the committee as a whole was the unit of analysis.

5. See chap. 3 for relevant definitions. Seventeen units were coded redistributive: three from the Senate Human Resources Committee; four from the House Education and Labor Committee; five from the House Ways and Means Committee; and five from the Senate Finance Committee.

6. Units were coded 1 on the basis of respondents' answers to the following questions. "Does the [sub]committee have many of its programs (or agencies) on annual or periodic reauthorization cycles? [Followup]: About how many? About what percentage of the total number of programs or agencies does this represent?"

7. See tables 5-1 and 5-2 for the scales and original numerical values attached to them.

8. Standardized variables are rescaled to have a mean of zero and unit variance.

9. For a sophisticated discussion of the use of regression analysis with ordinal data, see George W. Bohrnstedt and T. Michael Carter, "Robustness in Regression Analysis," in Herbert L. Costner, ed., *Sociological Methodology 1971* (Jossey-Bass, 1971), pp. 118–46. A different view can be found in John Aldrich and Charles F. Cnudde, "Probing the Bounds of Conventional Wisdom: A Comparison of Regression, Probit, and Discriminant Analysis," in Herbert B. Asher and others, *Theory Building and Data Analysis in the Social Sciences* (University of Tennessee Press, 1984), pp. 263–300.

10. All independent and dependent variables have the same variance.

11. It is conceivable, although very unlikely, especially given the coherent pattern of the results across the six equations in table 7-1, that the scores on the motivational and behavioral variables used in the analysis may be associated without there necessarily being a systematic link between the same motivations in particular cases and specific instances of behavior. This is because the variables in the analysis are summary estimates of motivations and behavior. The cautious reader, therefore, should regard the results of the analysis as highly suggestive, not definitive.

12. The mean of the absolute value of the nonsignificant regression coefficients is 0.08. The standard deviation is 0.06.

13. For this reason, Appropriations staffers were not asked the questions used to measure use of reauthorization and amendment hearings for oversight. Therefore, equations Y_5 and Y_6 do not include the Appropriations Committee dummy variable (X_5).

14. Comparison of the results presented in table 7-1 for equations Y_1 to Y_6 to results based on the smaller subsamples ($N=45$) used to estimate

equations Y_5 and Y_6 show similar coefficients. The smaller Ns, of course, do change the level of statistical significance of some of the coefficients.

15. The entries for R_2 separately sum to approximately the R_2 for the total variable equations in each case.

16. The semi-partial r^2 (sr_i^2) "equals that proportion of the Y variance accounted for by X_i beyond that accounted for by the other K-1 IV's [independent variables]. . . . [I]t may be thought of as the unique contribution of X_i to $R2$ in the context of the remaining K-1 IVs." See Jacob Cohen and Patricia Cohen, *Applied Multiple Regression/Correlation Analysis for the Behavioral Sciences* (Hillsdale, N.J.: Lawrence Erlbaum, 1975), p. 95. Cohen and Cohen, pp. 96–97, advise caution in using the semipartial to partition R^2. For the reasons they state, I have not relied solely on this technique. I thank Professor Robert Mare, my colleague at the Center for Advanced Study in the Behavioral Sciences in 1983–84 and Lynn Gale of the staff for bringing this technique to my attention.

17. These figures were compiled by summing the total unique contributions for each variable in each equation, calculating the percentage of that unique contribution represented by the objective characteristics, and then taking an average for the "approaches" and "hearings" equations.

18. I will say more about the weakest element in the generalization, staff approaches (Y_2), below. For now, note that when one breaks the staff index into its component parts and analyzes them separately, the item measuring program evaluations done by staff behaves more like the other "approaches" variables, while the staff investigations variable resembles the hearings variables. The objective characteristics predictors are key for the latter, the agenda-setting motives more important for the former.

19. The negative coefficient in equation Y_2 for the Appropriations Committee units indicates that, taking the other variables into account, they do less piecemeal review than the overall norm in overseeing the executive. This is particularly true of review of agency regulations, which the very busy Appropriations units usually leave to other committees.

20. Breaking the other indices in table 7-1 into component parts does not have a significant impact on one's interpretations.

21. This finding holds, incidentally, even when the equation is run with the Appropriations respondents (all coded 0 on reauthorization frequency variable) removed from the sample.

22. A positive coefficient indicates that oversight units use the type of oversight hearing more frequently than others; a negative coefficient indicates the opposite.

23. See chap. 3 and appendix C for definitions of the variable.

24. This is one case in which an interaction term in the model is justified statistically. Adding an interaction term for chamber (X_1) times redistributive policy issue (X_3) makes the coefficients for the two individual variables lose significance but yields a significant interaction term ($b = -0.42$, $p < 0.10$). This fact is fully consonant with the interpretation in the text.

25. For a forceful version of this perspective, see Barry R. Weingast and

Mark Moran, "Bureaucratic Discretion or Congressional Control? Regulatory Policymaking by the Federal Trade Commission," *Journal of Political Economy*, vol. 91 (October 1983), pp. 765–800.

26. Interview, December 7, 1979.

27. The significant connections of frequent use of primary-purpose oversight hearings (Y_4) and of amendment hearings (Y_6) for oversight and the assist favored programs variable (X_{10}) are the most noticeable relationships in this regard, but certain nonsignificant regression coefficients are also of interest. For piecemeal oversight (Y_1), staff (Y_2), and reauthorization hearings (Y_5), the regression coefficients are close to o (b = 0.03), suggesting that there is no tie between hostility to programs and use of these oversight techniques. The coefficient for the comprehensive approach index (Y_3) equation is negative, as one might expect, but even here the magnitude is low (-0.18), and the coefficient is insignificant. There seems to be little or no hostility necessarily implied by the use of any oversight technique.

28. Path analysis is the technique I used. For a good explanation, see Herbert Asher, *Causal Modeling*, 2d ed. (Sage, 1983).

29. Neither variable shows any significant indirect link, that is, through an approach, to oversight hearings.

30. Staff evaluations and investigations reflect more complex but easily interpretable patterns of use.

Notes to Chapter Eight

1. Joel D. Aberbach, Robert D. Putnam, and Bert A. Rockman, *Bureaucrats and Politicians in Western Democracies* (Harvard University Press, 1981) p. 241.

2. Aberbach, Putnam, and Rockman, *Bureaucrats and Politicians*, p. 113.

3. Interview, February 27, 1980.

4. Interview, February 12, 1980.

5. Interview, January 29, 1980.

6. Interview, February 4, 1980.

7. See, for example, R. Douglas Arnold, *Congress and the Bureaucracy: A Theory of Influence* (Yale University Press, 1979).

8. Interview, January 28, 1980.

9. Interview, February 12, 1980.

10. Interview, June 2, 1980.

11. Interview, January 21, 1980.

12. Interview, January 28, 1980.

13. Interview, March 31, 1980.

14. Interview, January 10, 1980.

15. In each instance the coder judged how the respondent felt based on the respondent's discussion of the committee unit's "most successful" oversight endeavor. The respondent chose the case, using his or her own judgment about what was successful, but the case was described from the perspective of the committee unit. Check coding was done by the author to

verify that scores on the sympathy/hostility and implementation approval/ disapproval codes reflected the respondent's views about the relationship of his or her committee unit to the program or agency that was the focus of the oversight endeavor. Not surprisingly, given that the most successful oversight questions focused on the committee unit, they did.

16. The correlation (Gamma) between the advocacy/opposition and the sympathy/hostility measures is −0.63. The two measures are coded in opposite directions.

17. Of the total respondents who could be coded on *both* the sympathy/ hostility and approval/disapproval measures, 74 percent were scored as sympathetic to the program's basic purpose while at the same time disapproving of some aspect of its implementation.

18. Some respondents, for example, described committee investigations of problems in society for which there was no relevant federal law or program in existence at the time of the study, that is, what I classify as an investigation rather than oversight.

19. The correlation (r) between a division of units into oversight/nonoversight and a trichotomous advocacy variable based on the data in table 8-1—grouping units into those scored as advocates, qualified advocates, or those taking a neutral or "it depends" stance (the latter two collapsed)—is 0.42. If the "depends" group (see table 8-1) is dropped from the trichotomous advocacy variable, the correlation remains essentially the same ($r = 0.45$).

20. Steven S. Smith and Christopher J. Deering, *Committees in Congress* (Washington: Congressional Quarterly, 1984), p. 105.

21. Smith and Deering, *Committees*, pp. 83–119, especially p. 117.

22. Following Smith and Deering, the Senate Commerce, Environment and Public Works, and Appropriations Committees and the House Education and Labor, Public Works and Transportation, and Science and Technology Committees were classified as constituency committees, the others not. See Smith and Deering, *Committees*, pp. 99, 112.

23. Incidentally, if the House Education and Labor Committee, which Smith and Deering place parenthetically in both the constituency and the policy categories, is moved to the nonconstituency group, then the final correlation (r) becomes negative ($−0.04$).

24. Recall that Smith and Deering classify Senate Appropriations as a constituency committee and even talk of its stance as shifting from one of "appeals court for agencies and affected interests that suffered cuts in House action to one of more actively protecting established programs." Smith and Deering, *Committees*, p. 117.

25. Smith and Deering classify House Appropriations as an "influence and prestige" committee, but they note that even for this venerable guardian of the Treasury, "reforms and agenda changes since the mid-1970s have affected . . . goals for Appropriations members. . . . Appropriations Democrats now openly choose subcommittee assignments they believe are valuable to them at home. Senior Appropriations members complain that this change has meant that during hearings and markups members more frequently are

advocates for, rather than critical overseers of, programs than they were in the late 1960s. Democrat David R. Obey of Wisconsin explained that 'now the pro-defense people go to [the] Defense [subcommittee], public works people go to Energy and Water, pro-health and education people go to Labor-HHS.' " Smith and Deering, *Committees*, p. 93.

With data from the top House Appropriations and all oversight unit staff excluded from the calculation, the percentage of strong or qualified advocates rises to 79 (N = 65) compared with 72 percent (N = 73) for the nonoversight units including House Appropriations (see table 8-1). Excluding all Appropriations staff (House and Senate) brings the percentage of strong or qualified advocates up another two points to 81 percent.

26. Those who indicate that their stance depends on the program obviously take an opposition position at times, but they would be coded in one of the opponent categories (see table 8-1) only if the balance tilted toward opposition, which it never did.

27. Separate analyses were carried out with the "depends" data deleted. These were compared to analyses in which "neutral" and "depends" were combined. Results indicated that combining the categories was a proper procedure.

28. For example, the correlation (r) between the frequency of use of reauthorization hearings for oversight—a behavior much influenced by unit type (oversight units very infrequently hold reauthorization hearings)—and advocacy is 0.40 with oversight units included. Advocates are much more likely to employ reauthorization hearings frequently, or so it appears. However, with the oversight units removed, the correlation drops to 0.14. The initial relationship, therefore, is the spurious result of including the oversight units.

29. Tables, as well as the correlations, were examined for indications of curvilinear or other notable relationships. None were of sufficient import to dwell on here.

30. The relationship between advocacy and scandal is negative as one might expect—for advocates, a scandal is less likely to be an important stimulus to placing an item on the oversight agenda—but it is very weak (r = −0.08).

When the advocacy and piecemeal approaches indices are correlated, the relationship is in the "right" direction—negative because of the coding of the variables—but the magnitude is trivial (−0.04). A negative coefficient indicates that advocates use piecemeal approaches more frequently.

31. Recall from chapter 7 that the use of comprehensive techniques is linked to oversight motivated by a sense of duty (commitment to the review of ongoing programs and agencies).

32. Neither is statistically significant at the 0.05 level. The p for the correlation of the advocacy and comprehensive approaches indicators, however, is 0.067. For purposes of comparison, the correlation (r) between the comprehensive approaches and duty (commitment) indicators is 0.33.

33. The low end of the commitment to review measure includes those

who rated commitment unimportant or of minor importance in leading to selection of programs or agencies for oversight. The high end contains those who score it of major importance. The low end of the comprehensive approaches index, a standardized average of scores on items measuring use of program evaluation techniques, groups those scoring more than one standard deviation below the mean of zero. Those at the high end of the index scored more than one standard deviation above the mean of zero.

34. Sixty percent of those who use staff investigations very frequently or frequently are advocates or qualified advocates, compared with 79 percent of those who rarely or never use them.

35. Eighty-seven percent of those who use oversight hearings very frequently or frequently are advocates, compared with 67 percent of those who rarely or never use them. Users of other types of hearings for oversight, incidentally, are slightly less likely to be advocates than nonfrequent users, but the relationships are small and insignificant. ($R = -0.04$ between advocacy and use of reauthorization hearings for oversight, and -0.12 between advocacy and use of hearings on proposed amendments for oversight.)

36. See table 8-2. A quotation from a senator who chaired an important subcommittee gives some of the flavor of this supportive attitude: "In most all of the hearings I conduct, well, we ask tough questions, but . . . I wouldn't say they're adversary. After all, we're working with them all the time. We're trying to find out from them how could the program be improved. And if we've got [a] criticism, we raise it with them and see what answers they've got. . . . We're working together on programs. We want them to execute more efficiently, and I assume most of them want to execute efficiently." Interview, n.d.

37. In describing why the case selected for discussion as "the most successful oversight case" of the unit was nominated, for example, many types of changes were discussed by top staffers, but only 14 percent of them talked about a "major change of substantive policy or policy direction." The modal discussion (26 percent) focused on improvements (adjustments) in a program or policy area, while others emphasized various improvements in implementation and management. This all fits quite nicely with the results presented in table 8-2.

38. See, for example, Martha Derthick and Paul J. Quirk, The Politics of Deregulation (Brookings, 1985). For an analysis of basic policy conflict between a congressional subcommittee and its agency, see Barry R. Weingast and Mark J. Moran, "The Myth of Runaway Bureaucracy: The Case of the FTC" Regulation (May–June 1982), pp. 33–38 (reprinted by Washington University, Center for the Study of American Business, August 1982).

39. Smith and Deering, Committees, p.93.

40. See Morris P. Fiorina, Congress: Keystone of the Washington Establishment (Yale University Press, 1977) for an articulate statement of this thesis.

41. See Herbert Kaufman, Are Government Organizations Immortal? (Brookings, 1976).

42. Some of the units in the interview study sample were involved in

deregulation. Responses varied, but typically the units were classified depends or qualified advocate on the advocacy/opposition measure. For an example of a qualified advocate, see the quotation from the interview cited in note 12. The following is an example of the "depends" classification: "Well, it depends—that's a mixed bag. We're an advocate of many of them; on the other hand, we're also an advocate of sunsetting the [agency]." Interview, February 29, 1980.

The lack of units classified as opponents or qualified opponents, including those active in deregulation, is instructive. Even the units active in deregulation were oriented to advocacy in at least half the program areas they cover because of the advantages and appeal of program promotion.

43. See Derthick and Quirk, *Politics*, pp. 238–252.

44. Derthick and Quirk, *Politics*, pp. 242–43.

45. See, for example, chap. 6, "The Limits of Deregulation," in Derthick and Quirk, *Politics*.

46. See Weingast and Moran, "The Myth," 1982, for an account of the situation facing the Federal Trade Commission in the late 1970s.

47. Remember that representatives and senators tend to seek membership on committees of benefit or interest to them and to remain on the committees in order to build seniority and, with it, the electoral advantages enjoyed by incumbents.

48. See Jean Peters, "Reconciliation 1982: What Happened?" *PS*, vol. 14 (Fall 1981), pp. 732–33, for a brief synopsis of events and precedents paving the way for the use of reconciliation in 1981 (fiscal 1982). For a complete account, see Allen Schick, *Reconciliation and the Congressional Budget Process* (Washington: American Enterprise Institute for Public Policy Research, 1981).

49. Peters, "Reconciliation 1982," p. 732.

50. Schick, *Reconciliation*, p. 12.

51. Peters, "Reconciliation 1982," p. 735.

52. Schick, *Reconciliation*, p. 38, says, "More than 75 percent of the reductions recommended by the Senate Budget Committee in 1981 were initiated by the Reagan administration."Indeed, in a remarkable example of credit given to others for a committee's recommendations, the Senate Budget Committee's March 23, 1981, report on the reconciliation motion contained the following statement: "In reaching its decisions the Committee considered a variety of sources. The primary source of proposals for spending reductions were the President's economic message of February 18, 1981, and his budget revisions submitted to Congress on March 10, 1981." (Revised Second Concurrent Resolution on the Budget, Fiscal Year 1981.) The report, pp. 20–156, contains a series of proposed reconciliation savings, by committee with jurisdiction and by budget function, and lists the source of each proposal.

53. These statements are based on a few interviews with Senate committee staff in 1982 and 1983, but I am confident of their accuracy.

54. Steven Smith, "New Patterns of Decisionmaking in Congress," in John E. Chubb and Paul E. Peterson, eds., *The New Direction in American Politics* (Brookings, 1985), p. 224. See also Lester M. Salamon and Alan J.

Abramson, "Governance: The Politics of Retrenchment," in John L. Palmer and Isabel V. Sawhill, eds., *The Reagan Record* (Ballinger, 1984), pp. 31–68. In "The Year of the Congress," pp. 52–53, Salamon and Abramson say, "By the time the administration submitted the FY 1983 budget in February 1982, opposition was running high even among Republicans, and the Republican dominated Senate Budget Committee rejected the administration's budget 21–0 in early April 1982."

55. David A. Stockman, "The Triumph of Politics: Why the Reagan Revolution Failed," *Newsweek*, April 21, 1986, p. 40.

56. Stockman, "Triumph," p. 57. Stockman's judgment is confirmed in more temperate language by the analysis of Palmer and Sawhill. They state that "it would be a serious mistake to conclude that a revolution has taken place. . . . The president exercised far less fiscal discipline than economic realities required and got only half of the domestic spending restraint he requested from Congress." See John L. Palmer and Isabel E. Sawhill,"Overview," in Palmer and Sawhull, *Reagan Record*, p. 24.

57. Stockman, "Triumph," p. 58.

Notes to Chapter Nine

1. Richard Hofstadter as quoted in James MacGregor Burns, *The Deadlock of Democracy: Four Party Politics in America* (Prentice Hall, 1963), p. 22.

2. John F. Bibby, "Congress' Neglected Function," in Melvin R. Laird, ed., *The Republican Papers* (Anchor, 1968), pp. 477–88; Seymour Scher, "Conditions for Legislative Control," *Journal of Politics*, vol. 28 (1963), pp. 526–51; and Morris S. Ogul, *Congress Oversees the Executive: Studies in Legislative Supervision* (University of Pittsburgh Press, 1976).

3. Ogul, *Congress Oversees*, p. 199.

4. See Mathew D. McCubbins and Thomas Schwartz, "Congressional Oversight Overlooked: Police Patrols versus Fire Alarms," *American Journal of Political Science*, vol. 28 (February 1984), pp. 165–79.

5. Ogul, *Congress Oversees*, p. 180.

6. Ogul, *Congress Oversees*, pp. 153–80.

7. For example, contrast Morris P. Fiorina, "Control of the Bureaucracy: A Mismatch of Incentives and Capabilities," in William S. Livingston, Laurence C. Dodd, and Richard G. Schott, eds., *The Presidency and the Congress* (Austin: Lyndon B. Johnson School of Public Affairs/Lyndon B. Johnson Library, 1979), pp. 124–42, with McCubbins and Schwartz, "Congressional Oversight." Fiorina is much more skeptical.

8. See the interchange between Richard Fenno and Representative John Culver in *Committee Organization in the House*, Panel discussion before the House Select Committee on Committees, vol. 1, 93 Cong. 1 sess. (Government Printing Office, 1973), pt. 1, pp. 15–16. Culver was distressed because academics stuck to the realpolitik notion that oversight was infrequent because of the lack of political incentives to do it, no matter how much some in Congress might wish otherwise.

9. Ogul, *Congress Oversees*, p. 199.

10. For a similar view, see the excellent article by Cooper and Young cited in chap. 1. They argue that "self-interest per se has no definitive or absolute meaning as a guide to action. . . . The concrete operational meaning of self-interest is always relative to context and informed by context." Joseph Cooper and Cheryl D. Young, "Bill Introduction in the Nineteenth Century: A Study of Institutuional Change," *Legislative Studies Quarterly*, vol. 14 (February 1989), p. 99.

11. James L. Sundquist, *The Decline and Resurgence of Congress* (Brookings, 1981), p. 482.

12. Richard P. Nathan, *The Plot That Failed: Nixon and the Administrative Presidency* (John Wiley, 1975); and *The Administrative Presidency* (John Wiley, 1983).

13. Herbert Kaufman, *The Administrative Behavior of Federal Bureau Chiefs* (Brookings, 1981).

14. Richard F. Fenno, Jr. *The Power of the Purse: Appropriations Politics in Congress* (Little, Brown, 1966); and Aaron B. Wildavsky, *The Politics of the Budgetary Process* (Little, Brown, 1964).

15. Interview, May 31, 1979.

16. Interview, July 21, 1979.

17. These figures exclude the Appropriations Committees because the question was not asked of their staffers. The wording of the question was as follows: "Do you usually follow up oversight hearings with: a) reports; b) communications with the agency; c) legislation?" Answers were coded on the following scale: 1) Yes, usually do; 3) Depends; 5) No, usually do not; 6) Never.

18. Interview, June 2, 1980.

19. Interview, May 24, 1979.

20. "Roundtable Discussion on Congressional Oversight," transcript (Brookings, June 5, 1979), p. 9.

21. "Roundtable Discussion," p. 15.

22. "Roundtable Discussion," p. 16.

23. National Academy of Public Administration, *Presidential Management of Rulemaking in Regulatory Policy* (Washington, January 1987), p. 21.

24. See James G. March and Herbert A. Simon, tenit Organizations (John Wiley, 1958); and Richard M. Cyert and James G. March, A Behavioral Theory of the Firm (Prentice-Hall, 1963).

25. Ogul, *Congress Oversees*, pp. 195–96, specifically mentioned bicameralism and the system of relatively autonomous standing committees.

26. Continued decentralization of committee decisionmaking will also contribute to this end, even when conditions are less favorable to oversight than they are now.

27. Ogul, *Congress Oversees*, pp. 181–202, especially pp. 183, 186.

28. Members and staffers, as well as bureaucrats, are probably open to studies that accept the basic premises of their programs and suggest ways to improve them. However, when the programs are threatened or important

clienteles are likely to be severely disadvantaged by the implementation of study evaluations, resistance occurs.

29. See Fiorina, "Control of the Bureaucracy."

30. For a case study on Sunset, see Michael J. Malbin, *Unelected Representatives: Congressional Staff and the Future of Representative Government* (Basic Books, 1980), chap. 4.

31. See Congressional Quarterly, *Congress and the Nation, 1977–80,* vol. 5 (Washington, 1981), pp. 842, 851.

32. The analysis in the text is based on interviews done by the author on Sunset in general and the Muskie proposal in particular.

33. For example, "The House Budget Committee (HBC) groups all federal activities into 279 major programs. Of the 279, 133 have no expiring legislation, and 146 at least in part expire." Congressional Budget Office memo, mimeograph (November 9, 1979), p. 2.

34. Most Sunset proposals exempt entitlements and revenue provisions of federal statutes, which is understandable in light of the way their threatened expiration would affect large constituencies or basic government finances. However, exemptions of important programs clearly undermine the basic purpose of Sunset.

35. See, for example, *Sunset, Sunrise, and Related Measures,* Hearings before the Subcommittee on the Legislative Process of the House Committtee on Rules, 96 Cong. 1 sess. (Government Printing Office, 1980), pt. 2, pp. 150–52.

36. James Davidson, "Sunset—A New Challenge," *The Bureaucrat,* vol. 6 (Spring 1977), p. 160. Davidson was the staff counsel for the Muskie subcommittee that had jurisdiction over Sunset.

37. For a full account, see Roger H. Davidson and Walter J. Oleszek, *Congress against Itself* (Indiana University Press, 1977).

38. *Committee Reform Amendments of 1974,* H. Rept. 93–916, 93 Cong. 2 Sess. (GPO, 1974), pt. 2, pp. 66–68.

39. See *Committee Reform Amendments of 1974: Explanation of H. Res. 988 as Adopted by the House of Representatives, October 8, 1974,* Committee Print, House Select Committee on Committees, 93 Cong. 2 sess. (GPO, 1974), pp. 58–59.

40. *Oversight Plans of the Committees of the U. S. House of Representatives.* H. Rept. 94-61, 94 Cong. 1 sess. (GPO, 1975), pp. 7–9.

41. *Oversight Plans of the Committees of the U.S. House of Representatives.* H. Rept. 99-25 99 Cong. 1 sess. (GPO, 1985), p. 2.

42. See, for example, Fiorina, "Control of the Bureaucracy." A recent, detailed consideration of the basic issues in U.S. constitutional reform can be found in James L. Sundquist, *Constitutional Reform and Effective Government* (Brookings, 1986). Numerous essays on the subject are collected in Donald L. Robinson, ed., *Reforming American Government: The Bicentennial Papers of the Committee on the Constitutional System* (Westview Press, 1985).

43. See Geoffrey Smith, *Westminster Reform: Learning from Congress* (London: Trade Policy Research Centre, 1979).

44. Clive Ponting, *Whitehall: Tragedy and Farce* (London: Hamish Hamilton Ltd., 1986), p. 155.

45. Michael Rush, *Parliament and the Public*, 2d ed. (London: Longman, 1986), pp. 100–101.

46. Ponting, *Whitehall, p. 158.*

47. Richard Crossman, *Diaries of a Cabinet Minister*, vol. 1 (Holt, Rinehart and Winston, 1976), p. 628, as quoted in Ponting, *Whitehall*, p. 153.

48. For a similar point, see Bert A. Rockman, "Legislative-Executive Relations and Legislative Oversight," *Legislative Studies Quarterly*, vol. 9 (August 1984), p. 434.

Notes to Appendix A

1. Joseph P. Harris, *Congressional Control of Administration* (Brookings, 1964), p. 9.

2. See, for example, John F. Bibby, "Committee Characteristics and Legislative Oversight of Administration," *Midwest Journal of Political Science*, vol. 10 (February 1966), p. 79, note 5; Cornelius P. Cotter, "The Concept of Legislative Government," in Alfred de Grazia, ed., *Congress: The First Branch of Government: Twelve Studies of the Organization of Congress* (Washington: American Enterprise Institute for Public Policy Research, 1966), p. 29; Genevieve J. Knezo and Walter J. Oleszek, "Legislative Oversight and Program Evaluation," *The Bureaucrat*, vol. 5 (April 1976), p. 37; Seymour Scher, "Conditions for Legislative Control," *Journal of Politics*, vol. 25 (August 1963), p. 528, note 8; Randall B. Ripley and Grace A. Franklin, *Congress, the Bureaucracy, and Public Policy*, 4th ed. (Dorsey Press, 1987), p. 17; and Mathew D. McCubbins and Thomas Schwartz, "Congressional Oversight Overlooked: Police Patrols versus Fire Alarms," *American Journal of Political Science*, vol. 28 (February 1984), p. 165.

3. Morris S. Ogul, *Congress Oversees the Bureaucracy: Studies in Legislative Supervision* (University of Pittsburgh Press, 1976), p. 11. See also Fred Kaiser, "Oversight of Foreign Policy: The U.S. House Committee on International Relations," *Legislative Studies Quarterly*, vol. 2 (August 1977), p. 257.

4. Ogul, *Congress Oversees*, p. 11.

5. Ogul, *Congress Oversees*, p. 11.

6. The language requiring committees to issue reports carrying out these provisions is regularly reprinted in the reports. See, for example, the *Legislative Review Activity Report of the Committee on Labor and Human Resources*, S. Rept. 100–29, 100 Cong. 1 sess. (GPO, 1987) especially p. iii, which quotes the language of sections 136a and b.

7. See chap. 2. See also James L. Sundquist, *The Decline and Resurgence of Congress* (Brookings, 1981), pt. 2.

8. David E. Price, *Who Makes the Laws? Creativity and Power in Senate Committees* (Cambridge: Schenkman, 1972), p. 10. See also Steven S. Smith and Christopher J. Deering, *Committees in Congress* (Washington: Congressional Quarterly, 1984), especially pp. 271–72.

9. This analysis extends work I did as a consultant on oversight to the Commission on the Operation of the Senate. See Joel D. Aberbach, "The Development of Oversight in the United States Congress: Concepts and Analysis," in *Techniques and Procedures for Analysis and Evaluation*, Committee Print, Commission on the Operation of the Senate, 94 Cong., 2 sess. (GPO, 1977), pp. 53–69. A revised (and properly edited) version of the commission paper, entitled "Changes in Congressional Oversight," can be found in Carol H. Weiss and Allen H. Barton, eds., *Making Bureaucracies Work* (Sage, 1980), pp. 65–87.

10. The *Daily Digest* of the *Congressional Record* was used as the basis for coding in preference to other committee calendars or other sources because it contains the most complete listing of committee hearings and meetings.

11. A detailed description of the clusters is available from the author. See George Goodwin, Jr., *The Little Legislatures: Committees of Congress* (University of Massachusetts Press, 1970), pp. 102, 114–15; Donald R. Matthews, *U.S. Senators and Their World* (University of North Carolina Press, 1960), p. 154; and Barbara Hinckley, "Policy Content, Committee Membership and Behavior," *American Journal of Political Science*, vol. 19 (August 1975), p. 547.

12. I used two classifications from the literature, one by Theodore Lowi and the other by Barbara Hinckley, as my guides. See Theodore J. Lowi, "American Business, Public Policy, Case-Studies and Political Theory," *World Politics*, vol. 16 (July 1964), pp. 677–715, and also "Four Systems of Policy, Politics, and Choice," *Public Administration Review*, vol. 32 (July–August 1972), pp. 298–310. Hinckley's classification can be found in Hinckley, "Policy Content," pp. 543–57. The Lowi classification is the renowned and, by now, widely criticized categorization of policy into types labeled "regulatory," "distributive," "redistributive," and "constituency." See George D. Greenberg, Jeffrey A. Miller, Lawrence B. Mohr, and Bruce D. Vladek, "Developing Public Policy Theory: Perspectives from Empirical Research," *American Political Science Review*, vol. 71 (December 1977), pp. 1532–43. I selected committees to cover the range of policy categories, using George Goodwin's breakdown, in Lowi's terms, of the types of issues handled by each committee. See Goodwin, *Little Legislatures*, p. 103. Confidence in this decision is enhanced because Goodwin's classification parallels the related breakdown of committees by Hinckley's panel of experts into those whose subject matter encourages either positive-sum (more or less) or zero-sum (competitive solutions) to problems. All of Goodwin's distributive committees are classified positive-sum when rated by Hinckley and those considered regulatory or redistributive are placed in Hinckley's zero-sum "scope" category. Hinckley, "Policy Content," p. 547.

13. See *Congressional Yellow Book, a Directory of Members of Congress, Including Their Committees and Key Staff Aides* (Washington: Monitor Publishing, Spring 1978, and various editions.) I consulted the *Congressional Staff Directory* (Mount Vernon, Va.: Congressional Staff Directory, 1977, 1978, and later editions), committee calendars and documents, House and Senate payroll records, informants on the committees, and the staff members who cover

the relevant committees for the *Congressional Yellow Book*. In three cases "substitute" top staffers were selected for inclusion in the top staffer group. See table A-1, note b.

14. For independent confirmation of this fact, see Christopher J. Deering and Steven S. Smith, "Subcommittee Government?" paper presented at the 1983 annual meeting of the American Political Science Association, p. 33. Deering and Smith used the *Congressional Staff Directory* as their primary source on subcommittee staffing rather than the *Congressional Yellow Book*.

15. For discussion of the interview method used, see Joel D. Aberbach, Robert D. Putnam, and Bert A. Rockman, *Bureaucrats and Politicians in Western Democracies* (Harvard University Press, 1981), pp. 33–35. The main interview instrument was pretested on five top staffers, three from the Senate Foreign Relations Committee and two from the House International Relations Committee.

16. The cases were done in varying degrees of depth. The programs involved were the Rehabilitation Services Administration, the Food and Drug Administration, the Economic Development Administration, the Federal Trade Commission, and the National Institute of Education. Thirty-one interviews were conducted in connection with the case studies.

17. A conference was also held with congressional staff people. See James L. Sundquist, *The Decline and Resurgence of Congress* (Brookings, 1981), p. 334, note 48, for a full description of the conferees. Sundquist and I jointly convened the conferences.

Notes to Appendix B

1. After making suitable adjustments for the hearings and meetings of the joint committees and so on, the data set reported in this study contained only 2.8 percent fewer hearings and meetings than the commission data. See *Legislative Activity Sourcebook: United States Senate*, prepared for the Commission on the Operation of the Senate, 94 Cong. 2 sess. (Government Printing Office, 1976), pp. 6–16. These commission data were coded by the Congressional Research Service.

2. This includes review that takes place during program and policy implementation as well as afterward.

3. *Committee Reform Amendments of 1974*, H. Rept. 93-916, 93 Cong. 2 sess. (GPO, 1974), p. 267.

Notes to Appendix C

1. The same operational definitions of the indicators were used in the analysis of data for the Reagan years reported in chap. 3.

2. The sources for these data are as follows: Norman J. Ornstein, Thomas E. Mann, and Michael J. Malbin, *Vital Statistics in Congress, 1987–1988*, (Washington: Congressional Quarterly, 1987), pp. 147–48; Paul S. Rundquist,

"House Committee Staffing and Investigations Funding, 1947–1977," (Washington, Congressional Research Service, June 8, 1978); *The Senate Committee System: Jurisdictions, Referrals, Numbers, and Sizes of Limitations on Membership, First Staff Report to the Senate Temporary Select Committee to Study the Senate Committee System,* 94 Cong. 2 sess. (Government Printing Office, 1976), pp. 198–202; *Committee Reform Amendments of 1974,* H. Rept. 96-916, 93 Cong. 2 sess. (GPO, 1974), pp. 357–58; and various reports of the *Clerk of the House* and the *Secretary of the Senate* on chamber expenditures.

3. For a similar view, see Steven S. Smith and Christopher J. Deering, *Committees in Congress* (Washington: Congressional Quarterly, 1984), chap. 5.

4. See George Goodwin, Jr., *The Little Legislatures: Committees of Congress* (University of Massachusetts Press, 1970), pp. 102–103. Redistributive issues are defined by Goodwin, drawing on Lowi, as "involving government manipulation with class overtones and resulting [in] especially hard-fought decisions." The committees listed as redistributive and coded 1 are as follows: Senate Finance, House Ways and Means, Senate and House Judiciary, Senate and House Banking and Currency, Senate Labor and Public Welfare, and House Education and Labor.

5. I wish to thank my colleague at the University of Michigan, Professor Mary Corcoran, for help in interpreting this information.

6. See David A. Belsley, Edwin Kuh, and Roy E. Welsh, *Regression Diagnostics: Identifying Influential Data and Sources of Collinearity* (John Wiley, 1980); and SAS Institute, Inc., *SAS User's Guide: Statistics, 1982 Edition* (Cary, N.C.: SAS Institute, 1982), pp. 39–83.

7. It also stabilized the residual variance, a crucial assumption for the pooled analysis. See Edward R. Tufte, *Data Analysis for Politics and Policy* (Prentice Hall, 1974), pp. 108–34, for an excellent discussion of the value of log transformations. Tests indicated that logging the counts of the relevant dependent variables—total days and staff—was unnecessary and actually detrimental.

8. The Senate Judiciary Committee had an exceptionally large staff during Senator Eastland's tenure as chairman, part of his effort to deal with committee liberals.

9. The log of the dependent variable (with one added to the count of committee oversight days to handle cases where the value was zero), actual counts of the relevant independent variables, percentages, or dummy variables (0 or 1) where relevant were used. See section on independent variables in this appendix.

10. The number of pages in the *Federal Register* variable was included in preliminary tests but later dropped.

11. See Samprit Chatterjee and Bertram Price, *Regression Analysis by Example* (John Wiley, 1977), pp. 96–100 on "Stability of Regression Parameters over Time;" and J. Johnston, *Econometric Methods,* 2d ed. (McGraw Hill, 1972), pp. 204–07.

12. Since the data are a "universe" of committee behavior for the first six

months of each year, marred solely by whatever measurement error is present, I only eliminated coefficients where p is greater than 0.5. The dummy variables dropped were chamber ($p=0.59$, $F=0.64$); redistributive policy issues ($p=0.56$, $F=0.69$); and the intercept adjustment ($p=0.74$, $F=0.42$). Those retained were committee decentralization ($p<.01$, $F=5.31$); oversight unit ($p=.02$, $F=3.37$); staff ($p=.04$, $F=2.71$); and total days ($p=0.41$, $F=0.74$). The total days slope dummies, the most questionable variables retained, have, as it turns out, some meaningful substantive interpretation. The dropped dummies are harder to interpret. This gives me confidence in the procedure followed.

Notes to Appendix D

1. The data in chaps. 2 and 3 cover only the first six months of each year. Data on the calendar year were gathered as well for selected years, including 1977. Therefore, data for the full 1977 calendar year were available for this analysis.

2. Appropriations units were excluded from the comparison because oversight data for them were not available in the *Daily Digest* data. Therefore, eleven committees formed the basis of the comparison.

3. See Hubert M. Blalock, *Social Statistics* (McGraw-Hill, 1960), pp. 179–81.

4. The scores for the minority are significantly lower than for the majority in each case, but the differences are not all that great. Both report frequent use and high effectiveness.

5. Incidentally, when comparable paired difference of means tests are done on the agenda-setting variables analyzed in chap. 5, there are no significant differences ($p \leq 0.05$) between the minority and majority for estimates of members' importance scores and only one significant difference for staff's scores. Majority and minority staffers see agenda setting for committee oversight in the same way.

Index